THE CHANGING ARCHITECTURE OF POLITICS

Structure, Agency, and the Future of the State

PHILIP G. CERNY

SAGE Publications

London · Newbury Park · New Delhi

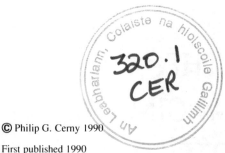

© Philip G. Cerny 1990

First published 1990

 SAGE Publications Ltd
28 Banner Street
London EC1Y 8QE

SAGE Publications Inc
2111 West Hillcrest Drive
Newbury Park, California 91320

SAGE Publications India Pvt Ltd
32, M-Block Market
Greater Kailash - I
New Delhi 110 048

British Library Cataloguing in Publication data

Cerny, Philip G., 1946–
   The changing architecture of politics: structure, agency, and the future of the state.
   1. State
   I. Title
   320.1

ISBN 0-8039-8255-0
ISBN 0-8039-8256-9 pbk

Library of Congress Catalog Card Number 89-63697

Typeset by Sage Publications
Printed in Great Britain by Dotesios Printers Ltd
Trowbridge, Wiltshire

Contents

For Alexander and Marcus

Introduction

If we are to understand the tremendous structural changes going on in the world today, we need to look at politics and the state through new lenses. Unfortunately, political science – the systematic study of politics – suffers from a deep-rooted ambiguity, almost a schizophrenia. That ambiguity concerns the role of institutions, both the formal institutional structures which we associate with constitutions and governments, and the more informal political structures with which they are inextricably intertwined. For whereas the empirical 'stuff' of politics revolves around such institutions and structures, the theoretical conceptualization of how institutions work and what sort of impact they have is severely underdeveloped. And the insufficient understanding of structures which this gap has entailed means that we may be in a very poor position to analyze and evaluate recent structural trends in politics, economics, and society in ways which will be relevant in the twenty-first century.

Much of this underdevelopment is the product of a reaction among political scientists earlier in the twentieth century to the perceived failure of attempts to build new formal–legal institutions of various kinds in the context of rapid change and deep social and economic upheavals. The failure of democratic constitutions to stem the tide of fascism in the 1920s and 1930s, the failure of the League of Nations and the impotence of the United Nations, the collapse of post-colonial constitutions in the Third World, more 'realist' interpretations of jurisprudence (with regard to the United States Supreme Court, for example), all of these and many other symptoms led to the association of institutional analysis with flawed institutional 'solutions' and to a fundamental shift in focus toward other levels of analysis.

It is the unsurprising thesis of this book – a thesis which will be developed at a theoretical level mainly in the first half of the book – that this shift left an important gap in the study of politics, one which has only partly (and unsatisfactorily) been addressed by some forms of organization theory and, in recent years, by some strands of neo-Marxist and neo-Weberian state theory. In trying to examine this gap more closely, however, I do not intend to go back to formal–legal institutional analysis; rather, I will try to synthesize certain of its common-sense insights – insights which practical political scientists and others still use as rules of thumb – with a variety of elements of institutional theory drawn from sociology, anthropology and economics. Indeed, each of the social sciences (and social science in general) is characterized by an institutional or structural *problématique* from which insights can be drawn.

The core of the problem is to ask whether institutions and structures develop and operate according to an independent dynamic, and, if so, how. In attempting to analyze how these structures work, and how they interact with other levels of society and economy, political scientists have tended to look outside political structures for first causes and for basic chains of explanation. Whether derived from individual or group psychology, social structures such as class or race, 'natural' economic laws or dialectics, or complex combinations of these, political structure is too often treated as *explanandum* rather than as *explanans*.[1]

There are basically two issues here. The first is the nature of *politics*. Definitions abound,[2] some of which are more specific than others about delineating what is distinctive about politics *per se*. But although political scientists, like social scientists in other disciplines, often tend to think that their own discipline is 'the master science' – that the study of politics provides a unique understanding of the overarching framework of society – their definitions and paradigms in practice frequently run counter to this claim. For example, politics is usually seen as a *process of action*, rather than as structure – action which is rooted in the motivations of individuals, groups or classes. Therefore although politics may be seen as a synthesis of social action, that action stems from other levels of explanation. Politics may indeed give a picture of the whole, but that whole represents a complex dependent variable rather than an independent one.

If theories of this kind treat politics as a whole as epiphenomenal, as a secondary phenomenon derived from other sources, then they implicitly treat political institutions and structures, in turn, as tertiary phenomena, as doubly derivative epi-epiphenomena. Cruder versions of this approach – versions which range across the ideological spectrum from economic liberalism* to variants of Marxism – derive political phenomena directly from such *a priori* socio-economic factors.[3] More sophisticated versions frequently posit a range of social, psychological, or economic factors which are of particularly political consequence, of which the most important have probably been notions of power or authority. We will

---

*The term 'liberalism' is used throughout this book in its European sense, the theory of free market economics and limited state intervention – what in the United States is often called 'nineteenth-century liberalism'. By asserting that human beings are subject to such 'natural' economic laws (enforced by Adam Smith's 'invisible hand'), the liberal paradigm can be just as 'economic determinist' as Marxism (and in some ways more so).

look more closely at conceptions of power and authority at various stages in this book. Yet more sophisticated has been neo-Marxist state theory with its attempt to carve out a realm for the 'relative autonomy of the state', although it still posits the determinism of the economic base 'in the last analysis'.[4]

Even these more sophisticated theories, however, remain ambiguous in terms of developing a structural or institutional theory of politics, for two reasons. In the first place, they usually describe a particular attribute of political structures, but not others. And in the second place, the factors seen as primary phenomena are characteristic of a wide variety of social, psychological, and economic structures, and processes besides politics. Thus the nature of politics as a whole, and of the role of institutional structures within it, is not specified or substantially theorized.

The second major issue is of course the nature of *institutions and structures*, political or otherwise. Both formal institutions and informal structures are problematic in any social science context. This is true in several ways. In the first place, there is often a tendency to 'reify' structures – to invest them with a capacity for action and even choice, a capacity for rationality analogous to that of individuals. This is more than mere *raison d'État*, and even borders on the metaphysical in some classical and modern political philosophy. It is as if when newspapers report that, e.g., 'France rejects American proposal', it is really some sort of eternal France which is acting and not specific state actors operating in a particular structural setting.

Now many social scientists who deny that states or governments can possess this sort of holism readily attribute similar subject-like qualities to families and other primary groups or to interest groups, classes, the structural–functional characteristics of social systems, and the like. That aside, however, the dividing line between autonomy and reification is a fine one and the theoretical linkages are complex, and this must be one of the major problems to be dealt with in this book.

In the second place, structural and institutional theories are often seen as static. If one is attempting to describe the structure of constraints within which action takes place, then it is also critical to have a theory of how structures change. In this book we will present structures not as static edifices, but as processes of *structuration*.[5] Structuration implies a process of continuing interaction between agent and structure, in which structures which are generally constraining can also change and be changed in certain conditions.

For example, there are some analogies between structuration as a coherent process of stasis and change, on the one hand, and the way that Thomas Kuhn describes paradigmatic change in scientific communities, on the other.[6] Structuration can also be seen as the interaction of a range of games, with different rules and stakes but linked within an overall 'structured field of action' in which outcomes are probabilistic rather than fully determined, and which has different levels, interstitial spaces, uncertainties, and the like.[7] Thus structures are inherently ever-changing; stasis is at the surface level of appearance, while the deep structure is one of both stasis and change in complex tension at all times.

In the third place, there is often a tendency to analyze institutions and structures not by looking at their internal dynamics but by measuring or estimating their overall impact – for example, by looking not at the structure of government but at the overall amount or 'degree of government'.[8] This approach, however, tends to neglect the role played by the form of the structure. Like Thomas Hobbes's *Leviathan*, it sees the overarching order itself as more important, at an *a priori* level, than the details of how the structures themselves work. Another, not unrelated approach which neglects institutional form is that of systems analysis, in which it is posited that social systems, like biological systems, must first of all survive and adapt to their environments. An understanding of what is functional is gained primarily through analysis of inputs to, and outputs from, the system, which is itself treated as a 'black box'. In contrast to both of these approaches, we argue that the most important aspects of structuration are to be found in the 'withinputs', or what goes on *inside* the black box; institutional form and the structuration process are the key variables.

In the fourth place, many traditional approaches to structural analysis, especially in political science, assume that structures such as the state have a basically hierarchical or centralized character, in contrast to more pluralistic exchange theory or markets. Max Weber saw this operating through the state's 'monopoly of legitimate violence'; traditional typologies of comparative politics run from authoritarian states to the 'political marketplace' of democratic regimes; some approaches to international political economy assume that the hierarchical state is in tension with the growth of transnational markets; neo-Marxist state theory regards the state as having the function of 'extra-economic coercion'; and public choice theory sees 'government' and 'market' as opposing modes of allocation. Here we will pay particular attention to structural mixes of market and hierarchy as a fundamental dynamic of the structuration process, taking our cue from such fields as institutional economics, currently enjoying a renaissance in reaction to the recent dominance of harder versions of neoclassical economic theory.

And finally, rather than just seeing structures as developing and operating within a particular societal field or endogenous systemic environment, we look more closely at the *external* field in which political structuration takes place and in which institutions form and change. There is too much of a divorce within the discipline of political science between the study of domestic politics, for example, and that of international relations. Political institutions are all too often seen as the sum of their internal parts, or at least of the internal parts of the 'society' or nation-state within which they exist. In fact, structures are as much, if not more, influenced by exogenous factors as by endogenous ones.

For example, the state – in the wider sense of the set of political structures associated with a territory recognized as 'sovereign' by other states – is as much a product of transnational processes and structures as it is of its domestic environment. It will be the final crucial task of the book not only to situate the existing structures of the state in the context of international developments, but also to relate the ongoing processes of state structuration in the contemporary world to changes in the transnational field.

The book itself will cover both theory and practice. The first part will develop the points briefly outlined above. Chapter 1 will look more closely at the problem of locating institutional and structural theory within political and social science.* Chapter 2 will describe and classify the main elements or building-blocks of political structures generally and the modern state in particular. Chapter 3 will examine basic patterns of agency – the ways that actors' choices interact and cumulate through basic modes of hierarchical control and the political marketplace – in a dynamic process of 'political allocation', which is at the heart of political structuration. Chapter 4 will analyze the structured action field which lies at the crossroads of the statics and dynamics of structuration: both different internal aspects and levels of the structuration process itself; and the centrality of the modern state in the wider structural environment – among other social and economic structures, between internal structures and the international context, and within the system of states which dominates the wider structure of world politics.

Part II of the book will look at certain core areas of political structuration in practice, including both how states work and how they interact with other social and economic processes, at both domestic and international levels. Chapter 5 will suggest ways that structural factors condition the constraints and opportunities within which personal leaders and political parties operate, shaping both the transformation of the 'raw materials' of social and economic resources and the patterns of power and control over decision-making processes in the state. Chapter 6 will look at the ways that the state interacts with a variety of socio-economic interests and groups – patterns of 'interest intermediation' – and at how the

---

*The words 'institution' and 'structure' will be used almost interchangeably in this book, as they are in much of social science. However, it will be assumed that 'institutions' are the more formal manifestations of the more general category of 'structures', and sometimes this distinction will be indicated.

structuration of the state shapes the context of such processes as pluralism, clientelism, concertation, corporatism, and the like.

Chapter 7 examines the way that state structures have become intertwined in new and complex ways with changing patterns of structuration in advanced capitalist society – and the way the state shapes, and is in turn shaped by, those processes, both internally and transnationally. Chapter 8 will discuss the implications both of changing patterns of state structuration and of contemporary processes of change at a transnational level; these are interacting to transform politics both domestically and internationally, through the emergence of the 'competition state' in an ever more interdependent world.

These developments taken together, we will argue, are leading to a situation which will transform not only the institutional structures of politics but also the dominant ideas of the twenty-first century. Changes in the architecture of politics will interact with and shape social and economic transformation in ever more complex ways. The challenge of the approaching decades will be to link more complex pressures and demands, which can only be catered for by new forms of structural decentralization, with ever more sophisticated forms of strategic monitoring and control at the macro level – monitoring and control of processes which transcend the distinction between the domestic and the international, such as the rapidly integrating global financial marketplace and the growing issue of environmental resource management.

These issues will not just transform the state, but will also themselves be transformed by structural changes in the nature not only of the central state but also of other political institutions. These include the formal and informal transnational regimes and structures in which the state is increasingly enmeshed, on the one hand, and various functionally and territorially deconcentrated apparatuses of the state such as local and regional government, development agencies, industrial and financial policy structures, and the like, on the other.

In this way, the process of political structuration, which has shaped the state as we know it, is continually both recreating the state and creating new, emerging political forms alongside and inside it. Both the traditional right and the traditional left are already feeling the impact, as their recognizable landmarks shift and alter. But the language of political discourse, mired in the neo-classical reaction of the 1980s and in the opposing tendency of social democracy and the welfare state to resist this assault, has not yet developed constructive ideological responses. This was vividly demonstrated in the United States presidential campaign of 1988, in which the categories of 'liberal' and 'conservative' appeared more caricatured and unreal than ever but dominated both rhetoric and voter perception of the candidates. We are not certain, either, just what the responses will be over the longer term. But it is hoped that this book will help identify the issues of an era in which the construction of new political edifices will require a deeper understanding of the architecture of politics.

Notes

1. See Andrew C. Janos, *Politics and Paradigms: Changing Theories of Change in Social Science* (Stanford, Cal.: Stanford University Press, 1986), chs. 1 and 2, for an insightful look at what he calls the 'classical' and 'neo-classical' paradigms which have dominated political science.

2. A survey of some (but not all) useful definitions can be found in Adrian Leftwich, ed., *What is Politics? The Activity and its Study* (Oxford: Basil Blackwell, 1984).

3. Cf. P.G. Cerny, 'State Capitalism in France and Britain and the International Economic Order', in Cerny and M.A. Schain, eds., *Socialism, the State and Public Policy in France* (New York and London: Methuen and Pinter Publishers, 1985), ch. 10, and Janos, *op. cit.*, pp. 7–11.

4. For a clear and thoughtful survey of these attempts, see Martin Carnoy, *The State and Political Theory* (Princeton, N.J.: Princeton University Press, 1984).

5. The notion of 'structuration' is familiar within European philosophy and social science, especially in sociology and linguistics. See Anthony Giddens, *Central Problems of Social Theory: Action, Structure and Contradiction in Social Analysis* (London: Macmillan, 1979).

6. Thomas Kuhn, *The Structure of Scientific Revolutions* (Chicago: Chicago University Press, 1962). For an application to institutional analysis, see Peter A. Hall, *Governing the Economy: The Politics of State Intervention in Britain and France* (New York and London: Oxford University Press and Polity Press, 1986), ch. 1.

7. See Michel Crozier and Erhard Friedberg, *L'acteur et le système: les contraintes de l'action collective* (Paris: Editions du Seuil, 1977).

8. As, for example, in one of the best-known recent attempts to revive institutional theories of political modernization: Samuel P. Huntington, *Political Order in Changing Societies* (New Haven, Conn.: Yale University Press, 1968).

Acknowledgements

In the long process of putting together the complex pieces which together constitute this book, I have been led in several directions in attempting to reconcile theory and practice in political science. Probably the most important elements can be described as follows. The first was the contrast which the study of comparative politics brings out between American notions of politics as a political marketplace, on the one hand, and the European state tradition, on the other – especially as revived in the Fifth French Republic by President Charles de Gaulle (about which I wrote a certain amount between the mid-1960s and the early 1980s).

The second direction has been to contrast cultural and symbolic interpretations of political change with the economic changes which have characterized the period since World War II, and especially since the economic crisis of the 1970s and early 1980s – reflected not only in the First World but also in the Third World. The *bricolage*, both symbolic and economic, of governments, political movements, and leaders faced with new constraints and opportunities has foreshadowed the developments analyzed here.

The third direction has stemmed from teaching both comparative politics and international relations, in different universities and in different countries, and by a shift in my own focus toward political economy as an academic specialism which embraces both levels. It has convinced me not only that an understanding of state theory and of the history of political structures cannot be gained unless both comparative and international analysis is pursued, but also that future directions can only be discerned through a prism which synthesizes both levels. This does not always make for an easy fit with the orthodox cleavages between established sub-disciplines of political science, and it is only to be hoped that these cleavages will be eroded.

It also goes without saying that each of these directions requires an attempt to cross the disciplinary boundaries of social science. Nevertheless, the underlying rationale of this study is clearly political, both in its focus on political structures and in its assertion that those structures possess an independent dynamic which in turn shapes society – not only national societies formed around the state, but also the complex transnational society which is beginning to emerge.

It would be impossible to mention all of the colleagues and friends who have had a direct or indirect impact on the development of my thinking as this book has taken shape over the past few years. I must mention first of all Martin Schain, with whom I have collaborated closely on other projects over the years, and who has been both supportive of my forays into theorizing and a valuable source of advice on this book. Youssef Cohen has also been a valued interlocutor during my year at New York University and has offered penetrating comments on the manuscript. Other friends and colleagues who have made significant, if less direct, contributions over the years include Jean Comaroff, Patrick Dunleavy, Jeffrey Freyman, Peter A. Hall, Christine Harrington, Ian Lustick, Jonas Pontusson, Peter Rutland, Vivien Schmidt, Susan Strange, Gerald Studdert-Kennedy, David Wilson, and Irene Wilson.

Fellow participants in various conferences and seminars of the American Political Science Association, the Political Studies Association of the United Kingdom, the International Political Science Association, the European Consortium for Political Research, the Socialist Scholars' Conference, the Universities of Sussex, Exeter, Birmingham, and Manchester, Dartmouth College, Columbia, Cornell, Wesleyan, and New York Universities, have been very helpful. And I am particularly grateful to David Hill of Sage Publications, who encouraged me to pursue this project from an early stage and who has been patient and supportive during its development. None of the above, of course, should be blamed for the result.

Philip G. Cerny
New York

PART I

THE PRINCIPLES OF POLITICAL STRUCTURATION: STRUCTURE, AGENCY, AND THE DEVELOPMENT OF THE MODERN STATE

1
Political Structuration and Political Science

The most important single fact about the evolution of politics over the past three centuries or so is that virtually the entire world has been progressively carved up into political units of a single broad type – the nation-state – to the exclusion of others. Whether one is looking at grass-roots politics or global politics, the world which went before looked very different. And yet, at the same time, we still have little idea what the world of politics would look like if the nation-state were to be transcended by some other predominant structural pattern.

States have evolved along two closely intertwined dimensions. On the one hand, they have undermined or replaced larger but often looser units, such as traditional empires. Within this process, of course, the more powerful states have usually developed by gaining and losing their own empires, which they had conquered on the way up and which have since split into successor states. On the other hand, they have consolidated smaller units, whether territorial – cities and regions – or kinship-based – clans, families, tribes, and the like – or both.

States come in many varieties, of course. They may be big or small, stable or unstable, more or less centralized, with strong or weak domestic institutions, and powerful or relatively impotent abroad. Nevertheless, their central institutions are far stronger overall than their predecessors', in two ways. In the first place, while states are less closely-knit anthropologically than many of the smaller units which were absorbed in the process of state formation, society itself has become far more complex economically, technologically and socially; far more is demanded in terms of the quantity and complexity of politics, of the tasks which institutions are asked to perform. And in the second place, they operate in the context of the competition and struggle of states both with each other and in attempting to manage often powerful transnational forces; the obscure frontiers of traditional empires have given way to the closely marked and jealously guarded borders of states, and the possibility of long periods of protected stasis, such as the Chinese Empire once enjoyed, are no more.

It must be emphasized, however, that states are not 'natural' entities, the product of an inevitable evolution. The division of the world into nation-states began in the then-peculiar conditions prevailing in one part of the world, Europe, and was either imposed upon or otherwise exported to the rest. And while it is quite likely that this division will someday be eroded or transcended (or both) by some other structural pattern, at the present time we might expect this either to take a very long time, given the predominance of the states system today, or to require major upheavals. The latter have often been heralded, but their supposed manifestations have so far generally either worked through or been absorbed into domestic state structures or the states system.

It is also clear that states, like all social categories, are never finished products, but are always in the process of formation, change and potential decay. Even where constitutions have a longer life – although a relatively short one would seem to be the norm – those constitutions 'evolve' in convention, interpretation and practice; legal structures, too, whatever the formal wording of the rules, also change. Thus the analysis of states does not mean just focusing on the continuities of structural patterns; it means seeing states, and the states system, as involving a process of structuration.

Structuration, Stasis, and Change

Structuration as a process involves both stability and change; indeed, the two are inextricably intertwined. Where stability seems to be the norm, it must be asked how that apparent stability is maintained. As in theories of relativity in physical science, political structures such as the state are only apparently solid and stable; the eternal movement of molecules and energy fields is the norm. Change would, of course, seem to be easier to explain in this perspective. But change is complex and differentiated throughout the structure; it is like a range of different games with different rules, stakes, and distributions of the resources of players, being played simultaneously.[1] Neither the players – the actors or 'agents' – nor the structures – the pattern of constraints and opportunities for action and choice – 'determines' the other. Both are, in the last analysis, independent variables, but they are inextricably intertwined in a dynamic process. In this process, choice is always constrained; the range of alternatives open to rational agents is limited. However, the actual pattern of constraint (and opportunity) is itself in dynamic flux, filtering and transforming the choices and actions of agents in ways which can either reinforce or modify existing structures (or both at the same time) in complex ways.

In this setting, the actions of agents are limited by the existing distribution of resources, stakes, and rules in the *particular* game (or games) in which they are enmeshed (and by their perceptions of these conditions); by the agents' own perceptions of *which* game they are playing within the complex of games; and by uncertainties about the *cumulative* outcomes of the whole range of perceived games being played by others as well.

(These various conditions and perceptions are inevitably filtered through the lens of a reductionist, and ideologically caricatured, image of the overall pattern of games.) Change at the micro level will thus tend to take place within the limits of the overall pattern or structure of games. The possibility of system-level change, in other words the probability that micro-level change will affect the working of the overall structure, would seem, therefore, to be limited.

These limitations, however, are only probabilistic. There are a number of sets of circumstances in which more widespread pattern change or structural change can take place. For example, there is the possibility that widespread analogous or coincidental changes in the microstructures can lead to wider patterns of change. This may occur incrementally over a relatively long period of time, on the one hand; or it could occur rapidly, almost spontaneously, because of a change in the conditions of the structure itself, on the other – for example if a factor or set of factors affected a wide range of agents simultaneously.

It is also possible that certain games may play a disproportionate role in determining, for example, the rules, stakes, and distributions of resources of other games. Strategic control of such nodal points in the structure would, in theory, enable certain agents to trigger off chain reactions in the structure. Of course, such nodal points are what revolutionary theorists have always sought to identify. Revolutions which have occurred in state societies, however, have virtually always led eventually to a strengthening of the state structure: whether because the early failure of the revolution reinforced the existing structure, or its subsequent failure led to counterrevolution; or because revolutionaries have attempted to use the state itself to carry out the revolution, absorbing revolutionary energy and enmeshing its agents in a variety of classic micro-level games.

Agents wishing to *maintain* the system will also seek to identify and control such nodal points. However, their task is easier, and it may not require active control so much as a capacity for veto power. Reformists will likewise aim at control of systemically critical games. Their task is harder, in two ways. In the first place, even providing that they can gain access to nodal institutional positions, their goals are always in danger either of being vetoed, or of being absorbed and enmeshed. And in the second place, they may find that the institutional positions which they have struggled to occupy are not so critical as they might have appeared to be, and again their energy is absorbed in a variety of relatively indecisive micro-level games. In effect, then, it can be argued that some institutional structures possess more *decisional capacity* than others – if there really are such critical games, or structural nodal points, to which access can be gained, and over which control can be exercised.

A third pattern of change, one which tends to be privileged in structural analysis as practiced by socio-linguists and anthropologists, results from the differentiation and even incompatibility between micro-level games themselves within the same wider structure. This is *deep-structural* change. Deep-structural change can occur when micro-level structures are characterized by clusters of games with fundamentally dissimilar dynamics – where different clusters have sufficiently opposing rules, stakes, and resource distributions so that tension, conflict, and even contradiction are present.

It may be, for example, that the predominance of one cluster of games, or dimension of deep structure, is undermined by contact and competition between agents involved in that cluster and agents involved in an opposing cluster. It may lead to uncertainty and confusion. It may lead to a creative 'dynamic tension' between different rationalities. It may lead to structural contradiction and even to the concept of an ongoing dialectical struggle, whether between the perennially conflicting requirements of power and justice – as for Plato – or between the class which controls the means of production and the class which includes all the others – as for Marx.

One such perceived tension or contradiction, again an issue discussed as far back as Plato's *Republic*, is that between 'culture and practical reason': the power of ideas and values of a moral or ethical kind, or even of just imagining alternative worlds and being able to orient one's actions to one's ideas, on the one hand; and the requirements of physical survival, material calculation, and cost–benefit analysis on the other.[2] Because the normative requirements on individuals and groups deriving from one set of precepts can conflict with those stemming from the other set, people and societies develop games which sometimes control and balance these requirements, devise rituals and symbols to explain and justify what otherwise might engender cognitive dissonance – or provide a safety valve such as ritual combat or team sports.

However, the tension between them, especially if ideational structures are challenged by changing circumstances or if economic conditions change, can be the cause either of evolutionary, adaptive change, or of crisis and contradiction, which must be resolved by the outcome of real conflict. For anthropologists, such a major – paradigmatic – cultural shift comes when cultures based on kinship relations, which, despite their variability, can be deeply legitimized and 'naturalized' through biological metaphors, come into contact and tension with societies with more developed and specialized state and economic class structures. Such a contradiction impacts upon fundamental conceptions of self, and, in particular, of the body itself. Body rituals and symbols change, represent-ing the deep-structural conflict itself, and potentially symbolizing either adaptation to change – or resistance to it, for those who lose identity, autonomy, or livelihood.[3]

In fact, as will be discussed shortly, many political scientists and sociologists regard processes and sub-structures linked with conceptions of power and authority, on the one hand – the Weberian tradition – to be in ongoing tension with those which derive from relations to the means of production, on the other – the Marxian tradition. On one level, the problem of class is characterized by internal tension or contradiction between classes *per se*; however, on another level, class as a structuring principle can also be seen to be in tension or contradiction with power as a structuring principle, as in much neo-Marxist and post-Marxist state theory and 'regulation theory' (more of which later).

Furthermore, many theorists have derived *both* the state and class from power relations – not only the traditional distinction between the rulers and the ruled which is the basis for the 'predatory theory of the state',[4] but also perspectives such as that of Michel Foucault. Foucault regarded class domination as essentially a system of power relations rather than economic ones, deriving from a substructure itself made up of micro-level power relations; thus he saw the development of modern technologies of surveillance and punishment (prisons, asylums, etc.) as the means of production of new forms of power itself, forms of power which constitute the base from which capitalist class relations spring.[5] Thus modern capitalist society, far from being one which effectively diffuses power through the market, instead effectively concentrates it through the technologies of power (rather than through the ownership of the means of production *per se*). Indeed, the role of technology itself, including such perceived imperatives as maximizing economies of scale, is a key issue running through both class and power analysis.

A fourth pattern of change is stochastic change, a concept from mathematics which brings a different kind of dynamic element into the equation. Stochastic change essentially boils down to the consolidation of luck. We have already argued that due to the complex dispersal of micro-level games, structures are 'sticky', as economists might say of wages and prices, which tend to move up more easily than they move down. In the theory of the firm, for instance, which we will say more about later, a quite dynamic and efficiently organized firm can suffer if that dynamism and efficiency reach their optimum at a time of market instability or falling demand. Once such a firm is down, it may be out; more likely, however, is that it will find its dynamism and efficiency compromised and its internal organization weakened. It may not be able to catch up when better times arrive.

Conversely, a firm which is taking off as good times arrive will find its structures strengthened and its growth stronger and more stable in relation to other firms. Indeed, firms which are successful in this way find their growth rates less likely to fall in bad times, increasing the level of concentration in the industry. Thus the more variability and fluctuations there are in the growth rates of the firm, 'the more rapidly concentrated industry structures will emerge, all other things being equal'.[6] Furthermore, variability is greater for smaller firms, speeding concentration; and industries as well as firms characterized by rapid innovation, design change, and luck with fashion, will leap ahead while, structurally, a miss is as good as a mile. As with firms, it can be argued, political and social structures can change stochastically too.

There are, in fact, many ways in which structures can change, despite the apparent tendency to a certain stability. One of the most widely noted, but most difficult to analyze, causes of social, political, economic, and technological change is what is called the 'demonstration effect'. Quite simply, the fact that change is seen to happen in one part of a structure (or outside the structure) may cause other agents who see the 'demonstration' to try to copy it. This is often remarked upon by analysts of Third World development and of change in Eastern Europe,[7] where Western prosperity has sometimes been referred to as capitalism's 'shop window'. And there is also idiosyncratic change, whether promoted or catalyzed by leaders, social movements, political parties, or whatever, which can include elements from any or all of the above categories. Thus as well as studies of patterns of structural change, old-fashioned 'event history' is needed too in order to study political structuration.

Political structuration, then, is a process in which stasis and change are themselves in ongoing dynamic relationship. It is, then, important to look at different ways in which different 'mixes' of stasis and change are produced. For example, if the games which constitute 'nodal points' of the structure are relatively easily controlled, and relevant agents and resources readily mobilized by strategically placed political actors, then the structure itself can be said to possess greater 'decisional capacity', as we have noted above. Decisional capacity may be needed for political actors to deal 'effectively' with shocks arising from change inside or outside of the structure itself. Generally speaking, we might assume that decisional capacity permits active management of stasis and change in order to optimize the mix (in the view of the controlling agents); of course, however, that depends on the quality of that management, which may actually, in contrast, activate internal or external tensions, create resistance, and the like. Decisional capacity is a potential, contingent on the circumstances: it is not the same as stability over time; and it may or may not actually be realized in practice.

Another state of relative stasis and change which is insufficiently analyzed is that of entropy. Entropy is defined in the *Concise Oxford Dictionary* as 'a measure [from physics] of the unavailability of a system's thermal energy for conversion into mechanical work'. What this means is that so much energy is absorbed by the complex game-playing which constitutes the structure that *although the structure remains stable,* its decisional capacity is reduced. In systems terms, so much energy goes into maintaining the bonds which link the parts of the system that the system remains essentially immobile.

A classic case of this is found, I have argued elsewhere, in the governmental system of the United States, which is characterized by 'Madisonian entropy', the primary cause of which is the complex system of checks and balances built into the constitutional framework – in other words, the complex and absorbing games of politicking at all levels. In a context – in this case, a system of states – where changing structural conditions make a certain degree of decisional capacity necessary to compete, entropy, on the other hand, can create a potential for stagnation.[8] An analogous argument has been made about the French Third and Fourth Republics.[9] Here, too, the problem is not the same as that of stability (or instability); an entropic system can be stable but immobile as well as fragile and vulnerable.

Stasis can thus be either dynamic, or *immobiliste*; change can be creative and dynamic, or disruptive and corrosive. But any of these apparent structural mixes or states of the system is a complex accumulation of withinputs representing both stasis and change at one and the same time – linked in a process where stasis is itself the result of ongoing changes which are articulated with each other, and change can actually represent the juxtaposition of relatively static elements. In all of this, choices made by agents, whether tactical or strategic, of limited or wide-ranging individual impact, can cumulatively exacerbate or absorb tensions, entrench or undermine existing patterns, and can orient and shape the continuing process of dynamic structuration. The concept of political structuration, in turn, will enable us to transcend some apparent paradoxes in political science, to articulate some key structural dynamics and to analyze how they work.

State Theory, Class, and Power

Political science, political sociology, and political economy are characterized by two contrasting traditions – not quite paradigms, but certainly alternative perspectives. The rest of this chapter will deal with them, and their relationship to the process of political structuration. This section focuses on those larger, collective actors which populate the sweep of social history – economic classes, power groups such as elites and masses, and organizational structures like states.* The subsequent section will deal

---

*Cutting across these categories are found other collective actors, more or less organized, such as corporations (especially multinational corporations), trade unions and broader working-class movements, or races and ethnic groups; each of these, interpreted somewhat differently, can of course also be conceptualized as 'interests' in a pluralist political marketplace.

with the concept of the political marketplace, looking both at the theory of pluralism and the opposing views which focus on the 'imperfections' of political markets. Although on certain levels the two traditions overlap, their fundamental assumptions and dynamics are different. Yet they are both necessary for a theory of political structuration.

Most of the theories of politics which are generally labelled 'structural' are those which root their explanations of stasis and change, of political action and outcomes, in specific large-scale 'structures'. Sometimes these structures are said to be perennial, ever-present characteristics of human nature or social order. Sometimes they appear at certain stages in history, whether accidentally (because of contingent or 'conjunctural' factors) or through evolution or revolution. These macro-structures include, in particular: territorial groupings; kinship networks and hierarchies; classes, in the general sense of groupings based on economic inequalities; power structures, or a tendency for society to be divided into 'rulers and ruled', based ultimately on violence and coercion; or cultural and symbolic structures, based on the ways that ideas, perceptions, and the 'rules of the game' themselves are generated, formulated, controlled, or manipulated. As we shall see, the state itself has sometimes been interpreted as constituting such a structure.

Such orthodox structural theories generally attempt to identify which of these macro-structural features or principles are predominant in political life, to argue why a particular one – or a combination of them – is predominant and how they interrelate with the others, and to show how a focus on the particular structural approach in question appears to explain what happens in the real world better than other approaches do. Like many political theories, these approaches often appear in a range of different guises, from more academic attempts at explanation, through doctrines meant to be proselytized in such a way as to lead to political action, to vaguer belief clusters which represent widespread attitudes. The latter two are reflected in different definitions of the word 'ideology'.

The power of such theories often lies not so much at the academic level in their capacity to explain complex phenomena in complex ways – as in their capacity to seem to explain complex things in simple ways. That is why orthodox structural theories frequently require 'health warnings'. One of the most powerful structural theories in history has been racism. Although racism has had its academic adherents and a certain theoretical apparatus, in particular in the study of 'eugenics' in Germany and elsewhere from the late nineteenth century to World War II, it has fundamentally been discredited both intellectually and morally. However, it retains some of its force at the ideological level, not only in terms of government policies such as *apartheid* in South Africa or the doctrines of racist movements in many places in the world, but even more so through widespread political and social attitudes. The idea that there is some sort of hierarchy of different races with unequal attributes (intelligence, moral character, etc.) can seem to explain complex events in a simple way, leading to tragedy and disaster, as has been seen all too often in history.

In attempting to develop an approach based *not* on the determining role of such large-scale structures, but rather on ongoing processes of political structuration, it is therefore necessary to start with some more health warnings. For example, this book will focus on the state as the core structure of political life. However, the modern state – as it has developed in post-feudal and capitalist society – is viewed here not as a reified, determining, large-scale structure analogous to, e.g., race, but as a contingent phenomenon. It is the product of a certain amount of historical accident, of circumstantial choices made by political agents, and of pre-existing structures being in flux due to a wide range of interconnected changes along all of the structural dimensions listed above: changing territorial boundaries and land use; changing kinship structures; changing patterns of economic inequality; changing forms of coercion and violence; changing ways of looking at the world culturally and symbolically; and, of course, classic forms of political conflict and change.

The state, then, can be seen as the crossroads or nodal point at which these changes have jelled. As states became more complex, legitimated, and institutionalized, state structures not only persisted, but came to constitute the overall pattern of games, the contextual framework within which games of other kinds were increasingly to be played. Seen in this light, a fundamentally contingent phenomenon such as the state can appear – and often has appeared, in many guises – as if it were one of the large-scale, deterministic macro-structures discussed above. It is an interesting paradox that the state as such is studied in a non-reified fashion not so much by political scientists as by anthropologists and sociologists, who see the state as one social structure among, and intertwined with, other social structures.

In recent years all social sciences, including political science, have witnessed a very important revival of explicit reference to, and theorizing of, the state. This revival of state theory was sparked off in the late 1960s by works such as Barrington Moore Jr's *Social Origins of Dictatorship and Democracy* or Ralph Miliband's *The State in Capitalist Society*.[10] These developments have for the most part occurred, however, in the higher reaches of political science – in research, at seminars and conferences, etc. – and are only just starting to trickle down to introductory-level teaching and to the conceptualization of the discipline *per se*.[11] Why has this been the case?

The main reason for the slowness of contemporary political science to assimilate the concept of the state has been the inadequacy of the way that contemporary state theory has itself conceptualized the state. State theory has primarily been a response to the dominance in much of Western, especially American, political science of the pluralist paradigm, in which a stable and efficient state consists of little more than a consensus on the rules of the game, a relatively neutral field in which a large universe of diverse and overlapping groups with different interests compete relatively peacefully for shares of power. In this context, the conception of the state as an autonomous structure or independent actor is essentially pathological – a distorting mirror at best, an authoritarian or even totalitarian aberration at worst. Real political stability was seen as analogous to the notion of a stable equilibrium in economics, the result of a complex process of individual or group interactions in a political marketplace, rather than the false stability of authoritative control.

Critics have always charged that pluralism's premium on stable competition was inadequate to explain both underlying structural imbalances of power (the ongoing dominance of particular groups), on the one hand, and large-scale political conflict and upheaval, on the other. Although the pluralist paradigm was at least in part intended to be more scientific and objective than earlier frameworks of analysis, it was actually primarily a normative conception, an attempt to provide a more realistic theory of political stability in general, and democratic stability in particular, than its legal–constitutional or *realpolitik*-based antecedents.

The new state theory was intended to stand in contrast to pluralism in several ways. It rejected the notion of stable equilibrium as either an empirical possibility or a desirable state of affairs; this was at best a façade for suppressed conflict, at worst a mechanism for domination. It focused on the organizational characteristics of the state itself and on how they were and might be manipulated; it saw groups in an unequal struggle to dominate a powerful state apparatus rather than in a game of consensual competition for easily divisible stakes. And it saw the state itself as at least a relatively autonomous structure, at most an independent actor, in this struggle.

State theories, however, in the debate in political science which has stemmed from the paradigmatic inadequacies of pluralism, have suffered from both of the main failings which we identified earlier, and which both involve a certain functionalism: either they tend to derive the state itself – its structure and its autonomous character – from other social structures; or they tend to reify the state, virtually personifying it, by giving it the character of a conscious, rational agent. In the first place, most of these treatments have continued to see the state as exogenously determined, or 'society-centered', deriving the structure and activities of the state in a functionalist fashion from first causes which lie outside of the state itself. There are various levels at which the state is seen as being 'determined' by social forces outside itself.

For example, state positions can be filled by members of particular groups, who continue to pursue the interests of those groups and are able to manipulate the organizational resources of the state to ensure that those interests would prevail and become entrenched in the workings of the system itself. This has been called the 'instrumentalist' thesis; eventually, the state itself becomes the instrument of a governing elite or ruling class. In this case, the autonomy of the state is limited. It may be absent altogether, if the social forces controlling it are also in control of mechanisms which are in the long run more important for overall social or economic control than the state itself, for example through a social hierarchy ('elitism') or through their ownership of the means of production (economistic versions of Marxism).

Or state autonomy may be said to have a somewhat greater scope, constituting one or more critical dimensions of control, without which the power of such exogenous social forces would be more indirect. These dimensions would include control over legal rules and dispute mechanisms (associated mainly with Max Weber's 'legal–rational authority'), control over 'extra-economic coercion' (compatible with both Weberian theory and Marxism), control over conditions of economic competition and profitability (especially important for Marxist and neo-Marxist state theories), control over ideology and culture (in both Weberian analysis and Gramscian neo-Marxism), or control over certain organizational apparatuses which themselves involve or reflect dimensions of social conflict or class struggle (crucial for the neo-Marxist theories of, e.g., Louis Althusser or Nicos Poulantzas). In these cases, state autonomy is only relative, determined 'in the last analysis' by the relationship of exogenous social forces. Thus in 'society-centered' approaches, the state is essentially a function of its social context.[12]

In the second place, in contrast, some new state theories derive the function of the state, in quasi-idealist fashion, from a first cause or basic drive which, as in some of the orthodox structuralist theories which were discussed earlier, make the state itself a fully autonomous, primordial structure. Some of these theories are basically revivals of older theories: that there is a special quality to *public* power, as in classical theories of *potestas*, which give the state a unique role to play in pursuing certain central collective social values such as justice or the common good;[13] that the development of the modern state reflects a quasi-metaphysical, historical progress toward the ideal community, as in Hegel's political philosophy; that the state constitutes a single collective actor in the international field, sometimes called the 'billiard ball school', derived from traditional theories of sovereignty or expressed in contemporary revivals of the notion of *Realpolitik*;[14] or that the state represents and embodies the functional requirement for all societies to have an overarching, cybernetic regulatory system in order to survive.[15]

In each of these cases, the state itself is defined as an essence; it becomes the manifestation of a first cause or primordial deep structure with a categorical imperative. This is difficult to disentangle from reification, the investing of an object with the qualities of a subject, or the confusion of agency and structure – which can lead in turn to a fetishism of the state. This leads to two contrasting problems. The first is that such reification can make it difficult to classify states or analyze the way states work without positing, explicitly or implicitly, that some states are more equal than others – that having a 'true state' is a limited blessing, bestowed only on some 'nation-states' but not on others.[16]

Other countries or political systems, i.e. the majority of what are termed 'states' in another context, more often than not will fall into a fuzzy alternative category such as 'weak states' or even 'non-state societies'[17] (a very different concept from what anthropologists, for example, would call 'non-state societies', i.e., societies lacking a political structure which is differentiated from relatively small-scale kinship hierarchies). Indeed, the main criterion for a 'true state' is usually said to be the effective centralization of power. This is a highly problematic notion to apply and, for example, one which leaves a state like the United States, which has a very strong, legitimate, widely diffused and high-profile state apparatus – but one which is not strongly centralized – as less of a 'true state' than France – with its traditions of upheaval and *anti-civisme* (as well as *étatisme*).

Other versions of this sort of reification pose a second problem, in contrast to the first. The alternative to setting up a category of 'true states', in contradistinction to the others, is to count all states as structurally equivalent or even equal, as in some versions of realist international relations theory. To posit that the formal sovereign equality of states has certain consequences for the operation of international relations is one thing; to assume that states are in a situation of 'anarchy' with respect to each other, and that they are all pursuing increased international power and increased authoritative control, is another.[18]

Given the inadequacies of society-centered and idealist/functional approaches, researchers have been attempting to develop more complex 'state-centered' theories, but these usually suffer either from a lack of clarity about the role of exogenous factors[19] or imply a return to essentialism with its dangers of reification.[20] This is less problematic for writers who are dealing with historical subjects, as they refer to actual historical state structures and not to theoretical constructs. They tend to criticize the application of theories, rather than to offer full-blown alternative theories, relying on a useful eclecticism and arguing for the contingency of historical phenomena, including the state.[21] However, they do not translate this contingency into a theory of state structure itself.

It is more problematic when what writers are doing is in fact merely shifting from one exogenously-derived theory to another while assuming that they are becoming more 'state-centered' in the process. This is what tends to happen when the focus is shifted entirely to 'state actors', who, it has been argued, are themselves autonomous actors, independent (or potentially independent) of the social groups from which they come.[22] Even in this case, however, the state *as structure* is neutralized once again, and the outcome is an even more pronounced behavioral pluralism than before – but based on the individual rationality and free will of state and political office-holders rather than on exogenous social forces. The same is true when the shift is to a Weberian perspective, for the notion of 'authority' or 'the monopoly of legitimate violence' as the basis for the state in fact returns us to a version of *potestas* or the 'true state'; we will return to this later.

In all of these approaches, however, there is an essential missing ingredient – a theory of how structures themselves originate, change, work, and reproduce themselves. Structures can be conceptualized in different ways, as we have to some extent seen already. Blau identifies three main approaches to structure in the sociological literature: structure as a pattern of interactions; structure as positing the prior existence of a structured substratum; and structures as a particular form or pathway for development, especially through the general principle of differentiation as seen by the 'founding fathers' of sociology or theories of organization.[23] But none of these deals with the problem here, which can be defined as attempting to analyze how particular structures – in this case, political structures – may act as independent variables, how they can operate autonomously. At the heart of any theory of structure, as Boudon has argued, is the notion that 'the whole is greater than the sum of its parts'[24] – a philosophical problematic of ancient lineage.

We have already mentioned a number of ways in which contemporary theorists have attempted to explain how the state works. Insofar as the state is seen as 'relatively autonomous', and not as a neutral field, simple instrument, or function, these explanations tend to privilege two sorts of factors: class and power. In the case of class, much neo-Marxist state theory argues (among other things) that while the notion of the state as a simple instrument of class (as in certain traditional versions of Marxist theory, for example) is not tenable, the state in capitalist society is none the less dependent upon the success of capitalism for its own existence, in particular through state dependence on a healthy tax base. Therefore, the state is necessarily driven to preserve, reinforce, and further the interests of capital in its own self-interest. Harder versions of neo-Marxist state theory assert that advanced capitalist society thus becomes characterized by an ever-closer alliance of an increasingly monopolized capital, on the one hand, and an interventionist state, on the other, referred to as 'state monopoly capitalism'.[25]

Another form of neo-Marxist theory sees capital as somewhat less unified, but characterized none the less by an indirect kind of unity-in-diversity. Particular capitalists are driven by the conditions for success of their own 'capitals' (or 'fractions of capital'), i.e., their particular firms or sectors, and are therefore incapable of perceiving or acting to fulfill the wider requirements for the survival and furthering of 'capitalism as a whole'. The latter requires a structure separately constituted from the market and able to control it through 'non-economic coercion'; thus the state 'was constituted' in order to fulfill that function, i.e., to be the 'ideal collective capitalist'.[26]

A third form of contemporary class theory of the state argues that the class struggle itself is reproduced and played out *within* the capitalist state (especially the democratic variety) according to a different set of rules, rules which are partly produced within and through the state itself. In other words, state actors – especially the growing group of lower and middle-level civil servants who constitute the 'new lower middle class' (or 'new petty bourgeoisie') of advanced capitalist society – are increasingly becoming key agents of class struggle, despite (and in some ways because of) the fact that they are situated in a 'contradictory class location' compared to economically-defined groups like capitalists and workers. State actors are becoming key agents because in the advanced capitalist state, state intervention in the economy is continually increasing in order to counteract the growing contradictions of capitalism itself. Therefore the state even becomes the primary 'site' of the class struggle; the relative autonomy of the state consists mainly in that the class struggle is displaced into the state itself and consequently played by the rules of the interventionist state rather than by the rules of an unfettered marketplace.[27]

All of these approaches are significant advances on the more instrumentalist and economistic versions of traditional Marxism, and they certainly support the view that the state in advanced capitalist society must operate very differently on some levels than the state in early capitalist, pre-capitalist or non-capitalist societies. Just as states existing within societies characterized by slave labor have key features reflecting (and reinforcing) that form of economic structure, so too do capitalist states have key features which are inextricably intertwined with capitalism. But there are two objections to the assumption that the nature of the state is therefore determined by capitalism *per se*, as these theories still posit, 'in the last analysis'.

In the first place, they still include a functionalist end-point. While they posit the 'relative autonomy' of the capitalist state, they also claim that the action of that state (as well as the limits on that action) must derive from the nature of the class struggle and capitalism; in other words, the state is only autonomous as a state because – and insofar as – it is a capitalist state. This means, in turn, that it is only possible for the state to act autonomously so long as it is functional to capitalism, and must founder when the contradictions of capital outstrip this relative autonomy. Thus they ignore the question raised by the fact that states with many structural and behavioral characteristics similar to those of capitalist states, but which are not capitalist states but pre-capitalist or non-capitalist states, have not always been constrained in this heavily determined fashion; indeed, states have sometimes maintained their core structures through extreme social transformations and upheavals, often re-emerging to claim the legitimacy of continuity.

In the second place, these approaches give too much coherence to the notion of class. Class is the most important category of stratification in capitalist society, but it does coexist with other forms of stratification; its delineation is not at all clear (as evidenced in the attention paid to the petty bourgeoisie by neo-Marxist theorists); the perception of class identity is often confused; and class is a most insecure basis upon which to predicate political and social activity much of the time. These issues cannot be explained away merely by referring to the coexistence of different modes of production, with capitalism only as the dominant mode, or by reviving intermediate classes, or saying that the economic base is determining 'in the last analysis', in order to force other categories of action and structure into particular pigeonholes. Thus the huge significance of class does not eliminate its weaknesses as the ultimate source of explanation for the operation of the state (among other things).

In the case of power, the other main category used to explain how the state works, sociologists and political scientists generally tend to fall back upon certain well-known perennial themes: the arguments of Thrasymachos in Plato's *Republic*; the 'Hobbesian problematic' of human survival and the need for order prior to the search for other values; or Weber's contention that the defining characteristic of the state (as compared with other social structures) is that in the last resort it can claim the 'monopoly of legitimate violence'. In the Weberian version, it is the combination of such ultimate power with the voluntary or internalized compliance called 'authority', rationalized through 'legitimacy', which is the state's core characteristic. Indeed, the modern state is seen as specifically characterized by a particular form of power/authority, the 'legal–rational' form, which has an internally differentiated and special-ized, and externally expanding, bureaucratic structure.

The notion of power is even more important, however, insofar as it provides perhaps the most important linking concept between the state and wider notions of 'politics'. Perhaps the most widespread working definition of politics involves the primacy of power;[28] if the defining characteristic of politics is seen as power, then a definition of the state as embodying 'legitimate power' or authority provides a key structural linkage in the uneasy conceptual coexistence of politics and the state.

However, the use of power as a core definition of either politics or the state is problematic in a number of ways. In the first place, the concept of power badly captures a number of aspects of politics itself – in particular, activities of cooperation, the search for values such as a better society or justice, and the like. To do something because people think that it is right, or because they think that they are involved in a positive-sum game and therefore cooperate spontaneously, may be intertwined with power relations too, but they are not the same thing.

In the second place, power, although often seen as a defining characteristic of politics, is also frequently seen as a fundamental characteristic of social relations generally, as in much sociological theory; it is in fact characteristic of an immensely wide variety of activities and structures in society. One might, of course, conclude simply that politics is everywhere, but this rather begs the question of the specificity of politics. Given that politics is, at the very least, much more than mere power, and that power is, at the very least, much more than mere politics, it may of course be necessary to look to other definitions.

And finally, this also leaves the concept of the state as the repository of legitimate power, or authority, in limbo. Even if we merely take the 'monopoly of legitimate violence' to be a key characteristic of the state, as Weber does, it reflects only a limiting case, and a questionable one at that. The state involves much more than sanctioning or coercing those within (or outside) its jurisdiction; it comprises activities of much greater range, scope and depth, whether in terms of the production of culture or the promotion of social and economic activities. These may serve to legitimate power structures too, of course; thus cooperation and acquiescence can be internalized, which is cheaper and more efficient than widespread repression. But again, they are not the same thing. All in all, then, despite the perennial problematic which the concepts of power and authority reflect, they are ultimately rather blunt instruments for the analysis of political structuration.

Therefore class and power are both too general and too specific to be the determining characteristic of political structuration. In basing their rejection of the pluralist paradigm on these conceptual alternatives, the more recent state theorists have provided an inadequate basis for a theorizing about political structures and institutions in a non-society-centered, non-functionalist and non-reified way. This has led to a revival of pluralism, not only among the traditional liberal-democratic variety of pluralists, but also among anti-statist radicals who see the future of socialism in capturing civil society, rather than the state, through 'new social movements',[29] or among those Marxists and 'post-Marxists' who see a truer pluralism, not distorted by domination of class or power, as something which not only must be achieved in a future socialist society but also in the present, in order to point the way forward.[30]

Pluralism and Political Structuration

The state theories which we have criticized above have been in the tradition of what we have called 'orthodox' structural theories, positing the presence and the explanatory power of large-scale underlying structural phenomena which directly or indirectly determine the long-term pattern of constraints and opportunities affecting the behavior of individual or group agents. Whether the state itself is seen as the 'primary' structure, or as an epiphenomenon of class or power, history is seen as shaped by large forces, which may be static or changing, but in which the autonomy of agents is generally closely constrained. The strategic and tactical choices of agents are limited to jockeying for place or position within the structure (usually called 'relational power') – except under highly specific structural conditions, such as exploiting weak points or even contradictions embodied in the structure, or expressing symbolic resistance. Pluralism, which has been primarily – and consciously – concerned with relational power,[31] has often been dismissed as missing the forest (wider structures of power, sometimes called 'meta-power')[32] for the trees.

Nevertheless, alternative approaches have not mounted the effective paradigmatic challenge which they seemed to promise just a few years ago. But this does not mean that the weaknesses of pluralism have been surmounted. On the one hand, pluralism as a paradigm seems regularly in crisis, as its ideological predisposition to liberal democracy and its straightforward methodology of the study of easily identifiable groups have continued to experience problems with explaining deep and persisting disparities in group power. On the other hand, alternative approaches have had continuing difficulties in coming to terms with the robust multiplicity and variety of active groups and interests in society, a multiplicity and variety which tend to undermine the explanatory power of large-scale structures.

Pluralism owes its durability and revival – its capacity to 'bounce back'[33] – to its central conception of politics as a market, in which people and groups with different interests compete. Of course, a market is also a structure. But it is somewhat different from what we have called an orthodox structure, i.e., a large-scale structure characterized by features which determine the broad outcomes of agents' choices (generally falling into Blau's second and third categories – a structured substratum or a particular form or pathway with which structures must conform as they develop). Rather it is like one version of Blau's first category, a pattern of interactions. Ideal-type markets would be built from the bottom up through a cumulative process in which separate, discrete choices based on individual (or group) preferences are supposed to aggregate into patterns of collective choice – although both theory and reality are in fact much more complex.*

How those patterns of collective choice work – how stable or unstable they will be, or how efficient or inefficient they will be – will differ from interpretation to interpretation. In classic liberal democratic pluralism, the difficulties associated with attempts to ground the political marketplace on participatory democracy (a perennial problematic of democratic theory in both ancient and modern times) were thought to be at least partially remedied; this was done by grounding political markets not in individuals, but in voluntary associations, interest groups, and other social categories with common points of identification. Individuals would choose the groups which they wished to associate with; they could enter, participate (or not), and leave, an overlapping or cross-cutting mix of groups in accord with their personal preferences.

However, at a second level of political market interaction, the groups would then compete (or combine, or conflict) with each other in a 'second circuit of representation'; this would not involve the direct representation of individual preferences, but would, at least in theory, be more linked to ongoing interests and preferences than classic representative democracy was. Rousseau's dictum that the English were free only once every five years was to be transcended through an indirect, but more responsive, market for the representation of groups.[34]

This sort of approach marked a particular kind of paradigmatic shift in democratic theory and the role of groups within it. Just as merchants and financiers were widely regarded as greedy and pathological parasites and usurers prior to the development of eighteenth-century capitalist economic theory by Adam Smith and others, groups had traditionally been regarded, from Plato to Rousseau and Madison, as 'factions'. Factions, because they were seen to be seeking power (and usually wealth too) at the expense of competing or conflicting groups, were thus similarly seen to be inherently dangerous to the common weal.[35]

Madison sought to tame them through enmeshing them in an institutional separation of powers and federal structure.[36] Pluralism saw them as incorporating principles of voluntary cooperation and collective values as well as greed and self-interest, and sought to enmesh them in a relatively open political marketplace in which their enlightened self-interest could be maximized and their misanthropic tendencies harnessed. However, such a political marketplace could only work in a stable and efficient way if it could be assumed, as in classical economic theory, that markets

---

*In fact, the institutionalization of market systems requires the authoritative establishment of rules of the game which are meant, again in theory, to maximize the range of choices that agents can make, simultaneously maximizing market efficiency while circumscribing alternatives which undermine the market system itself.

characterized by genuine (if not ideally perfect) competition would tend to move toward a state of stable equilibrium – that pathological claims would cancel each other out, and that a sort of political price mechanism could operate efficiently. In such a process, the structure of the market would emerge spontaneously from free political exchange and the aggregation of preferences.

It is this problematic conceptualization of politics as a market which has been the crucial point of attack for critics of pluralism. On the one hand, pluralism's orthodox structural rivals – such as elitism, class analysis, corporatism and state theory – assert that the political marketplace is fundamentally skewed because of structural asymmetries in society and the economy. These structural biases not only limit the scope for individual rational choice, but also prevent the emergence of stable equilibria grounded in the spontaneous aggregation of individual or group preferences. On the other hand, recent developments in rational choice analysis and public choice theory have focused on other problems of bottom-up collective choice, following up a number of paths which analyze various difficulties which emerge in the aggregation of private choices into public choices.[37]

We have already argued that orthodox structural theories have problems with the multiplicity and variety of agents which characterize the political bazaar. At the same time, rational choice analysis is having to question a number of postulates about the nature of choice which have usually been assumed away both in economic theory and in much public choice theory: issues such as the bounded nature of rationality; the amorphous, fluctuating, and incommensurable nature of preferences; the presence of highly imperfect information; or the biases and manipulability of decision-making procedures, are coming to the fore.

For even relatively 'efficient' markets are not peopled by atomistic, competitive individuals, engaged in ongoing processes of cost–benefit analysis. Markets in the real world generate organizational structures characterized by institutionalized collaboration or cooperation as well as competition and conflict. These organizational structures are therefore characterized by problems of control as well as by problems of choice, and it is the mix of problems of choice and control over a *range* of game-like structures and substructures which constitutes the 'structured field of action'.[38] Furthermore, economic markets are themselves made up of hierarchical organizations – firms – and not just market-rational individuals. Thus the dividing line between market behavior and organizational behavior is more complex than a simplistic notion of individual choice permits.

It is possible, then, to analyze interest groups in the political marketplace – the core subject matter of pluralism – not in the paradigmatic context of a self-regulating liberal-democratic ideal type, but rather in a fashion analogous to the way institutional or organizational economic theories approach the activities of firms and cartels in the economic marketplace. Theory of the firm and cartel theory not only provide more satisfactory explanatory hypotheses for the behavior of political groups than do orthodox structural theories with their exogenous variables or functional imperatives; they also provide better and more interesting explanations than do many interpretations of the market-*versus*-government problem in current public choice theory, which, as we shall see, often involves a number of manichean assumptions about structures of allocation.

Thus it ought to be possible to consider hypothetically how the dynamics of a plural universe of interest competition can result in a limited universe of structured collaboration and control, because of, and not in spite of, the way markets work. What is needed, then, is, again, an approach to the theory of groups based neither on orthodox structures nor on the mere aggregation of individual choices – but grounded in an ongoing process of political structuration. After considering in the next chapter some of the core structural elements and field patterns which are characteristic of such a process, we will in Chapter 3 focus more closely on the dynamics of political structuration and at the insights which can be gained by borrowing and adapting certain concepts from institutional economics and some recent public choice theory, in order to construct a typology of processes of political allocation.

Conclusions

In summary, then, the emergence and expansion of state structures has been the dominant characteristic of political development in recent centuries. In order to understand this development, it is necessary to have a theory of structural and institutional formation and change. On the one hand, however, orthodox structural approaches have suffered from a number of problems. Structures do constrain the process and impact of choice, but many of the most compelling are overly simplistic, positing the deterministic role of *a priori* large-scale structural features and principles; they can often be too static in practice. Furthermore, these large-scale structures either are usually too society-centered, and treat the state as an epiphenomenon; or they overly reify the state in functionalist fashion. On the other hand, pluralist approaches, which take their cue from the ideal-type concept of an 'efficient', self-regulating political marketplace, have difficulty explaining structural biases and control mechanisms. What is needed is an analysis which looks at political structures such as states as processes of structuration – as complex patterns of ongoing but uneven interactions between agents and structures, and as complex mixes of stasis and change.

Notes

1. Crozier and Friedberg, *L'acteur et le système*, *op. cit.*

2. See Marshall Sahlins, *Culture and Practical Reason* (Chicago, Ill.: University of Chicago Press, 1966). In sociology, somewhat analogous concepts are the basis of the mainstream tradition represented by, e.g., Durkheim, Weber and Tönnies; cf. Ferdinand Tönnies, *Community and Association* (East Lansing, Mich.: Michigan State University Press, 1957 [originally published as *Gemeinschaft und Gesellschaft*, 1887]).

3. Jean Comaroff, *Body of Power, Spirit of Resistance: The Culture and History of a South African People* (Chicago, Ill.: University of Chicago Press, 1985).

4. See Margaret Levi, 'The Predatory Theory of Rule', *Politics & Society*, vol. 10, no. 4 (1981), pp. 431–65. Predatory theories also contribute to variants of Marxism, for instance seeing the predatory state as the product of the need, in late feudalism/early capitalism, for the 'primitive accumulation' of capital, with the role of the state undergoing a fundamental later transformation into a full-blown capitalist state, first under mercantile capitalism and then under industrial capitalism; debates in Marxism on the role of imperialism, as well as of the role of the state as 'collective capitalist', often see the predatory phase as simply an earlier functional version of the 'extra-economic coercion' which capitalism requires from the state.

5. See Michel Foucault, *Power/Knowledge: Selected Interviews and Other Writings, 1972–1977*, edited by Colin Gordon (New York: Pantheon Books, 1980).

6. F.M. Scherer, *Industrial Market Structure and Economic Performance* (Boston: Houghton Mifflin, 2nd edn, 1980), p. 48.

7. Janos, *Politics and Paradigms, op. cit.*, pp. 84–95.

8. P.G. Cerny, 'Political Entropy and American Decline', *Millennium: Journal of International Studies*, vol. 18, no. 1 (Spring 1989).

9. Stanley Hoffmann, 'Paradoxes of the French Political Community', in Hoffmann *et al.*, eds., *In Search of France* (Cambridge, Mass.: Harvard University Press, 1963), pp. 1–117.

10. Barrington Moore Jr, *Social Origins of Dictatorship and Democracy: Landlord and Peasant in the Making of the Modern World* (Harmondsworth, Mddx: Allen Lane, 1967); Ralph Miliband, *The State in Capitalist Society* (London: Weidenfeld and Nicolson, 1969).

11. In American political science, the questions raised by state theory are only now coming to be addressed by those in the behavioralist and formalist mainstream; see the symposium on 'The Return to the State' in the *American Political Science Review*, vol. 82, no. 3 (September 1988), pp. 853–904.

12. For a critique of 'society-centered' theories of the state, see Gordon L. Clark and Michael Dear, *State Apparatus: Structures of Language and Legitimacy* (London: Allen & Unwin, 1984).

13. Theories which accompanied the consolidation of the modern state in France and Germany often involved the renewal of Graeco-Roman philosophies of the *res publica*, transferring this responsibility for defining and pursuing the public good from the king and/or the church to the state apparatus; see Kenneth Dyson, *The State Tradition in Western Europe* (Oxford: Martin Robertson, 1980).

14. As in contemporary 'realist' and 'neo-realist' theories of international relations; see Stephen Krasner, *Structural Conflict: The Third World Against Global Liberalism* (Berkeley and Los Angeles: University of California Press, 1985).

15. See David Easton, *The Political System* (New York: Knopf, 1953).

16. This is the trap which theorists such as Pierre Birnbaum tend to fall into; cf. Bertrand Badie and Pierre Birnbaum, *The Sociology of the State* (Chicago: University of Chicago Press, 1983), and Birnbaum, *La logique de l'État* (Paris: Fayard, 1982).

17. Badie and Birnbaum, *op. cit.*, use the category of 'weak states'; Dyson, *op. cit.*, uses that of 'non-state societies'.

18. For an excellent critique of the terminology of contemporary neo-realism in international relations, see Helen Milner, 'Anarchy and Interdependence', paper delivered at the annual meeting of the American Political Science Association, Washington, D.C., 1–4 September 1988.

19. Clark and Dear, *op. cit.*

20. Despite her devastating critique of other theories, Theda Skocpol would seem to be vulnerable to this charge; see 'Bringing the State Back In: Strategies of Analysis in Current Research', in Peter Evans, Dietrich Rueschemeyer and Theda Skocpol, eds., *Bringing the State Back In* (Cambridge: Cambridge University Press, 1985), pp. 3–37.

21. E.g., R.J. Holton, *The Transition from Feudalism to Capitalism* (London: Macmillan, 1985), or Geoffrey Ingham, *Capitalism Divided? The City and Industry in British Social Development* (London: Macmillan, 1984).

22. As is so well argued in Eric A. Nordlinger, *On the Autonomy of the Democratic State* (Cambridge, Mass.: Harvard University Press, 1981).

23. Peter M. Blau, 'Introduction: Parallels and Contrasts in Structural Inquiries', in Blau, ed., *Approaches to the Study of Social Structure* (London: Open Books, 1976).

24. Raymond Boudon, *The Uses of Structuralism* (London: Heinemann, 1971).

25. See Bob Jessop, *The Capitalist State: Marxist Theories and Methods* (Oxford: Martin Robertson, 1982), especially ch. 2.

26. See John Holloway and Sol Picciotto, eds., *State and Capital: A Marxist Debate* (London: Edward Arnold, 1978), especially ch. 5, 'The State Apparatus and Social Reproduction: Elements of a Theory of the Bourgeois State', by Joachim Hirsch.

27. See Nicos Poulantzas, *Classes in Capitalist Society* (London: New Left Books, 1975); cf. Carnoy, *State and Political Theory, op. cit.*

28. See Peter Nicholson, 'Politics and Force', in Leftwich, ed., *What is Politics?, op. cit.*, ch. 2.

29. Alain Touraine, *L'après-socialisme* (Paris: Grasset, 1980).

30. See Paul Q. Hirst, 'Retrieving Pluralism', in William Outhwaite and Michael J. Mulkay, eds., *Social Theory and Social Criticism: Essays Presented to Tom Bottomore* (Oxford: Basil Blackwell, 1987), pp. 154–74.

31. The classic presentation of this position is often seen to be Robert A. Dahl's *A Preface to Democratic Theory* (Chicago: University of Chicago Press, 1956).

32. Cf. the discussion in Krasner, *op. cit.*, pp. 14–18; the more complex classic treatment in Steven Lukes, *Power: A Radical View* (London: Macmillan, 1974); the extrapolation of the argument to the dimension of powerlessness, in John Gaventa, *Power and Powerlessness: Quiescence and Rebellion in an Appalachian Valley* (Urbana: University of Illinois Press, 1980); and the recent reformulation of the argument in Walter Korpi, 'Power Resources Approach *vs.* Action and Conflict: On Causal Intentional Explanation in the Study of Power', *Sociological Theory*, vol. 3, no. 2 (1985), pp. 31–45.

33. A. Grant Jordan, 'In Defence of Pluralism, or Why it Keeps Bouncing Back', paper presented to the annual conference of the Political Studies Association of the United Kingdom, Plymouth Polytechnic, 12–14 April 1988.

34. See David A. Truman, *The Governmental Process: Political Interests and Public*

Opinion (New York: Knopf, 1951); also Arthur F. Bentley, *The Process of Government: A Study of Social Pressures* (Chicago: University of Chicago Press, 1908).

35. Giovanni Sartori, *Parties and Party Systems* (Cambridge: Cambridge University Press, 1976).

36. Alexander Hamilton, John Jay and James Madison, *The Federalist* (New York: New American Library, 1961 [originally published 1788]), papers 10 and 47.

37. See Mancur Olson, *The Logic of Collective Action* (Cambridge, Mass.: Harvard University Press, 1971).

38. Crozier and Friedberg, *op. cit.*; see also Peter A. Hall's concept of institutional analysis, in his *Governing the Economy op. cit.*, ch. 1; Oliver E. Williamson, *Markets and Hierarchies* (New York: Free Press, 1975); Peter M. Jackson, *The Political Economy of Bureaucracy* (London: Philip Allan, 1982); and James G. March and Johan P. Olsen, 'The New Institutionalism: Organizational Factors in Political Life', *American Political Science Review*, vol. 78, no. 3 (September 1984), pp. 734–49.

2

The Elements of Structure

Developing a theory of political structuration requires the articulation of several different kinds and levels of analysis. One can start from a number of angles. First, one can take the macro level of political structures and break them down into their component parts. It is then possible to look at the ways that those parts cluster, to distinguish the different levels on which they operate, to locate the uncontrollable 'spaces' and tensions within and between those parts and levels, and ultimately to attempt to evaluate the extent to which political outcomes are structurally *indeterminate*. To the extent that outcomes are structurally indeterminate, they are potentially manipulable by agents.

A second, alternative angle, would be to start with the problems presented by the concepts of individual rationality and rational choice, to look at the limits of agents' understanding and potential leverage – and the sets of possible alternative choices with which they are presented in both hypothetical and real situations – and to see how particular patterns emerge, reproduce themselves, and change over time. A third angle of approach would be to identify various structural 'fields' which may hypothetically surround and link both particular structures and relevant agents (as geographers do). It would then be possible to describe and analyze over time the ways in which specific observed structural linkages change – whether in response to wider structural changes, or to the ongoing effects of agents' choices, or to certain observed characteristics of the fields themselves. Agents' actions can thus be seen in strategic and tactical terms.

All of these angles of approach, of course, are basically focused on the same phenomena – but each of them tells us something different about those phenomena. In the rest of Part I we will look at these angles in turn. In this chapter we will look at different elements and building blocks of political structure from the 'top down', focusing on the variety of those elements, the explicit and implicit tensions and ambiguities which exist within the interstices of those structures, and the ways in which change can occur at a structural level. In Chapter 3 we will look at the dynamics of choice and control, and in particular, at the dialectic of market and hierarchy as principles of action – how agents act and choose different options in a range of structural situations. And in Chapter 4 we will look at the 'structure of structuration' of the state: the different ways that state structuration actually works; and how the state itself has developed as the central linkage mechanism and set of channels for shaping agents' choices in relation to both the external or transnational field, on the one hand, and the internal socio-economic field, on the other.

Causes and Consequences of State Formation

It is essential to the argument of this book that political structures are not viewed simply as the functions of primordial deep structures, nor of atomistic rational choice, nor of their internal and external fields *per se*. Rather, we see them as essentially *contingent* phenomena, resulting partially from historically specific combinations and configurations of all three of these angles on the structuration process. Structures arise from non-replicable, unique mixtures of historical accident, coincidence, precedents (reinterpreted and refashioned in new circumstances), and design. Once established, however, structural patterns tend, in a probabilistic fashion, to be reproduced, whether because of biases built into the structures themselves, or the expectations held by agents, or the linkages built into structural fields. They build into coherent processes of development.

However, these structural patterns are ever-changing under the surface. They can evolve in an incremental fashion, whether from structural tendencies or because they are 'steered' in certain directions by the intentional actions of agents (or the unintended consequences of such actions). They can decay or even collapse – whether they fall of their own accord, or are pushed by agents. And, in certain relatively rare circumstances and conjunctures, they can be refashioned, or even transcended, through internal developmental trends, by external forces, by the design of agents, or by a process of accident and coincidence – just as they emerged in the first place. Structure cannot exist without history, and history takes place within – and reacts back upon – specific structural contexts.

The emergence of the state, whether in more general terms, as in the 'early' state,[1] or in the modern version,[2] exemplifies the way that an essentially contingent and polycausal generation process can result in a relatively coherent, homogeneous, and structurally durable result. In fact, empirical historical and anthropological studies of the state seem to indicate that there is no single class of exogenous causes or primordial imperatives of state formation and development. Instead, states manifest and develop certain complex analogous characteristics of an *existential* and situational, rather than essential or functionalist, kind. Anthropological studies of the origins of particular states, for example, have tended to cluster around two contrasting forms of explanation which are generally familiar in political science and sociology: on the one hand, conflict between unequal social strata can lead to one group's domination, which then becomes institutionalized, and subsequently tends to reproduce itself; and on the other, patterns of cooperation develop out of activities which have to be performed in concert, and those patterns likewise reproduce themselves.

The first type focuses on class and power, and conflict and domination; the second on the emergence of a common interest or consensus. What is perhaps even more interesting than these and other views about early state formation, however, is Cohen's conclusion from his own work, and from surveying the literature, that whatever the causes of state formation in particular cases, the *results* are not dissimilar.[3] Identifiable political structures emerge, at least partially separated out from all-embracing kinship structures; they comprise embryonic sets of specialized offices and positions the holders of which carry out a range of tasks and activities including rule-making, dispute-settling, social and economic steering, administration, or war-and-peace-making. Thus the most interesting aspect of state formation is the suggestion that early states, once in the process of formation, develop an analogous internal logic; they come to behave like each other to some extent, regardless of the social context in which they were formed and in which they operate. In effect, different contingent origins lead to comparable structural consequences.

The concept of the 'early state', however, is a very general one, as we have pointed out earlier; it includes any relatively centralized apparatus ruling over and, especially, combining pre-state and/or non-state groups into a single political unit. Most early state formation, however, was in some way related to external contact between pre-state or non-state groups, or between such groups and other groups already having some form of state,* rather than deriving solely from internal factors. In the modern state, which began to emerge in the post-feudal period in Europe, external contact was central to the formative process.[4] Such external contact has been significant on at least four levels: (1) dynastic and military conflict between emerging European states themselves in the post-feudal period; (2) conquest of other parts of the world by European states or colonizers, imposing state-like apparatuses on other societies (eventually leading to independence movements and a host of 'new states'); (3) economic interaction between states, leading to rivalry and competition promoted by state apparatuses themselves; and (4)

---

*The concept of 'tribe' in anthropology is as contested as the concept of 'state'. Tapper, among others, points out that the term 'tribe' has been used to cover a wide range of very different structural forms, and that the label is one which only comes into use when it is applied to a group by outsiders – in particular, by state administrations seeking to control the activities of previously autonomous groups which fall within a state's self-defined jurisdiction. Richard Tapper, 'Anthropologists, Historians and Tribespeople on Tribe and State Formation in the Middle East', in Philip Khoury and Joseph Kostiner, eds., *Tribe and State Formation in the Middle East* (Cambridge, Mass.: M.I.T. Press, forthcoming).

the 'demonstration effect', or conscious and unconscious copying of seemingly 'successful' or 'effective' state forms by elites (and masses) in other areas.

State formation, then, involves the complex interaction of internal and external factors. It is shaped by actors operating strategically in historically specific circumstances – aware of a limited range of existing structural possibilities, concerned with exploiting their room for maneuver, and, in some cases, seeking to explore new possibilities. The particular structural forms which emerge then constitute: (1) the psychological and physiological environment in which they make strategic and tactical choices (their awareness of and capacity to process the vast amount of potential information which flows around them); (2) the physical environment in which such choices are made (the limits of the technology made available by and through the structure, and the availability of many resources); (3) the sociological environment (whether other agents, consciously or unconsciously, act individually or collectively to constrain the range and scope of choice); and (4) the external environment discussed above. State structures have systematic, if not wholly determining, consequences for future action. They can be expected to reproduce themselves to the extent that they in turn shape these various environments in which strategic and tactical choices are made.

The Elements of Structure: What States and State Actors Do

What states and state actors do, in effect, is to create conditions within which other actors, and future actors, make choices which *re-create* the main lines of existing structures under changing historical conditions. They cause actors to make choices which have the effect of reproducing those structures. They do this by working to shape the various environments set out above. State structures and state actors are not, of course, the only forces working to shape these environments; the development of communications and information, of technology and economic structure, of social stratification, and of transnational structures, all shape these environments too. But the choices of state actors and the structural biases or internal logics of state structures have a particularly important role to play – especially as they occupy a unique strategic position at the 'crossroads' of social life and between domestic social life and the states system.[5]

State structures can be broken down into a number of structured tasks and activities. In this section we will briefly consider four sets of these tasks and activities, and will try to show how they, the actors performing them, and the structured linkages between them, all have an impact on each of the environments listed above. Together, therefore, these structured tasks and activities play a major role in shaping social choice and reproducing existing structural patterns, albeit in changing circumstances. However, as we have already pointed out, these structured tasks and activities involve a number of different 'games', often with different structural logics. In real historical circumstances, there are tensions between games, between actors, and between the state and other structural forces. Where the games are closely linked, by common habits and preconceptions, by strong controlling mechanisms, by common external pressures to conform, etc., then the tendency for state structure to reproduce itself will be more likely to manifest itself. Where the spaces and tensions between the logics of different games are wider and stronger, other forces, whether manifested through specific agents or through structural crises, will be more important in shaping society.

The four sets of tasks and activities (or of games) which we will focus on are: (1) the definition of 'society' itself, i.e., the boundaries and the character of the community or social unit; (2) the process by which different individuals and groups gain access to office and influence in the state (what is usually referred to more narrowly as the 'political process'); (3) the mechanisms by which the internal organization of the state is controlled and resources allocated, i.e., the 'state apparatus'; and (4) the way that specific decisions by state actors and specific biases in allocation processes impact on the wider society. The first includes what is sometimes referred to as the 'legitimation function' of the state, but this is much too narrow; we are talking about shaping the social bond itself. The second, as we have said, covers 'politics' in the limited sense of competition for 'political power' (rather than for social or economic power, for example). The third concerns not just bureaucracy and administration as such, but also many regularized processes in which state actors and organized social actors bargain over the allocation of resources and values which are more or less in the gift of the state. And the fourth concerns not only state intervention in the economy, but also its wider 'steering capacity' in terms of shaping the structure of social stratification; affecting the distribution of values, rewards, and power between individuals and groups; and manipulating expectations about future options.

The Modern State and the Construction of Society

The idea of 'society' is characterized by a central ambiguity. At one level, it involves the notion of a 'social bond', a set of interlocking relationships between individuals and groups which comprise a rich texture of interactions whether based on a drive for survival, or power and authority, or exchange, or 'natural' relationship structures such as kinship, or structures of class and stratification, or language and symbolism, etc. This is the 'fabric', 'stuff', or 'warp and woof' of society, an often-used metaphor evoking images of textiles, with their individual threads being integrated and shaped into an identifiable collective cloth. This social fabric not only has tremendous strength (in contrast with its separate threads) but also a clear pattern which can be compared to other patterns, an aesthetic design which evokes deep responses, and key forces in its creation and production – from the implied existence of designers, weavers, pattern-makers, etc., through the ways in which textiles are themselves used and exchanged, to notions such as faults, renderings, holes and splits in the fabric, as well as the possibility of mending and renewal.

This sort of metaphor – like another of the central metaphors used for society, that of health – focuses on the internal constitution of society. At the same time, however, the idea of society in the modern world has another level which is partially obscured by an emphasis on the social fabric: that is the notion of 'society' as a particular social *unit*, a frame or set of boundaries within which the society is contained. This is not simply society, but 'a' society or 'the' society. The latter also implies a system of 'societies' in the plural, seen not only as differently structured social fabrics (which can be compared), but also as an environment in which other societies, taken as discrete units, are themselves at least partially unitary actors. So when we talk about Britain, or France, or China, or (more problematically, of course) Lebanon, as 'a society', we are implying that they have not only different social fabrics, but also clearly-bounded collective identities and capacities for unified action. Furthermore, we are implying that the internal limits to social action, and the character of the society as a unit, are to a significant extent created and formed in and through external action and, consequently, by the nature of interaction between societies and the character of the wider intersocietal environment.

These two different dimensions of society, as fabric and as unit, are not merely different dimensions of the same concept, but are in many ways different concepts, referring to different kinds of reality. In the language we have used earlier, they are different sets of different kinds of games, with different logics. There are gaps or interstitial spaces between them; there are different dynamics to their development; and there are built-in structural tensions between them. Therefore the ways that they are articulated with each other in real historical situations are not given, but problematic. Within these situations, agents have varying possibilities for action in different historical circumstances. The formation of social structures involves the active structuration of linkage mechanisms – through which boundaries are established, channels constructed, gates kept and goals pursued – (a) between the fabric of society and the unit level, (b) between different kinds of social fabrics in cross-cutting 'transnational' contexts, and (c) between different social units. In the modern world generally – the long period stretching from the post-feudal period to today – the central linkage mechanism between the social fabric and the social unit, and between different social units, has been the state, and state actors have had an integral capacity to influence that process in a variety of circumstances and conjunctures.

On one level, this means that we have to question the common idea that 'states' are superstructures which arise or are formed out of and on top of the base or substructure of the social fabric – that political systems are a function of underlying social inputs. For in many ways, the state, in and through its own process of structuration, itself produces, or is a key factor in producing, the 'society' itself – especially *as social unit*. Buzan notes that we are perpetuating a misconception by using the term 'nation-state', for this implies that the 'nation' (as social unit) emerges from a natural process of social formation, out of which a 'state' develops. Instead of the 'nation-state', he argues, although it may jar the eye or ear, it might be better to refer to the 'state-nation'.[6] We will examine the nature and consequences of this kind of conceptualization in more detail in Chapter 4, looking at the ways that the state interacts with both other societies/states and with other endogenous socio-economic structures. For the moment, however, we are concerned only with suggesting that states, and state actors, have an ongoing, central, and autonomous influence upon the construction of 'society'. In fact, this influence means not only that the state has an integral impact on the construction of the social unit, but also that by thus setting the boundaries to, and influencing the fundamental design of, several principal dimensions of the 'social fabric', the state also shapes the internal structure of that fabric. It does this not just by imposing its power or its supposed monopoly of legitimate violence; it does this by influencing the structuration of society itself in particular historical situations.

States do this in several ways. In the first place, the structural biases which particular states develop historically, and the state actors which populate those state structures, shape several fundamental and salient dimensions of the psychological environment in which micro-level games are played. For example, as state structures emerge and develop, they are involved in structural rivalry with other socio-economic structures – the church, families or clans, existing regional or local loyalties, social elites and dominant economic classes, and the like. A key part of this rivalry is competition for the emotional loyalty of contested groups and individuals, especially those which possess and represent key resources. In this competition, probably the most important resource which the state can develop and build upon is the way in which cultural orientations are themselves formed and manipulated. Thus the state is, for instance, in competition with churches for control of the moral and ethical preconceptions which ordinary people apply every day.* If people regard the state as the legitimate source of a value such as justice – and not a church hierarchy or the patriarchal head of a clan – then it does not require so much physical force or economic inducement to spread spontaneous state-supportive behavior more widely and to root it more deeply. The state will be seen as rightly sovereign rather than as predatory, thus economizing on physical resources and drastically reducing costs.

The important thing is to influence the language and symbolism of legitimacy, in other words to shape the internalized responses of individual and group agents *before* they have to make specific choices on how they play specific games. State structures can therefore be made to appear as natural, and not as the contingent constructions that they really are. By making the symbolism of state sovereignty central to the language of societies, by allying the emotional power of *Gemeinschaft* to the 'objective' rationality of state-sponsored *Gesellschaft*, and by including and integrating wider groups and individuals through ideological concepts which have been associated with the language of the state rather than the languages of competing structures – concepts such as the common interest, progress, freedom, equality before the law, the rights of the individual, etc. – the state can become not only valued directly, but also quite simply taken for granted.[7]

As well as influencing the psychological environment of social formation, the modern state, in ways which are perhaps more obvious, influences its physical and material environment too. Although the development of technology in general is the result of a complex process involving a number of different structural influences, none the less key technologies which have been fundamental to the construction of the social order have been developed under the aegis of, or promoted for the purposes of, the state. Perhaps the most obvious of these have been the technologies of war, or those which have derived from military technology (today called 'spillover'). The development of metal and textile production, of ship-building, of communications technology, of energy technology, and the like, have all been shaped at key points by state promotion, whether directly for war or for civilian purposes. Another area is, of course, the technology of surveillance and the physical control of people, which has been seen as the core of the modern state by writers like Jeremy Bentham and Michel Foucault.

The main structures of land use and development – whether the consolidation of borders, as in Europe, or the opening of frontiers, as in the United States – have been the result of state policies. European states were built on conflict stemming from the relative scarcity of

---

*In this competition, states may attempt to control churches, collude with them, limit them to a separate religious sphere, establish civil religions, or abolish religion altogether.

land; the United States was built on the availability of cheap or free land (and government distribution of that land in land grants or the Homestead Act); and the shaky foundations of Third World states have been built on the conflict between colonizers, who believed that land was free for the taking, and indigenous peoples, who could only get it back by adopting the alien trappings and structural forms of the state. And the structures of financial exchange have been fundamentally shaped not only by the state's need for a solid and expanding tax base (and for the loyalties which rising living standards can reinforce), but also by the way in which taxation systems have themselves been structured. General tax levies, or 'confiscatory' taxes, for example, can often depress production and therefore reduce the viability of the tax base itself, as raising taxes can cause revenues to shrink in a vicious circle; in contrast, transaction taxes and customs duties (of the revenue-raising rather than the protectionist kind) can grow automatically as economic activity increases, creating a virtuous circle. Thus the general availability of resources in society is shaped fundamentally by the manner in which the state seeks to support itself. And the way that the state uses and distributes the resources it collects is an obvious dimension of the capacity of state structures and state actors to affect the form that social development takes.

As well as influencing the psychological and physical environments of social formation, the state shapes the sociological environment – the way in which agents themselves, consciously or unconsciously, act collectively in groups and social categories to constrain the range and scope of other agents' actions. In the post-feudal period in Europe, aristocratic families competed and fought to become dynastic families and to consolidate their territories into emerging state structures in order to control internal conflict and deal with external threats and opportunities. The history of state structuration is often dominated by the conscious attempt to integrate and mold locally and regionally based reference groups, religious groups, etc., into the framework of the state – with, of course, extremely variable results – and of these groups to resist absorption, bargain for influence, or even seek to control the state in turn. The example of Northern Ireland, which has still not been successfully integrated into one of the oldest of the European nation-states, Britain, indicates the ongoing problematic nature of regionalism and sub-state nationalism. The reverse process, 'balkanization', has been resisted by existing states, usually with some success but without any total resolution of the issues.

In addition to the persistence, revivals, and reformulation of local or regional loyalties, of course, the formation of a wide range of what are usually thought of as 'modern' social categories has also been structured by and through state development. The development of classes and elites is inextricably intertwined with changing patterns of state structuration and their consequences for control over the power and economic resources of society. The 'power elite' is not merely a social category, but rather a stratum which is inherently constituted through the task of controlling the state apparatus; a 'ruling class' is intrinsically stamped with requirements of ruling.[8] Furthermore, perhaps one of the most problematic sociological categories, the very definition of which is central to the notion of the underlying unity of the state, is, of course, that comprising race and/or ethnicity, which provide a continuing source of conflict over the most fundamental sort of political and social identity. Finally, the organization of contemporary interest and pressure groups is obviously designed for the strategic purpose of gaining access to and control over the allocation of resources and values within and by governments.

For all of these categories, a central problematic has been the extent to which a variety of social and economic processes, even when they are not directly controlled or managed by the state, pass through and interact with the structural filter and withinputs of the state – the structural biases of the institutional apparatus and the influences of state actors. Individuals and groups must define themselves strategically and maneuver tactically in the context of the logic of the state, whether conforming to legal rules, competing for resources distributed or regulated by the state, or attempting to resist or avoid the influence or control of other state and non-state actors. Thus the state, and state actors, are involved in a continuing process of interaction with other social and economic structures; the nature and development of these structures, however, is frequently shaped directly or indirectly by the state, by state actors, and by the process of state structuration.

Finally, of course, state structures and state actors, in their interactions with other states, are continually shaping the external environment in which the social unit exists. We have already discussed some of the implications of this for state structuration, and will do so again later in much more detail.[9] Whether in terms of state formation (especially in the post-feudal European setting), conquest and military confrontation, economic conflict and competition, or the spread of ideas which put the state at the core of concepts such as modernity and development, the state has become the hegemonic concept for ordering the modern world. Where the internal structures of the state are deeply rooted in social values, robust, and possess a high degree of decisional capacity, then those states tend to be more successful in external influence and international competition. But even where the effective sovereignty of the state is contested and its structures fragmented or entropic, external statehood and internal state-building are still seen as the ideal rule or norm by which socio-political effectiveness (and ineffectiveness) are measured; even dissident individuals, categories seeking to resist the existing ruling elites or state structures, and countercultures, usually seek either to control the state or to build a new state (or states) to replace the old. And, of course, the development of international norms, transnational structures, and patterns of interstate competition and cooperation has generally been viable only where the state and state sovereignty have been implicitly or explicitly accepted and adopted as the basic building-block of informal game-playing and formal decision-making.

Inclusion, Access and Control: The 'Political Process'

The state, then, has been a central feature of the formation of society itself, both shaping the social unit as a whole and comprising an intermediary linkage mechanism which structures the social fabric too. However, as we have argued earlier, it is crucial not to see 'the' state as a holistic reified entity. For the state itself is constituted by a range of middle-level and micro-level games, which are also characterized by contrasting logics, interstitial spaces, structural dynamics, and ongoing tensions. Some of these are more salient and obvious than others. For example, we will deal later with structural elements which include the bureaucratic organization of the state, which in its complexity remains an arcane mystery to most people. In this section we will look at what appears to be the most obvious and 'public' face of the modern state – both the competition for (and conflict over) appointment or election to state offices, on the one hand, and problematic nature of the control which such access gives to these officeholders in wider processes of political decision-making, the pursuit of influence, and the allocation of values and resources, on the other.

The development of a structure of public offices has been the central focus of the dialectic of political conflict and control throughout political history. How officeholders ought to be chosen, and what the scope and range of their powers should be, has been the main concern of political philosophers down the ages. In late- and post-feudal Europe, as more powerful nobles broke the bonds of vassalage and challenged for monarchical power, they developed more complex and extended forms of control, from the embryonic central administrations of the French kings and the Domesday Book of William the Conqueror to the more formalized administrations of Richelieu and Frederick the Great. The military and economic power of the European monarchies created new groups competing for shares of that power and the fruits of agricultural productivity, urban prosperity, and expanding world trade. New upper classes, middle classes, urban workers, and peasant groups, cross-cut by local, religious, and personal loyalties and interests, separately and in a variety of alliances, sought to wrest political power from their newly-sovereign monarchs and once-warrior aristocracies. Political power was a means to economic power (or a barrier to that power), a way for new individuals and groups to alter or better their station in life, or to resist new injustices. But it was also an end in itself; from it, in theory, would flow greater distributive justice and the common good – and, in later formulations, rights, dignity, liberty, equality, and fraternity.

Both traditional power-holders and newer power-seekers, then, were faced with a twofold problematic: the expansion of the scope and reach of the state, both externally and internally; and the inclusion of new strata and competitors for power. The expansion of the state nurtured and was nurtured by the growth of capitalism, despite the suspicion of traditional elites. And the spread of production and economic exchange was enabled and underpinned by the state's elaboration of a legal and administrative framework which undermined the diffuse property rights and the tradition of common lands characteristic of feudalism, replacing them with freehold land tenure, exclusive property rights (rediscovered from Roman law), and the sanctity of contracts. Despite the continued power and influence of both old and new aristocracies, and despite philosophical attempts to turn the clock back by making the king into a pseudo-divine patriarch, the state's power underpinned and was inextricably intertwined with both the growing market and a new class structure. Together, the spread of state administration and the spread of capitalism brought more complex and extended political and economic interactions and social exchange relationships to groups which had previously been 'subsumed' in more organically constituted extended family and corporate occupational categories.[10] These new constituencies – whether potential allies or competitors – were now an integral part of the political scene. They had either to be controlled or included.

From this problematic of inclusion and control arose the range of political institutions which we are familiar with today: from authoritarianism, and its contemporary extreme, totalitarianism, at one end of the scale; to democracy and ultimately anarchism at the other. This sort of regime typology was of course familiar prior to the formation of the modern state (especially within the Graeco-Roman tradition); however, the range of possible intermediate alternatives became far more problematic in the more socially and economically complex, and more geographically extended, context of European national state formation and emerging world dominance from around the sixteenth century. The spread of civil and military bureaucracies, of taxation systems, of communications, of trade and production both at home and abroad, and of ideological claims on the state, meant that the problem of control became ever more complex, and the range of groups which were pressing to be included expanded rapidly, especially with the coming of commercial agriculture (and the dislocation of the remnants of feudalism at the base) and of industry. Expanded monetary exchange, underpinned by the state, brought both a freedom for those with resources and a new discipline for those without.[11] The dialectic of inclusion and control reflected, and in turn unleashed, more complex and problematic political forces and processes as the state developed.

The 'political process' which has emerged in the modern state, then, consists of two sets of games, with different logics, but inextricably intertwined with each other. This structural mix of inclusion and control is predominantly seen as an endogenous, or internal, structural feature of the society or state. Of course, however, the exogenous interaction of states and societies has also been a crucial factor in its evolution. In the early and middle periods of capitalist industrialization, the expansion of empire and a world division of labor allied authoritarian structural forms in transnational relations with pressures to provide more inclusive channels of representation at home.[12] More authoritarian alternatives came to require the continued deepening and expansion of techniques of control, such as Nazism and Stalinism, in order to manage pressures for inclusion. Paradoxically, it was as much the military victories of the older democratic powers – Britain, France, and the United States – in the two world wars of the twentieth century, as any internal evolution, which spread one particular mix, liberal democracy, in the contemporary world. But the problematic of inclusion and control is alive and well today, whether in the Third World as states attempt to break the vicious cycles of military coups and economic underdevelopment, or in Gorbachev's Soviet Union, where regional nationalisms and ethnic clashes have been unleashed by *perestroika*, or in the developed West, where the new poor created by deindustrialization coexist uneasily with the new lower middle classes of the service society and the new yuppie rich.

This imbricated process of inclusion and control has become the public face of the modern state. Politics is seen by most people first and foremost as a process by which constitutions are made and evolve in practice, leaders and representatives are selected and/or elected, demands are transmitted through intermediary groups like political parties and pressure groups, laws are passed, policy outcomes determined, and officeholders held accountable. The state becomes a gridiron, and the stuff of politics a contest. In authoritarian systems, the outcomes may be more visible than the processes, requiring analyses of ideology and kremlinology; in liberal democratic states, the contest is judged by election results, and, in between, by opinion polls. Of course, critics throughout the ages have sought to look behind the mask of this public face. But the public face of inclusion and control is most often perceived not only as the central focus of politics, but also as what politics ought to be about – especially in liberal democratic states. In this sense it has a wide-ranging structural impact upon the psychological, physical, and sociological environments in which strategic and tactical choices are made. The game which involves the largest and most varied number of participants is, of course, that of inclusion.

At the broadest level, this includes citizenship and enfranchisement. It means being covered by the basic rights and privileges of the system, particularly in the voting process. In return for inclusion, it is expected that citizens will conform to the rules of the game, whether or not they derive any specific personal benefits in the way of private goods from the system. Even here, the perception of alternative choices is highly constrained. For example, in a world composed of nation-states, such broad inclusion is assumed; people living in a particular territory are presumed, in Locke's phrase, to be giving their 'tacit consent' to the system by remaining there. But for groups and individuals who feel excluded, or who are *de facto* or *de jure* denied certain of the rights and privileges of the system, a struggle for inclusion may be a two-edged sword, replacing a capacity for resistance or the leverage of independent resources with the constraints of acquiescence to the rules of the game; they may, however, have little practical alternative. Inclusion may be of more relevance to the stability of the system than to the interests of the included. But inclusion may also open the door to greater leverage in some circumstances.

The potential for that greater leverage is usually seen as coming at a second level of the political process, that of obtaining access to direct officeholding and/or indirect influence within the system. The structure of access constitutes a linking mechanism between the logics of inclusion and control; it is essentially an interface between the structure of officeholding, on the one hand, and 'included' individuals and groups, on the other. It can also be conceptualized as a *condensation* mechanism – in which a broad and multidimensional profusion of tasks, demands, and activities are cut down, transformed, and reshaped into forms which officeholders perceive as legitimate, recognizable, and manageable. The potential of 'included' individuals and groups for exercising leverage is therefore constrained not only by the social and economic resources which they may bring to the access process, but also by the structural constraints built into that process. Individuals, loosely organized social categories, corporate interests, organized interest groups, political parties, and other competitors and collaborators seeking leverage, are themselves structured around the limited room for maneuver rooted in the structure of access itself. The predominant forces in this input-reduction-and-transformation process are the constraints constituted by different levels of the access structure.

These levels of constraint are (a) the formal and informal 'rules of the game', which have a disproportionate impact on the access game by constituting the channels through which inputs are processed; (b) the bounded rationality of the officeholders, and the logistical constraints inherent in the tasks in which they are involved in carrying out; and (c) the *de facto* pattern of interaction among offices and officeholders themselves

– the number of 'access points' into the structure of control, the different levels of potential influence which they represent, and the range of pre-existing patterns of interaction between them and their holders. In this context, social and economic actors seeking leverage and influence on the structure of control must in effect pass through a system of gates, gates which have *de jure* and *de facto* requirements for passage. What is crucial, is the capacity of agents on both sides, officeholders and socio-economic actors, to operate effectively in strategic and tactical terms – to manipulate resources in ways that are relevant to the requirements of the access structure, to turn the constraints in the structure into opportunities in particular situations, and even to exploit the interstitial spaces and tensions in the structure in order to modify aspects of the structure itself.

The problematic of access is usually seen from the perspective of pluralism, in the context of liberal-democratic political systems. The main normative claim of such systems is that they enlarge access and consequently increase the leverage of included individuals and groups (in addition, making it easier for the non-included to seek to operate within the system). One of the main criticisms of the working of liberal-democratic systems, however, has been that rather than effectively increasing access, they channel pressures through structural filtering mechanisms which fragment the most substantial resources possessed by non-elite groups and subject them to manipulation by officeholders and by the social and economic interests with which officeholders are most closely tied by social origin, personal contact, political self-interest, class, etc.; this is the main appeal of approaches such as elite analysis, class analysis, corporatism, and the like.

This structuring can be manifested in a number of ways: (1) through decentralization and dispersal of points of access, thus dividing individuals and groups against themselves, fragmenting their resources, and engaging them in extensive processes of politicking for low stakes while taking advantage of their structurally-imposed weaknesses to block and/or veto their demands (a frequent criticism of the American governmental process); (2) through the centralization and concentration of the 'real' centers of decision-making power, whether in 'corporate elites' (a critique often applied to the United States), a 'ruling class' (more often applied by European social scientists), or a powerful, cohesive, and autonomous bureaucracy capable of marshalling the resources of a strong state apparatus (as in studies of the 'strategic state' in France or Japan), thus requiring included groups to confront the state either as equals (only the strongest socio-economic groups, companies, trade unions, etc., can do this) or as subordinates/opponents, i.e. as 'insider' or 'outsider' groups; or (3), through a combination of (1) and (2), coordinated through an articulated structure of elite, class, etc., domination – of power and powerlessness.[13] Even in 'democracies', then, access structures pay heed to the logic of control.

If, on the one hand, outwardly pluralistic processes and liberal democratic systems can often be seen as effectively constraining, imposing what those concerned with the 'public face' of politics might see as a counterintuitive 'top-down' structure of access, on the other hand the public face of outwardly authoritarian systems generally conceals a complex structure of access which, while still extremely limited in scope, goes against many of the most simplistic assumptions.[14] Whether through the simple enormity of the task of enforcing effective control from the top down within a complex bureaucratic apparatus,[15] or through competition between different apparatuses (the Nazi or Communist party versus government bureaucrats, the economists, the military or the intelligence agencies, etc.),[16] or through the porousness of local and regional structures (the need for regional officeholders to conform to the norms and deal with the grievances of the community for a variety of reasons), access may be much more extensive and substantial than commonly assumed. Even in authoritarian regimes, access structures are exploited and manipulated, but also must be nurtured and pay heed to the logic of inclusion.

The structure of access, then, like the other structured games in the political arena, is to some extent continually in the process of structuration; however, the structuration of access is more constrained than political structuration in general, because it is limited by the interaction of elements which make up the wider structure of the state. The densest layer of the structure of inclusion and control is that of control by political officeholders themselves – from formal decision-making, such as legislation or executive policy-making, to informal problem-solving, bargaining, or manipulation. Nordlinger has convincingly shown how state actors (including both political and administrative officeholders) can operate autonomously of their socio-economic origins and affinities.[17] However, their potential power as agents is constrained more by the decision-making and control structures within which they are situated than by their socio-economic associations. Huntington, for example, claims that the core structure of political modernization – linking the logics of inclusion and control – lies in the development of political parties.[18] However, the capacity of party in general (including both parties as organizations and party systems) to influence or control actual policy-making, implementation, and control varies widely with the formal and informal institutional structure of the state, in ways which are usually far more important over time than the 'raw material' of the socio-economic resources of parties themselves.

American parties may help to shape voter perceptions of candidates and to constitute some levels of linkage between officeholders and their supporters (financial contributors as well as voters), but they are notoriously weak in controlling patterns of media attention, legislative votes, group influence (especially insider influence) on policy-making, policy outcomes, etc. This is due primarily to the fragmentation of the American state and its entropic character. British parties seem much stronger, but this is true only insofar as members of the cabinet or 'Government' (drawn from the otherwise relatively powerless parliamentary parties) orient their undoubted policy-making control in ways that reflect wider party policy stances or interests; there is remarkably little control on the controllers, and what constraints do exist have tended to come from the cautious habits of the civil service and its 'logic of negotiation' rather than from democratically elected officeholders *per se*.[19] The nature of policy outputs in Britain is shaped much more by the structure of the executive and the civil service than by the party system. The same could be said in most contexts, although parties – as well as other intermediary structures and individuals, firms, etc., possessing strategically or tactically relevant resources – are also often capable of exploiting interstitial spaces and tensions in the structure; control structures are also in a continuous process of structuration. But even the *most* 'public' face of political control, the selection and/or election of national leaders (especially presidents, prime ministers, etc.), is for the most part strongly constrained over time. This is evidenced by the well-known fact that the President of the United States of America, supposedly 'the most powerful man in the world', is severely restricted in his actual capacity to control political processes and outcomes and must fall back upon his 'power to persuade'.[20] National leaders must operate and navigate within a structural context which they may seek to transform, but this is rare, as we will argue in Chapter 5. It is often said that the capacity of Mikhail Gorbachev to transform the political structure of the Soviet Union depends paradoxically upon his ability to utilize and exploit the very authoritarian structures which he seems to wish to transform, in order to impose a *perestroika* which has thus far had severe economic consequences as well as encountering political, bureaucratic and even some social resistance. The structure of 'games' which underpin the logic of control belies the predominant focus of political analysis on the 'public face' of the political process. This public face is for the most part a façade, not for a conspiracy of rapacious interests, but for a complex process of structuration. And this process covers not just the activities of inclusion and political control, but those of the construction of society itself (as we have argued above), of organizing and controlling the wider state apparatus and of steering certain key socio-economic processes (as will be argued below).

The Apparatuses of the State

While the 'political process', with its logics of inclusion, access, and control, is normatively the most public face of the state and has embraced most of what most political scientists (as well as ordinary people) have focused on, the apparatuses of the state are less well-known but perhaps more crucial to the shaping of policy outcomes. They comprise the core 'withinputs' of the state as a whole. Through them – and through the impact which their structures have on the filtering of inputs into, on the day-to-day and long-term operations of, and on the outputs of, the state – these apparatuses tend to predominate over other elements of the state structure. They constitute the more constant and durable features on the map of the state – its endogenous structured field of action.[21] And yet they, too, consist of a range of games with their different logics and indeterminacies – their historical specificities, their conflicting and cooperating agents, their uncontrollable interstitial spaces, and their inbuilt structural tensions.

These interlocking games can be seen as composed of the interaction of several different levels of structure: control by the political executive; the character of the higher civil service; the expansion of activities, tasks, and personnel at the lower and middle levels of bureaucracy; the regularized structures of interest intermediation, with the state as regulator and/or 'social partner'; the problematic of certain organizations formally outside the state, but which nevertheless function at least partly as virtual extensions of the state apparatus; and those activities which link domestic and transnational issues, not just foreign policy or the military, but social and economic interactions too. Although the 'administration', in normative theory, is supposed to be subordinate to the authoritative decisions reached through the 'political process', influence tends to be the other way around, as most studies of substantive public policy issues clearly demonstrate. Nevertheless, there are significant exceptions, for example, during times of structural change, or when the apparatuses are fragmented or stalemated, or when the weight of conjunctural pressures alters the balance in particular circumstances – whether in favor of groups and individuals working through the channels of the 'political process', or in favor of political officeholders, or, in potentially the most critical situation, both together. The apparatuses of the state, too, are in a continual process of structuration.

The political executive is ostensibly both the dominant linkage mechanism between the political process and the apparatuses of the state, and the source of legitimate authority and control exercised on behalf of the former over the latter. And yet its capacity both to act as an effective link and to control the state apparatus depends not merely upon its political legitimacy or legal authority but upon its cohesiveness and its ability to marshal the relevant resources to play the bureaucratic game effectively.

In order to do this, it must usually be able, first of all, to mobilize a range of socio-economic actors and political officeholders to support its goals; a groundswell of public opinion, an electoral mandate, party discipline and other signs of effective consensus within or top-down control of the 'political process' are transformed from ends in themselves into instruments for controlling bureaucratic games. Clear and coherent policy formulation, and a range of supportive signals to promote policies once adopted, can create a *fait accompli* which the various levels of the state apparatus must deal with.

Such requirements for effective, top-down political control, however, are rarely met. When they are not, then various interpretations of policy intent can be formulated within the bureaucracy itself; often these stem from pre-existing perspectives already functioning in the form of a bureaucratic ethos, ideology, or set of working assumptions. Once such orientations are present, these in-house interpretations constitute the operational criteria for dealing with the issue-area in question. When the political process is itself fragmented, as is so often the case, then the various apparatuses of the state have considerable discretion in construing their own mandate, scope, and range of activities; even relatively strong executive leadership can quickly run into the sands.[22] Political control then depends upon the effective manipulation of formal and informal institutional controls in an uncertain environment. The two most important levers of control which the political executive can exercise over the state apparatus are control of the purse strings and control of personnel appointments (and firings). Such institutional levers are often clumsy to control and indirect in their effects, and the strategic and tactical conditions for their success depend upon the precision and consistency with which they are targeted and applied, and/or the availability of trained and effective alternative personnel who have not been, or will not be, socialized into pre-existing bureaucratic perspectives. Changes in bureaucratic ideologies are more likely to come from changing social attitudes among bureaucratic state actors themselves than they are to develop from political control *per se*.

Much of this problematic of ineffective political control derives from the fact that civil servants are quite simply playing different games than are their supposed 'political masters', and the interlocking structure of these games is difficult to penetrate, even from the formally authoritative position of the political executive. Civil servants, in interacting with political executive officeholders, are often concerned with structural maintenance: defending their status as experts, whether as administrative generalists or as specialists in a particular sector; maintaining their career ladders; maximizing the share of expenditure appropriated to their departments or agencies; and applying policy (effectively or not) without destabilizing or undermining existing structures. At the same time, however, their sense of mission allied with their specialized knowledge may make civil servants into policy formulators or advocates, believing that their internally generated approach stands 'above politics', free from the sordid horse-trading and oversimplified gridiron contests of the 'political process'.

Therefore there is a complex but robust structural dialectic of stasis and change within the civil service, often deeply embedded in the ethos of the professional elite of higher civil servants,[23] the norms and rules of which severely constrict the interstitial spaces in which executive officeholders can exert leverage. Of course, higher civil servants are also structurally enmeshed in a range of structured games at other levels too: with elite strata in the wider society, including a variety of regular interlocutors in the media, major interest groups, 'policy communities', and the like; with middle- and lower-level civil servants; and with each other, in conflicts over both 'turf' and policy substance. Because most civil servants, especially in states with low rates of personnel turnover,* deal with each other in a regular and sustained fashion, such that their interlocutors are likely to change more quickly than they do, these games taken together over time produce a tight structure, in which games are frequently repeated (or 'iterated', in the language of game theory). The scope which remains for non-bureaucratic actors and structures is limited. However, it is everywhere true, in both liberal-democratic and authoritarian systems, that individual political officeholders can penetrate various levels of the bureaucratic hierarchy in pursuit of favorable treatment for individual constituents, local interests, special interest groups, etc.; however, their favorable reception by civil servants is usually part of a trade-off of individual services in return for the implicit assurance of political non-interference in more substantial matters which may challenge existing structural practices.

Similar comments can be made about the middle and lower levels of the bureaucracy. Lacking the prestige and institutional control of higher civil servants, middle- and lower-level bureaucrats find their independence more tightly constrained, and their dependence on routine much greater. Routine makes games at this level even more difficult to penetrate, although some changes in routine can be imposed from the top down, especially where higher civil servants and political officeholders are in agreement on such structural changes. Middle- and lower-level civil servants, however, are also enmeshed in a range of other structural games, the logics of which focus their attention and dominate their objectives.

---

*For example, where 'permanent' career ladders are sufficiently attractive to keep existing personnel and recruitment is constrained, or where a 'spoils system' is allied to continuous political control by the same groups.

These include the special social position of these civil servants as a major section of the fastest-expanding social stratum of contemporary society, the new lower middle class or *petite bourgeoisie* of the service sector. The fact that such an important group, whether defined as a class or not, is so numerically strong within the state apparatus, is often seen as a major influence on the changing role of the state in advanced capitalist society.[24]

Furthermore, this bureaucratic stratum is the one which staffs many of the agencies which interface most closely with the public, whether in terms of administering the welfare state, operating public services and state-owned industries, assessing and collecting taxes, enforcing economic or environmental regulations, disbursing grants and loans to businesses, homeowners, etc., staffing the police, running prisons, or myriad other tasks and activities. These activities can breed attitudes and orientations which cut across the left–right spectrum in a specific way: they often reflect a social conservatism, a support for law and order or social discipline; but this is usually mixed with support for the maintenance and expansion of public sector activities and social services. Thus middle and lower civil servants have their ethos and 'mission', too – to support the activities of the welfare state.

The most salient structural tension which this engenders is, of course, precisely that these groups have a particular combination of strong right-wing views and a sympathy with the established order, on the one hand, and what are often seen as strong left-wing views, and a sympathy with an expanding state apparatus and the growth of the social and economic 'reach' of that apparatus, on the other. Combined with the routine orientation of many of their tasks, and activities, the special class position and the ethos of middle- and lower-level civil servants create a relatively tight structure which is, again, difficult to penetrate. Social policies, in particular, tend to be implemented in ways which conform to the structural logic of this level of the state apparatus: it is relatively difficult to initiate radically new forms of policy implementation; and the structures are 'sticky', resisting the effects of deregulation, spending cuts, and other attempts to reduce the size, tasks and activities of the welfare state in general (as has been evidenced in many countries, including the United States and Britain, in the 1980s). Once again, it is the withinputs of state structures and of state actors which have the greatest ongoing impact on policy outcomes at this level, and they are in a continuous process of structuration.

Other levels of the state apparatus which involve particular closely-linked games and processes of structuration include systems of interest intermediation, i.e., the ongoing, organized bargaining processes which are situated at the interface of state institutions and a range of the more significant social and economic interests. These bring the state together on a regular, structured basis, both with organized 'groups', such as the trade associations which represent business or the trade unions which represent many workers, and with individual firms, etc. We will deal with this aspect in more detail in Chapter 6, where it will be argued that interest intermediation structures can be analyzed most effectively by seeing them as more fundamentally shaped by the structures of the state than by the socio-economic environment.

Furthermore, the apparatuses of the state can be located outside formal state institutions. For example, it has been a central argument of neo-Marxists such as Louis Althusser that many organizations which are usually seen to be independent of the state and representative of the socio-economic structure, such as trade unions and churches, are actually *de facto* arms of the state, quasi-state apparatuses, or 'ideological state apparatuses' (as distinct from 'repressive state apparatuses').[25] And finally, many businesses and other organizations are closely linked to the state because the state's primary role in foreign and defense policy can be seen as integrated with the state apparatus. Perhaps the best-known of such close linkage structures is the 'military–industrial complex' which President Eisenhower warned Americans against in 1960, and which has been identified in virtually all state societies (except perhaps Costa Rica). Intelligence agencies also frequently not only work through but also create ostensibly private organizations and associations. One might also put into this category industries dependent on tariff or non-tariff protectionism, private universities and 'think tanks' with regular government ties, banks and corporations which operate internationally and often act as instruments of foreign policy, and the like.

Thus there is not one, monolithic, state apparatus, but several levels and layers of structured games both within and between the different apparatuses of the state. However, these games are inextricably intertwined and continually repeated. Both political control and socio-economic influence are limited by the relatively tight structure constituted by this cluster of games. Nevertheless, there is no single hegemonic game within the state, nor is the configuration of games patterned in precisely the same way in different contexts. In different countries and in different circumstances, different levels of the state apparatus and different combinations of state actors produce somewhat different – historically-specific – configurations. The dominance of a tightly-knit and highly-institutionalized elite of higher civil servants in countries like Japan and France makes that level more important for shaping political outcomes; however, Japanese and French higher civil servants also have to deal with the structural problems of political and socio-economic pressure from outside, the entrenched routines of middle- and lower-level civil servants, and the demands made within interest intermediation structures. At the same time, some issues require greater coordination even within relatively fragmented and entropic state structures like that of the United States; *ad hoc* structural solutions like the Gramm–Rudman–Hollings Act to deal with the budget deficit, or the referral of key structural issues to the Supreme Court, come into play. States which cannot resolve these problems, like the Lebanon, risk fragmentation and outside control. Structuration is an ongoing process within the apparatuses of the state, between them and the political process, and between them and the socio-economic environment with which they are both directly and indirectly linked through both inputs and the coordination and steering of socio-economic development.

Economic and Social Activities Pursued by the State
States throughout history have carried on a range of important direct and indirect activities involving the initiation, managing and promotion of production, wealth creation, social engineering, and the like. In Anglo-American political culture, however, such activities are often seen as supplementary and even deleterious to the 'real' functions for which government was ostensibly set up; these, in the tradition of the English philosopher John Locke, are believed to be based on the establishment of a social contract among individuals – who are thus seen as forming a 'civil society' which takes precedence over the state – for the protection of individual rights to life, liberty, and property. The implication of the Lockean view is that the right of private property, and the allocation of the resources of society to individuals as their exclusive property, either predated, or ought to have moral precedence over and protection from, the activities of the state (as well as from the activities of other individuals). The only major admitted exceptions to this rule are, firstly, that the state, in order to defend individual property, must have the resources to do so, i.e., the tax base (and other material resources) and the legal power to defend property-holders against external and internal enemies, and, secondly, that the protection of property (which is the logical consequence of combining life, liberty, and the material environment) must be weighed against the morally prior commitment to protect life and liberty, when there is a conflict. In general, however, state intervention in the economy is seen as philosophically pathological, and ought to be avoided wherever possible.

In fact, as we have pointed out earlier, the establishment of a state structure has usually preceded the formation of a recognizable 'civil society', rather than the other way around. Indeed, early states were generally not based on the precedence of private property at all, but either on the dominance of a ruling stratum or on the organization of collective activities (irrigation is a classic if controversial example); and the modern state developed out of the diffuse and imbricated property structure of feudalism and church-sustained or clan-based corporatism. The system of private property rights was elaborated principally by state elites as they sought to promote and control the benefits of commerce and manufacture in order to create wealth for the state – often for the purpose, in turn, of promoting and financing state-controlled or state-fostered economic undertakings and social projects, from mines to roads and bridges to factories to poorhouses. The principle that exclusive ownership of property should be granted to individuals is the *consequence* of state formation and development – the need for wealth creation to swell the tax base or for political support from the wealthy* – and not its *raison d'être*. This is not to say whether exclusive private property rights are a 'good thing' or not; it is merely to argue that they do not necessarily take precedence over the state.

The consequence of this short philosophical detour is simply to make the point that the social and economic activities of the state, or 'state intervention' as they are inaccurately labeled,† in fact seem to be both ubiquitous and normal features of political life, and are not pathological in principle, at least. Indeed, such activities often appear to be central to both the rationale and the actual working of virtually all states. Along with providing for external defense and maintaining civil order, the economic activities of states – especially the sizable range and scope of public works projects which all states have either directly carried on or indirectly promoted throughout history – have perhaps been the most characteristic and salient of all state activities. They have frequently been the main motive for taxation, the greatest source of organized employment, and the largest object of expenditure in the state and even in the economy as a whole. The carrying on of economic activities, again along with defense and order, has always been a core *raison d'être* of state formation and development. This has been true not only of virtually all kinds of state forms, but also of all economic systems characteristic of state societies; it remains true in the capitalist era.

What is unique about the capitalist era is that many states, especially the leading economies and dominant military powers, have for the most part systematically encouraged and supported the growth of an economic system rooted in private self-interest, individual property rights, and the

---

*Early stock and bond markets, for example, were set up not by entrepreneurs seeking to invest their capital in private enterprise, but by governments seeking finance when the tax base was weak (during costly wars, in particular) and by those who sought to gain safe future returns at the expense of the taxpayer or who wanted favors and social connections at court.

†Such activities are inextricably intertwined with economy and society generally, and not the external interventions of a separately constituted state; nevertheless, we will use the term 'state intervention' in its colloquial sense in this book.

private accumulation of capital.* As the predominant economic system or 'mode of production' of the modern world, capitalism is usually regarded as having developed from a dynamic combination of three elements: the spread of private property rights as the dominant form of control of goods and services; the spread of market systems as the way in which goods and services are allocated and transferred; and the spread of the wage system as the mode of organizing and allocating the value of labor.† The process of capitalist development has been seen, by both traditional capitalist economic theorists and by Marxists, as structurally deriving from, and acquiring its underlying dynamic from, the motive of private profit as pursued by entrepreneurs (or the bourgeoisie). Each of these dimensions of capitalism, however, has been enabled to function and develop through the activities of the state: the legal entrenchment and physical protection of private property rights; the integration of national markets, the enforcement of contracts, and the international economic predominance of states with policies which supported the development of the market sector (the Netherlands, Great Britain, and the United States);[26] and state enforcement of the wage labor system, from the early suppression of peasant and worker unrest to legislation limiting trade union activities in Britain in the 1980s.

Capitalism may not be the product of the state, but its development has been closely intertwined with that of the state, and the state has consciously and in many cases systematically nurtured capitalist economic processes for a variety of reasons since at least the Mercantilist Era.[27] This has not meant, however, that states have not engaged in economic activities or have done so less. Indeed, the main structural conflict *between* capitalist states has been between those states which have promoted 'open' capitalist economies, on the one hand – based on relatively free trade and the enforcement of market norms, even within their imperial spheres of influence, such as (with considerable historical variation) Britain and the United States – and those which have promoted 'closed' capitalist economies – organized more around direct and indirect state promotion and control of industry and trade (including

---

*It can also be argued that so-called 'socialist' states, in pursuing capital accumulation and not abolishing wage labor and the money system, are really not so different – just a different form of capitalism; see Adam Buick and John Crump, *State Capitalism* (London: Macmillan, 1986).

†Sometimes the last two are seen as dimensions of the same phenomenon, the market system. However, theorists who would see the value of the goods and services produced in the production process as deriving from the labor put into those products (including Marxists) would see the market system with its price-derived values as an epiphenomenon of the labor process; in contrast, theorists who attribute value to the exchange process, as is the case with traditional capitalist economic theory, would see the labor process as just another kind of market.

direct manufacture; the systematic organization of links between state, finance, and industry; planning; protectionism; autarchic imperialism; etc.), such as (again with considerable historical variation) Germany or Japan, on the other.[28] France is an interesting mixed case.[29] Indeed, it is exactly this structural conflict which Krasner believes to lie at the heart of the contemporary problematic of North–South relations.[30] And recent developments in the Soviet Union, Eastern Europe, and China may indicate that, just as it is not impossible to make a relatively peaceful transition from autarchic/authoritarian 'closed' capitalism to 'open' capitalism (as the example of postwar Spain indicates), it may not be impossible for 'socialist' states to make a similar transition from autarchic authoritarianism to openness, although not without severe difficulty.

Even within relatively 'open' capitalist systems, furthermore, states have not been idle in their direct involvement in and indirect promotion of economic activities and social engineering. These activities involve several analytically discrete but interlocked dimensions. They include: the economic impact of a range of typical state activities which require and cost money, labor, etc. (just paying salaries to state officials, for one thing); the provision of a range of public goods such as defense, policing, or infrastructure; the production and/or promotion of the provision (e.g., through subsidization) of a range of private goods which are seen to be in the 'public interest', involving public ownership of land and other property, operating factories, etc.; the pursuit of 'macroeconomic' policies in order to regulate economic activity in general through fiscal and monetary policy; the regulation of specific economic activities, whether to control prices, support employment, promote environmental protection, or pursue a variety of other objectives; central, indicative, regional, or sectoral planning; the establishment and operation of public and social services for welfare purposes; protectionism and/or the promotion of international competitiveness; and the formation and manipulation of social attitudes in order to produce particular forms of thought and behavior, including the promotion of what have been called 'wealth-oriented values'.

The key question for state structures and state actors in 'open' capitalist systems, then, has not been whether or not the state should be involved in economic and social activities, for such involvement is inevitable. It is what sort of activities to be involved in, and what form that involvement should take. For the various activities of the state have different logics. On the one hand, states, in line with their traditional character as structures for the organization of collective activities and the pursuit of common goals, still quite naturally undertake a wide range of traditional activities such as public works. It is quite in character for state actors – and for the public, for interest groups, etc. – when they perceive a task which they think needs doing, such as building a bridge or keeping a military base open to support local employment, etc., to simply set out to go ahead and accomplish that task through the organizational capacities and structures of the state itself. And the norms and game structures characteristic of other dimensions of the state reinforce this tendency. Whether attempting to maintain and manipulate the social fabric, dealing with the demands of included groups and the logics of access and control, or sustaining and managing the apparatuses of the state, states and state actors in capitalist societies, like those in other socio-economic contexts, find it normal to engage in and to expand the economic and social activities of the state.

On the other hand, however, states in the capitalist era have come to depend for key aspects of their legitimacy (because of the need to 'include' economic groups which have developed through capitalism) and their financial health (because of the need for expanding wealth and competitiveness in order to maintain the tax base) on the health of capitalism. They feel the need to support and promote capitalist structures and processes: private property and profit to keep the virtuous circle of accumulation and reinvestment going; the market system to allocate resources efficiently in a complex and uncontrollable world; and the wage labor system to keep costs down and to impose labor 'discipline' without having continually to enforce physical sanctions on a large and politically enfranchised workforce. Thus state actors are continually faced with the dilemma of choosing what sort of socio-economic activities to engage in, and how to engage in them, while *at the same time* promoting the sorts of private activities which create wealth generally, drive economic growth, build up the tax base (so that the government can engage in other economic and social activities), and create conditions for increased international competitiveness in a capitalist world economy.

The structuration of state economic activities, then, reflects the competing logics of the games of collective organization, on the one hand, and the promotion of a self-sustaining and growing capitalist economy, on the other. Each of the dimensions of contemporary state economic activity listed above can be seen as an arena within which the state and the capitalist system have become closely interlocked in a variety of historical circumstances; sometimes trends have been circumscribed within a particular country or time period, and sometimes they have been genuinely transnational and secular. In each case, however, state activities have involved a process of structuration, and each of the dimensions is composed of yet further complex clusters of games, with their gaps and indeterminacies. Together they constitute a major element of political structure and structuration, which not only involves the structuration of the state, but also, of course, has shaped economic development – and the structures of capitalism itself. Now we have dealt with these structuration processes in less detail in this chapter, because they will become the focus of later chapters, especially Chapter 8. But the underlying argument of this book is that the process of state structuration in capitalist society is coming more and more to reflect the fact that the complex mix of both state structures and the structures of capitalism is becoming ever more internationalized. The competing logics of collective organization and the promotion of capitalist development are shifting the focus of 'state intervention' from forms which 'decommodify' those activities pursued by the state (which organize essentially domestic socio-economic activities along non-market lines) to those which 'commodify' or 'marketize' both state economic activities *and the other elements of state structure too*. The contemporary state is shifting its structural focus from being a 'welfare state' to becoming a 'competition state'.

Conclusions

What is conventionally referred to as 'the state' is in fact a complex but robust structure of iterated games, with a variety of different logics. Early state formation, and, indeed, the development of the modern state, manifest a certain similarity among state structures, although the specific form they take is contingent rather than determined. These indeterminacies, which represent the competing logics of complex clusters of games and the interstitial spaces and tensions which those competing logics represent, permit – even necessitate – both stasis and change.

The mechanism for the mixing of stasis and change is the ongoing interaction of structure and agency. We can see this interaction at work inside the state structure, and in the relationship between the state structure and the wider society and economy, by focusing on four key elements or dimensions of state structure: the way that state structures and state actors create, construct, and manipulate core aspects of the social unit, and through it, the social fabric; the way that state structures and state actors react to and manage the 'political process', or the problematic of inclusion and control; the way that the apparatuses of the state develop and operate; and the way that contemporary states carry on economic and social activities, especially in the context of capitalism.

In the next two chapters we will look first at the problematic nature of agency and how the dynamics of agency can contribute to the structuration of a range of processes of political allocation spanning the elements of state structure; and we will then turn to the process of structuration itself, to the way that structured action fields are constituted, and to the central but problematic position of the state in the contemporary world.

Notes

1. Henry J.M. Claessen and Peter Skalnik, eds., *The Early State* (The Hague: Mouton, 1978).

2. Gianfranco Poggi, *The Development of the Modern State* (Stanford, Cal.: Stanford University Press, 1978).

3. See Raymond Cohen, 'Introduction', in Cohen and Elman R. Service, eds., *Origins of the State: The Anthropology of Political Evolution* (Philadelphia: Institute for the Study of Human Issues, 1978).

4. Cf. Holton, *Transition from Feudalism, op. cit.*; Douglass C. North, *Structure and Change in Economic History* (New York: Norton, 1981); Perry Anderson, *Lineages of the Absolutist State* (London: New Left Books, 1974); E.L. Jones, *The European Miracle: Environments, Economies and Geopolitics in the History of Europe and Asia* (Cambridge: Cambridge University Press, 1981); and Paul Kennedy, *The Rise and Fall of the Great Powers: Economic Change and Military Conflict from 1500 to 2000* (London: Unwin Hyman, 1988).

5. See Chapter 4.

6. Barry Buzan, *People, States and Fear: The National Security Problem in International Relations* (Brighton and Chapel Hill: Wheatsheaf and the University of North Carolina Press, 1983). We will in fact, however, use the traditional term in this book.

7. See Murray Edelman, *The Symbolic Uses of Politics* (Urbana: University of Illinois Press, 1964). The way in which a political system can be taken for granted, in a 'rain-or-shine' fashion, has been called 'system affect' by Gabriel Almond and Sidney Verba in *The Civic Culture* (Princeton, N.J.: Princeton University Press, 1964). For a specific application of similar concepts to a recent case, see P.G. Cerny, *The Politics of Grandeur: Ideological Aspects of de Gaulle's Foreign Policy* (Cambridge: Cambridge University Press, 1980).

8. Cf. Poggi, *op. cit.*; Eugene Anderson and Pauline Anderson, *Political Institutions and Social Change in Continental Europe in the Nineteenth Century* (Berkeley and Los Angeles: University of California Press, 1967); Perry Anderson, *op. cit.*; Badie and Birnbaum, *op. cit.*; C. Wright Mills, *The Power Elite* (New York: Oxford University Press, 1956); G. William Domhoff, *The Higher Circles: The Governing Class in America* (New York: Random House, 1970); and Carnoy, *State and Political Theory, op. cit.*

9. See above, pp. 28–9, and below, especially Chapters 4 and 8.

10. Peter Laslett, *The World We Have Lost* (London and New York: Weidenfeld and Nicolson and C. Scribner's, 2nd edn 1973).

11. William M. Reddy, *Money and Liberty in Modern Europe: A Critique of Historical Understanding* (Cambridge: Cambridge University Press, 1987).

12. Eric J. Hobsbawm, *Industry and Empire* (Harmondsworth, Mddx: Penguin, 1969).

13. See Gaventa, *op. cit.*

14. Some authors have gone so far as to consider such systems as less 'political' than pluralist democracies: Bernard Crick, *In Defence of Politics* (Chicago, Ill.: University of Chicago Press, 2nd edn 1972).

15. Peter Rutland, *The Myth of the Plan* (London: Hutchinson, 1986).

16. Ghiţa Ionescu, *The Politics of the European Communist States* (London: Weidenfeld and Nicolson, 1968).

17. Nordlinger, *On the Autonomy of the Democratic State, op. cit.*

18. Huntington, *Political Order, op. cit.*

19. Cf. A. Grant Jordan and Jeremy Richardson, 'The British Policy Style or the Logic

of Negotiation?', in Richardson, ed., *Policy Styles in Western Europe* (London: Allen and Unwin, 1982), and Hall, *Governing the Economy, op. cit.*

20. Richard E. Neustadt, *Presidential Power* (New York: Wiley, 1976); see discussion in Cerny, 'Political Entropy and American Decline', *op. cit.*, and in Chapter 5, below.

21. Crozier and Friedberg are, in fact, sociologists of organization, and focus primarily on state bureaucracies; *L'acteur et le système, op. cit.*

22. As one well-known insider argues was the case with Reaganomics, in David A. Stockman, *The Triumph of Politics: Why the Reagan Revolution Failed* (New York: Harper and Row, 1986).

23. Cf. John A. Armstrong, *The European Administrative Elite* (Princeton, N.J.: Princeton University Press, 1973), and Michel Crozier, *The Bureaucratic Phenomenon* (London: Tavistock, 1964).

24. Cf. Poulantzas, *Classes in Capitalist Society, op. cit.*, and Erik Olin Wright, *Class, Crisis and the State* (London: New Left Books, 1978).

25. See Carnoy, *The State and Political Theory, op. cit.*, for a review of this debate.

26. Cf. Angus Maddison, *Phases of Capitalist Development* (Oxford: Oxford University Press, 1982), and North, *op. cit.*

27. See Michel Beaud, *A History of Capitalism, 1500–1980* (London: Macmillan, 1984). For a brief survey of contrasting approaches to the relations between state and capitalism, see P.G. Cerny, 'State Capitalism in France and Britain and the International Economic Order', in Cerny and Martin A. Schain, eds., *Socialism, the State and Public Policy in France* (New York and London: Methuen and Pinter, 1985), ch. 10.

28. The classic treatment is Barrington Moore, *Social Origins of Dictatorship and Democracy, op. cit.* See also Robert Gilpin, *The Political Economy of International Relations* (Princeton, N.J.: Princeton University Press, 1987).

29. See P.G. Cerny, 'Modernization and the Fifth Republic', in John Gaffney, ed., *France and Modernization* (London: Avebury/Gower, 1988), ch. 2.

30. Krasner, *Structural Conflict, op. cit.*

3

Patterns of Political Agency:
Markets, Hierarchies, and Political Allocation

The concept of structure implicitly puts the emphasis of the analysis – the priority for what must be explained – on constraints on individual agents' choices. In contrast, the concept of agency implicitly puts that weight on those very choices. This means that the analytical focus turns to the elements making up the process of choosing: the alternatives available; the agents' objectives and the resources at their disposal; and the rationality by means of which they organize and deploy those resources in order to maximize the attainment of those objectives. This kind of cost–benefit and ends–means analysis at the micro-level obviously implies that such choices are meaningful – perhaps the most meaningful building-blocks of the real world of society and politics. In order for such choices to be so significant, it must be assumed that alternatives, too, are real.

If the elements of structure in fact do constrain choices in critical ways, then it may be that what agents perceive as their real alternatives are actually misperceived or just imagined. Or if the complexity of structure makes it impossible to know just what the outcomes of perceived alternatives will be, then the consequent uncertainties – whether attributed to the complexity of the structure *per se* or to the 'bounded rationality' of agents – may render agents' choices quite irrelevant to the real working of the structure. Rational choice analysis takes as a working assumption that choices are rational, but cannot demonstrate that fact without locating those choices within a structured field of action within which alternatives are real, outcomes are in fact determined by those rational choices, and rationality is not undermined by uncertainties.

For rational choice analysis to be meaningful, then, it must be situated in a wider analysis of structures – in a process of structuration. And it must, of course, be assumed that those structures are sufficiently indeterminate in critical ways that agents' choices are in fact meaningful. This, in turn, implies that agents themselves must have a range of different preferences (or 'utilities') and resources to bring into play in the games in which they are rationally involved. Without such differences between agents, outcomes would also be predetermined. Rational choice analysis therefore implies that society, or economics, or politics, is composed of a plurality of agents. These agents then make strategic and tactical choices to compete or to cooperate in particular game situations. Their choices are made real not only by structural indeterminacy, but also by the assumption of pluralism – in the case of politics and the state, by the assumption that politics is fundamentally characterized by a plurality of actors engaged in something like market competition over scarce political resources.

There are two particular problems with this presentation of the issue of agency. The first is that markets are themselves not merely composed of aggregated individual choices, but are also structured fields of action, as we will argue in the first main section of this chapter. The very existence of markets can be seen as requiring the existence (and ongoing guarantee) of a favorable structural setting and of procedures for the enforcement of market norms, in order to prevent destabilizing conflict and predatory domination. The dividing line between market behavior and structured organizational behavior is more complex than a simplistic notion of individual rational choice permits. The requirements for the institutionalization of markets themselves will be the first issue examined in this chapter.

The second is that among the choices which are open to agents, even in an open and efficient market, may be the sort the outcomes of which in turn have the effect of limiting the nature of future choices, either for the agent making the original choice, or for his or her competitors/collaborators, or for future agents making similar and related choices. Actions have structural consequences, and those consequences are clearly essential to the concept of structuration. Thus structure can arise from the *de facto* impact of repeated patterns of choice – an issue which game theorists have been increasingly grappling with in recent years, especially since the publication of Robert Axelrod's *The Evolution of Cooperation* in 1984.[1] But it can also arise from choices which lead to structures of *control*. An agent or group of agents may seek to achieve outcomes which, in turn, give them (and/or others) control over the range of future outcomes and the capacity to manipulate those outcomes. (Such control can, of course, arise inadvertently too.) Control structures – hierarchies – can be partial or general: the former could still lead hypothetically to a kind of mixed, organized pluralism, with choices restricted but still assumed to be real in significant ways; but the latter might generate patterns of structural domination, such as authoritarianism, elitism, class domination, corporatism, or even totalitarianism.

Thus it is possible to consider hypothetically how the dynamics of a plural universe of individual and group agency can interact with elements of structure in an ongoing process of structuration. After considering the existing debate on pluralism and the major structural critiques of pluralism in more detail, this chapter will focus on four analytical levels of market structuration derived from institutional economics and recent game theory: the analysis of industrial market structure, the theory of transaction costs, the notion of semiprivate goods, and recent institutionalist variations of public choice theory. We will attempt to show how a plural universe of individuals and groups with different preference schedules and resource bases can give rise, not just intentionally but also inadvertently, to more structured forms of limited competition and control, meshing with state structures in processes of political allocation. Finally, a more complex taxonomy of political allocation processes will be derived from these strands.

The Problem of Political Markets: Rational Choice and its Limits

The concept of an economic market requires the existence of a set of 'rules of the game' and common measures of value. These generally include: legally enforceable, exclusive property rights; the principle of 'free' yet binding contracts; an integrated (usually national) market applying the same rules everywhere; and a common currency for the setting of prices. Without such an overarching framework, conflict over who owns what, the threat of promises broken, and chronic uncertainties over the actual value of that which is being traded or allocated, all crowd out orderly competition. A political marketplace similarly requires a 'consensus' on rules of the game: political property rights, such as civil rights and the vote; a legal system based on binding, universalizable rules; a sovereign state; and a political currency, or rather currencies – i.e., 'normal' methods of mobilizing and transforming raw political, social, and economic resources into insider influence, votes, protest, and a range of other kinds of access, control, and policy outcomes.

However, while these are necessary conditions for the establishment and functioning of a political marketplace – though problematic and controversial enough in themselves – it is none the less fairly obvious that they are not sufficient. Just as economic theorists base their analyses on the assumption that people can be seen as what has been called 'economic man' – with a natural propensity 'to truck and to barter' – political theorists must presume that people are also 'political animals', who wish to argue, to compete, and to take some part in decision-making processes. It must also be assumed, of course, that the currency of political exchanges is not too asymmetric, imposing discipline rather than choice (as Reddy argues is the case in what he calls 'asymmetric monetary exchange').[2]

But perhaps the most important question is whether conditions exist for an 'efficient' political marketplace. In an efficient economic marketplace, there must be a sufficient number of buyers and sellers to permit a price to emerge through comparisons of a range of alternatives, with clear market signals about the relative values which the parties each place on the good or service being traded, with sufficient knowledge on the part of actors about their competitors and about a range of exogenous and endogenous conditions pertaining to the transaction, and with the capacity on the part of those actors to process this information and to arrive at a price which clears the market.[3] These conditions are, of course, highly problematic, even in an economic market. They are much more so in political markets. In this environment, traditional pluralist approaches involve a number of analytical leaps which are not fully explained or explored. The main problem is the relationship between (a) the (hypothesized or real) existence of a genuinely 'plural universe' of competing interests, reflected in individual agents' behavior or that of latent or manifest groups in society, on the one hand, and (b) the actual conditions for equilibrium in a political marketplace, or the ultimate capacity for those interests to check and balance each other in a stable and ongoing way (rather than stalemate, collapse, or oligopoly/monopoly control), on the other.

It is all too often presumed in pluralist thinking that in the absence of exogenous imperfections, an equilibrium is possible: not only that the political consensus and the legal framework of the state provide a sufficiently strong yet open framework of 'rules of the game', i.e., that 'political man' is sufficiently autonomous and active, and that political processes are fair and neutral rather than disciplinary or controlling; but also that there is a sufficient range of alternative bids and offers, sufficient (true) information, sufficient certainty and sufficient rationality for political market efficiency. Now each of these points is arguable; more importantly, they are rarely argued systematically and in conjunction with each other. An example can be seen in the confusion surrounding the very word pluralism itself.

In the first place, 'pluralism' is sometimes used, especially by specialists on 'segmented' societies (e.g., in the Third World), to mean simply that a plural society exists *per se*, and not to denote the other characteristics of a political marketplace. This sometimes leads to the mistaken connotation that the groups in such societies have a potential for achieving a stable equilibrium (even if it is a non-cooperative equilibrium) despite fundamental power asymmetries. But this is merely one example of a kind of Western ethnocentrism which is a common problem in social science. More significant perhaps is the tendency to deny that 'pluralism' has much to say about the efficiency of markets at all,[4] or even to posit that political marketplaces are inherently imperfect anyway.[5]

The dropping of the assumptions of potential market efficiency in effect denies the paradigmatic quality of pluralism (as we have described it above), but simply sees the assumption of plurality as a useful tool for generating better hypotheses than its rivals, which overly restrict the universe of significant agents. Lindblom's attempt to identify market imperfections does, in fact, focus realistically on the constraints on efficiency in political markets, and asserts correctly that these imperfections are the result of the coexistence within political systems of two paradigmatic principles, the market and authority. But it does not go far beyond the juxtaposition of opposites, and it is never fully clear what are the sources of these two paradigmatic modes and how they actually interact systematically; 'polyarchy' ends up falling between two stools. Finally, there is the continuing confusion between pluralism as empirical paradigm and as normative standard, as we argued in Chapter 1.

The main alternatives to pluralism have gone somewhat further in denying the validity of the market analogy. Elitism, class analysis, corporatism, and state theory are all examples of what we have called orthodox structural theories. In such theories, the idea of a political marketplace is little more than a misleading façade for the dominance of a particular deeply rooted process of structural dominance. We have already discussed some of the inadequacies of class theory, elitist power structure analysis and the more reified structural versions of state theory in Chapter 1, and we will look more closely at more recent neo-corporatist analysis in Chapter 6. These approaches view the *a priori* power of the structure in question as invalidating the premises upon which markets and rational choice are based in the first place: whether the natural division of society into leaders and followers; the unnatural division of society into antagonistic classes of the owners of the means of production vs. all the others; the functional solidarity of certain groups such as capital, labor, and state actors at the core of the political and economic processes of advanced capitalist society;[6] or the autonomy and primacy of the state and state actors in pursuing unique common functions (a kind of neo-organicism) or the common interest.

In each case, however, the more rigid version of the approach has been challenged – successfully, in general – by a revised version which attempts to take into account the competition of a wider variety of groups and individuals, the presence of a plural universe and at least some sort of political marketplace: the emergence of 'democratic elitism';[7] neo-Marxist theory focused on the 'cultural hegemony' of capitalism as a system, the competition of fractions of capital, the importance of the 'new petty bourgeoisie' in 'contradictory class locations', and various versions of the 'relative autonomy of the state';[8] the existence of bilateral corporatism,[9] the distinction between those more corporatist groups organized around the 'production function' vs. a more pluralist set of interests linked with 'consumptionist' interests,[10] and different levels of macro-, meso- (or sectoral), and micro-corporatism;[11] and a re-focusing on conflicts within a more diversified state structure, the differences of interest between state actors, and the ways in which diverse alliances between state actors and socio-economic interests vary in different historical circumstances.

One interesting recent attempt to link individual rational choice with a range of underlying limitations on the political marketplace has been public choice theory. Public choice theory begins with individual rational choice analysis and depends upon the existence both of an *a priori* plurality of interests and of the equilibrating effects of the market; it then, however, astutely develops the notion that many 'public' choices involve criteria which partly distinguish them from 'private' choices, creating a class of specific dilemmas peculiarly characteristic of political markets. Although public choice theory does look at the implications of a series of logical conundrums, such as the impossibility of reaching any collective decision in certain circumstances when people have different orders of preference, the most influential and suggestive version of the approach looks mainly at the things to be allocated – 'public goods' vs. 'private goods'. In both cases, however, public choice theory looks at the process of choosing, at aspects of its internal logic, rather than at the impact of external structural constraints, leaving significant gaps in terms of a theory of structuration. Nevertheless, it raises a number of useful questions about the dynamics of rational choice which will help to conceptualize how the 'agency' side of the structuration coin works.

Public choice theory attempts to restate certain traditional dilemmas of political theory in terms of economic concepts. Unlike elitism, class analysis, corporatism, or orthodox state theory, however, public choice theory starts from the market, looking at the implications of individual rational choice for the public sphere. But the results have been uneven. The range of premises of public choice theory has been extremely limited even in economic terms. Its applications of economic theory have sometimes suggested explanations of political behavior which are far less plausible than orthodox political and sociological approaches would suggest. And the process of testing hypotheses, even in formal mathematical terms, is still in its infancy, so that contradictory findings rise and fall in fashion; creative insights alternate with reinventions of the wheel, sometimes not as well-rounded as earlier versions.

One of the best examples of this is found in the area of pressure group theory, which looked as if it might be revolutionized following the publication in 1965 of Mancur Olson's *The Logic of Collective Action*.[12] Olson argued that individuals did not cooperate in pressure groups out of simple common interest (as pluralist theory took for granted that they did) even if they would gain from the benefits of successful collective action, because the logic of their self-interest would lead them to 'free-ride' on the contributions of others. The key element is that the public nature of certain 'goods' which people wished to secure – goods which can only be provided to all at the same time, and which individuals who have not paid for them cannot be prevented from consuming – define the limiting criteria for choice. If the public good which interested individuals (and others) were seeking could be enjoyed without paying the costs of participating in providing the goods, then there would be little reason to pay these costs. In consequence, Olson argued, large, 'latent' groups – even those representing a clear sectional interest valued by all potential members, such as labor unions – were in fact the least likely to become manifest, active, organized pressure groups. Small groups had certain advantages, such as face-to-face relationships in contexts where social incentives and sanctions could apply directly, and especially where a few actors (or even one actor) could bring disproportionate resources to bear. Perceiving one's own contribution as a 'drop in the bucket' (rather than a 'little drop of water, little grain of sand'), or the reducing gains from 'rival' goods, have been seen as reinforcing Olson's logic.[13]

Of course, large groups such as trade unions, professional associations, farmers' organizations, etc., have not exactly been missing from the political scene. One explanation, put forward by Olson himself, has been called a 'finessing' of collective action problems.[14] As Olson writes: 'The large and powerful economic lobbies are in fact the by-products of organizations that obtain their strength and support because they perform some function in addition to lobbying for collective goods.'[15] These other functions include the provision of 'selective incentives' to members (not only magazines and discounts, but also, in the case of trade unions, the power to deal with employers exclusively on wages and conditions . . .), the capacity to punish non-joiners by excluding them, the oligopolistic nature of many industries, government promotion of groups in order to avoid backlashes, promoting certain cause groups low on economic 'rationality', organization of political patronage through party machines, etc. One might be forgiven for thinking that perhaps Olson may have drawn the category of public goods in too narrow and idealized a fashion – a theme which we will return to later.

The second set of explanations has involved borrowing the concept of the 'political entrepreneur' from other aspects of public choice[16] and making the case that entrepreneurs – in theory working for their own career interests rather than for collective goods as such – play a crucial role in changing the rationality equation for interest groups. They can control information in such a way as to manipulate the bounded rationality of potential and existing members through a kind of false consciousness which helps keep potential free-riders in line.[17] While very plausible, this is hardly an advance on Michelsian or Weberian forms of elite and organization theory. A third set of explanations is more interesting, but again fraught with the problem of fashion: the iterated Prisoners' Dilemma game.[18] Olson's conclusions about the rationality of free-riding may have stemmed from an elementary misunderstanding. The temptation to free-ride may, as increasing experience with repeated games seems to indicate, be limited to the equivalent of a 'one-shot' game. In contrast, the more that a player knows the game is to be repeated with the same opponent on a long-term basis with no predictable cut-off point, the more effective are cooperative, carrot-and-stick strategies. An efficient dyadic cooperation strategy, called 'Tit-for-Tat', can be extended through networks of dyads (two-player games) to form societies relatively safe from 'invasion' by non-cooperative strategies (although there are reducing returns when large-numbers, non-dyadic games are involved).

Thus one of the key issues studied by public choice analysts, interest group formation and maintenance, seems to have been left in a muddier state by the assumption of widespread free-riding. This leads us to question more closely a range of assumptions used in public choice theory. As we have already pointed out, the distinction between public and private goods is such a crude one that to assume that politics is somehow essentially about public goods seems almost Hegelian in its abstract artificiality. Politics is, and always has been, about private goods, public goods, and a range of in-between categories. Indeed, one attempt to specify the latter as 'semi-private goods' is an essential feature of contemporary cartel theory, which we discuss below in more detail. A further assumption concerns the structural alternatives which public choice theory presupposes. McLean asserts that: 'There are four ways of allocating goods that involve at least partial cooperation: altruism, anarchy, markets, and government.'[19] (Of these, we are of course concerned mainly with markets and government.) And Lane argues that: 'Fundamentally, there are only two mechanisms for collective choice: voting, politics and bureaucracy on the one hand, and the variety of markets on the other.'[20] (As with neo-pluralism, 'government' means authority, and authority means compulsion.)

The problem with this is that most of what goes on in politics involves *neither* pure markets nor pure 'government', but a dynamic organizational mix of the two – what we have called structuration. Neither organization nor structuration is listed by McLean, for example, as a discrete mode of allocating scarce goods; but organization is at the core of how elitism, class analysis, corporatism, and state theory work. Organization might be seen just as a prudential mixture of market and government, but its dynamic principles are different from both. It rejects the pure concept of market allocation and the efficiency of market pricing within its orbit; and it is based more on the coordination of complementary tasks through voluntary compliance and cooperation than on coercion, which is at best a last resort (and which rarely involves Weber's 'monopoly of legitimate violence'). Organization does not replace either markets or government; it is the inextricable intertwining of both. Seeing organization as a discrete mode of allocation, for one thing, helps to discriminate between the main rivals to pluralism, for whereas elitism and class analysis are seen as deriving from 'natural' *a priori* structures, neo-corporatism and state theory tend to be more a matter of organization.

The central problem with pluralism, then, seems to be an ambiguity embedded within the market concept. The robustness of a plural universe of groups makes it difficult to reject the market analogy *in toto*; however, individual rational choice, even in its public choice version, is so hedged about and watered down by constraints and qualifications that models based on generalizable rational choice processes lack credibility. But economic theory has also experienced difficulties with the market analogy. By this I do not mean only the issue of pathological 'market failure' – in which organized and authoritative solutions are seen to be rational only when *a priori* market processes fail in particular circumstances. The issue goes much farther than this. In fact, the problem with much economic theory (especially the kind of neo-classical theory fashionable in the 1970s and 1980s, which presumes that 'rational expectations' usually prove to be correct and that the attainment of equilibrium is due to the unalloyed benefits of competition) is that it, too, does not explain organizational formation and maintenance in the economic sphere, and that consequently it cannot explain outcomes.

And yet organizational formation and maintenance, it can be argued, may be just as characteristic of economics as of politics – if we take into account (a) the nature of the firm and (b) the question of cartel-like collaboration. Both of these are already rather better served by political theory, for example in the theory of groups,[21] whereas economic theory often takes the firm as a given, a fictitious individual in a frictionless market.[22] None the less, this gap has to some extent been filled in recent years by both a revival of theories of the firm and the rediscovery of efficient cartels.[23] In seeking to fill in the gaps in the pluralist political marketplace, then, it may be more fruitful not simply to posit alternative first principles, but to look more closely at the ambiguous nature of markets themselves. We will first of all consider some of the elements which are seen to enter into a calculation of the costs and benefits of hierarchical modes of organization, to reconcile individual rational choice with hierarchy and control – elements such as market structure, transaction costs, and semiprivate goods. Then we will look at organizational form: first, the limits of both decentralization and unitary structures in large organizations; and then the fashion for multidivisional organization, 'nested structures', and efficient cartels. Finally, a typology of political allocation structures will be presented taking into account the costs and benefits of organizational form.

In conclusion, it will be argued that even the *a priori* existence of a 'plural universe' of interests pursued by rational individuals and groups will lead, paradoxically, to the consolidation of a more restricted organizational universe. In this epiphenomenal universe, intermediation processes reproduce themselves through bounded rationality and socialization, except when either (a) internal stresses upset the cost/benefit calculation enough to produce a critical number of dissenters and/or free-riders, or (b) exogenous changes – in, e.g., the calculi of economies of scale, the requirements of technology, the impact of information on rationality, the number of market actors, or the demand for relevant goods or values – undermine existing organizations and thus lower barriers to entry. The result is the other face of structuration from the elements of structure discussed in Chapter 2, the other side of the same coin.

The Dynamics of Organization

Economic markets are everywhere characterized by the development of organizational structures when the number and rate of transactions exceeds what a single market actor can deal with on his or her own. Although the relationship between individuals within such an organization will be regulated by an original market transaction embedded in a contract such as an employment contract, that original contract does not itself have to be renegotiated each time the individuals interact. The basic contract will normally prescribe that both parties will conform to decisions made in a discretionary manner within a hierarchical relationship or command structure – for example, that disagreements about the nature of the obligations of the parties will be settled by fiat rather than by haggling – and the basic contract itself will prescribe or imply that the overall relationship is constituted by a range of sub-relationships, such as different tasks to be performed and/or the sequential execution of such tasks over successive time periods.[24]

The presupposition is, of course, that organization saves costs and confers benefits – that the market would not otherwise be a very efficient form of socio-economic organization, as it would quickly seize up from the logistical impossibility of spontaneously coordinating such a huge range of individual choices, rational or not. However, the premise of institutional economics is not that organization is inherently superior to markets (this might lead to the prescription of a central planning system); it is that in certain circumstances markets are more efficient allocators than hierarchies, while in other circumstances hierarchies are more efficient. The issue is to ascertain the nature of the circumstances. Thus firms are organizational structures, but they operate in markets; at the same time, as we argued earlier in this chapter, markets themselves may require organizational underpinnings in order to work efficiently in the first place.[25] Economic 'market structures', like political structures, are in a continual process of structuration.

Three sorts of factors are generally seen as particularly significant in the constitution of economic organizations. The first concern economies of scale and capacities for coordination. Economies of scale arise when economic processes require the simultaneous or serial carrying out of similar or identical tasks (or use of the same technology or materials in bulk), such that tasks can be carried out more efficiently if done virtually automatically. It is usually the case in industrial production that an integrated labor process or a machine which must be set up and operated for one unit of product to be produced, requires the identical or little additional input (except in terms of raw materials) in order to produce n units. Thus operation is only profitable if the process is run beyond a certain threshold of units produced, and beyond that threshold costs are drastically reduced. Capacities for coordination concern similar principles applied to the process of organization itself – information processing, managerial economies of scale, etc. The greater the economies of scale, the more the production must be organized and run as a single integrated unit, minimizing the economic equivalent of interstitial spaces and tensions, and requiring the adoption of a single structural logic; this can only be done, in a complex environment of competing utilities, by establishing a command hierarchy.

The second set of factors, related to economies of scale, are called transaction costs. These refer not to the positive logic of organization itself, but to the negative logistical and strategic costs of dealing with a multiplicity of transactions. Cost savings on eliminating the continual negotiation of contracts, the information costs required to determine prices in an uncertain context, and the monitoring of agents' performance, can in specific situations outweigh the benefits of the marginal savings which may be gained from haggling. The third set of factors, in a way which is analogous to Olson's 'selective benefits', concerns the provision of semiprivate goods. These are goods which may be private goods as regards allocation between firms (or sectors, or other levels), but which have the character of collective or public goods within firms (or sectors, etc.). Thus hierarchical organization – whether within firms or through cartels and the like – may be more efficient at eliminating 'free-riding' or 'chaotic competition', and therefore maximize the resources available for producing the desired outcomes. Of course, each of these gives rise to analogies with political allocation and structuration processes, although difficulties of quantification, bad enough in economics, are worse in politics.

Economies of Scale and the Capacity for Coordination
Scherer identifies four main determinants of what he calls 'market structure', i.e., conditions which can be more or less conducive to organizational integration or diffusion.[26] These are: economies of scale; mergers and concentration; the impact of government policies; and

stochastic determinants. Each of these, we will argue, has a political analog. In effect, to study the role of choice in the process of structuration, one must see individuals and groups not only in terms of the logic of participation – through exit, voice, and loyalty – but also with regard to the overall impact of the outcomes of the choice process in terms of pursuing and achieving objectives. The basic principle of group economies of scale, for example, is the classic 'unity is strength'. Political economies of scale can be seen, therefore, at three levels – analogous to the main types of economies of scale for industrial firms discussed by Scherer: 'product-specific' scale economies, plant-level economies, and multi-plant economies of scale.

The first of these can be compared in political terms with the category of single-issue pressure groups, a category which has often been seen to be increasingly salient and significant actors in the political marketplace of advanced capitalist societies.[27] In terms of the logic of participation, the cost–benefit calculus is different for single-issue groups from that relevant for the multi-dimensional, 'sectional' interest groups which are most often analyzed in economic terms. Whereas for the latter, in Olson's argument for example, costs are more readily perceived than benefits, for the former the perception of benefit is heightened by the greater clarity of the goal; such groups are likely to be more single-minded. If the goal is a public good, then various social incentives, from altruism to honor, are activated, and such groups are often structured in a relatively decentralized way: contributions are fundamentally self-monitored. If the objective is a semiprivate good, then benefits through selective incentives will be relatively specific and possibly of high perceived value to members. If it is a private good, then members will only join if they benefit directly, in a quite calculable or at least perceptible way.

Costs, in turn, may be perceived to be low in relation to other uses of resources, time, energy, etc. – whether because benefits are highly salient and valued ('well worth the trouble'), or because they can actually *be* low when activity touches only one aspect of a member's social existence. By not involving what public choice analysts call 'full-line supply' – i.e., the achievement of several different (even competing) goals at the same time – such groups can avoid the potential conflicts of interests both between members and within individual members' own preference schedules which can raise perceived costs relative to their other goals. Furthermore, advantages of unity are perhaps more obvious in such groups. They are less likely to be undermined by specific conflicts of interest; they are more likely to achieve scale economies in information gathering and processing, through specialization, given their restricted terms of reference; and thus they are more likely to be listened to both by the public, and within policy communities, even when their goals are opposed by others, and more likely to play perhaps pivotal roles in debate. And they may be cheaper to organize, being self-monitoring and self-mobilizing. On the other hand, they may be vulnerable to changes in fashion, technology, market conditions, etc., precisely because of their narrowness.

At the next level, the analogue of plant-level (and plant complex-level) scale economies is quite straightforward. Increasing group size, whatever other dysfunctions it may entail in terms of complexity and difficulty of control, does provide a higher absolute level of resources to the group itself, resources which go into such obvious uses as staffing, information processing, providing office space, publicity, the capacity to carry out membership drives or expand on a regional basis (similar to transportation costs in industry), and the like. And this may, as Moe argues, attract the elite 'political entrepreneur', who can coordinate the activities of the organization, making it both more efficient at reaching old members and in recruiting new ones, on the one hand, and more effective in targeting policy communities, state actors, the media, etc., in pursuit of group goals, on the other.[28]

As with plant-level economies, there may in effect be what Scherer has called a 'minimum optimal scale' or MOS,[29] linking (a) the technology of running a group (capital and operating costs), (b) the particular population of state actors, etc., being targeted, and (c) the requirements of communication and recruitment *vis-à-vis* the rank-and-file. Examples include hiring a minimum headquarters staff and local permanent staff; renting offices in a visible and 'respectable' part of town; purchase of word-processing and data-processing equipment; capacity to solicit and collect dues and donations; capacity to mobilize a sufficient number of specialized lobbyists to deal with a range of government departments, political officeholders, legal processes, etc.; capacity to mobilize a minimum visible amount of grass-roots pressure at short notice (letter-writing, demonstrations, etc.); and managerial capacity to coordinate the above.

The marginal utility of expanding beyond the MOS may be limited, unless a quantum leap is made. On the one hand, if a number of exclusive centers of power must be pressurized – say, different state governments in the United States – then something analogous to multi-plant economies may occur, in step-level fashion. These may not introduce new overall scale economies, but may maximize those realizable in each unit. On the other hand, where the equivalent of vertical integration occurs – where, for example, certain common functions are integrated (strategic management, research, production of selective incentives such as magazines, etc.) – further scale economies can be achieved. And if the group is expanded to include a wider range of 'interests', the possibilities are greater, although larger size often introduces coordination problems as well as scale economies if the linkages between infrastructure, base, and targets become overloaded. In all of these cases of economies of scale, however, it is clear that the achievement of group goals can be enhanced if the greater resources which come with size can be effectively coordinated.

Even the provision of 'inclusive' collective goods may be made so much more feasible where size problems are successfully overcome (i.e., decentralized cooperation in the case of cause 'movements') as to significantly reduce perceived private costs of participation. And when other categories of goods are considered, free-riding becomes less attractive and collaboration more the rule. Indeed, cooperation feeds back, through practice, experience, and socialization, to become a social norm or expectation, raising the 'discount parameter' (i.e., encouraging the deferment of gratification). Such a norm is less likely to be broken unless benefits fall below an expected threshold, or unless private costs rise above a certain threshold. Organizations develop resources to maintain thresholds as well as to pursue ultimate group goals, i.e., to pursue system maintenance goals as a bottom line.

Scherer's next two determinants of market structure – mergers and concentration, and the impact of public policies – can be seen as extensions of the above arguments. In particular circumstances, where the conditions for linkage between the group's infrastructure, base, and targets are insufficiently achieved or are disturbed by endogenous or exogenous shocks (internal conflict, changing values, economic hard times, and the like), then the effective pursuit of group goals may require changes in organizational form, by expansion or consolidation.

A good recent example of the issues of merger and concentration is the trend in British trade unionism toward what has been called the 'new realism', including a number of converging elements: mergers between unions themselves, as old craft and industrial demarcation lines become unsustainable in a shifting environment of global competition and technological change (changing product-level scale economies within the unions); single-union agreements at plant level (changing plant-level scale economies for unions in general); and the crisis in the Trades Union Congress itself (as inter-union coordination breaks down due to the decentralized nature of the common organizational framework). On the one hand, the more traditional unions, such as the Transport and General Workers' Union (as in the Spring 1988 inter-union conflict over the abortive Ford electronics plant in Dundee, Scotland), accuse the 'new realist' unions such as the electricians and the engineering workers of breaking solidarity and/or of seeking semiprivate gain; while, on the other, the latter accuse the former of free-riding by winning higher wages (again, a semiprivate gain), while other workers are not employed at all!

The impact of government policies has obvious effects on scale economies of pressure groups, as Olson conceded.[30] Another striking example is the defense industry, in which the presence of the government as monopoly purchaser is the key determinant of economies of scale.[31] Indeed, the plausibility of neo-corporatism as an alternative to pluralism rests largely on the argument that *societal* corporatism – corporatism built upon the natural solidarity of socio-functional categories – as well as state corporatism,[32] results from the state's 'licensing' of groups with the intention of making them into monopolistic or oligopolistic collaborators in a harmonious, cross-class cooperative venture. *Dirigisme* and clientelism, in which the state either controls, or is in turn captured by, private interests, rest largely on the symbiosis (although not necessarily a synergy) of groups and the state.

Scherer's last category, stochastic factors, brings a dynamic time element into the equation. These factors essentially boil down to the consolidation of luck. In effect, as we pointed out in Chapter 1, structures are 'sticky'. A quite dynamic and efficiently organized firm can suffer if that dynamism and efficiency reach their optimum at a time of market instability or falling demand. Once such a firm is down, it may be out; more likely, however, is that it will find its dynamism and efficiency compromised and its internal organization weakened; it may not be able to catch up when better times arrive. Conversely, a firm which is taking off as good times arrive will tend to find its structures strengthened and its growth stronger and more stable in relation to other firms; indeed, firms which are successful in this way find their growth rates less likely to fall in bad times, therefore increasing concentration. The more variable are the growth rates of firms, 'the more rapidly concentrated industry structures will emerge, all other things being equal.'[33] Furthermore, variability is greater for smaller firms, speeding concentration; and industries as well as firms which are characterized by rapid innovation, design change, and luck with fashion, will leap ahead, while, structurally, a miss is as good as a mile.

Such factors will affect interest groups also. Successful structuration entrenches patterns of behavior which have the benefit of inertia. It is often accepted in game theory, too, that: 'Once the system gets there, it stays there. . . . Which history unfolds may depend on idiosyncratic events, e.g., an unlucky early defeat that creates widespread suspicion of shirking. Consequently, explaining why patterns persist may be more amenable to theoretical analysis than explaining how they arose.'[34] But while it may be difficult to explain particular *configurations* of events other than historically, it is not impossible to specify the terms of the perceptual calculus applied by actors. Scale economies and coordination capacities, in non-economic contexts where costs and benefits depend more upon unquantifiable perceptions than on specifiable prices, constitute a major element in the efficient organization of political interests – and, obviously, in the structuration of the state itself.

Transaction Costs

Economies of scale and coordination capacities mainly concern structural 'indivisibilities'. They are top-down factors – essentially micro-economic, of course, but at the 'macro' end – which organization either conforms to, by design or by luck, or does not. Transaction costs are even more micro-economic, concerning not given indivisibilities but the critical interface or threshold where markets – even without orthodox scale economies – interface with organizational forms. Williamson[35] argues that the difference between markets and hierarchies in terms of efficiency can actually be explained better, and in a more dynamic fashion, by relative levels of transaction costs than by indivisibilities such as economies of scale. Markets and hierarchies are thus not *opposing* principles of efficiency, but complementary ones, mutually reinforcing each other.

The image, then, is one of a multidimensional threshold where markets and hierarchies meet and overlap. Where the cost of market transactions is too high, it can often be brought down by the savings on transaction costs which can be found by adopting internal organizational decision-making processes for resource allocation, internal pricing, broad contracts covering a variety of the aspects of the employment relation, and the like. Thus cumulative, bottom-up cost savings can be made within organizations which cannot be made in markets. Making these savings depends on the presence of a number of conditions which can make market transactions particularly expensive. However, it should be noted that the most powerful form of internal organization is one which will both maximize the benefits of economies of scale and minimize transaction costs – while at the same time allowing the organization as a whole to operate as efficiently as possible in the wider marketplace.

According to Williamson, the prerequisites which make internal organization more efficient than markets by saving on transaction costs consist of three pairs of linked conditions. The first of these is the pair which includes (a) uncertainty, which, in the terms set out in the first part of this chapter, means the lack of clear market signals, and (b) bounded rationality. The combination of these two means that if 'it is very costly or impossible to identify future contingencies and specify, *ex ante*, appropriate conditions thereto, [then] long-term contracts may be supplanted by internal organization'. Internal organization allows the process of adapting to uncertainty to unfold sequentially 'rather than to attempt to anticipate all possible contingencies from the outset . . . [when] prices are not "sufficient statistics" and uncertainty is substantial'.[36]

The second pair comprises (a) 'opportunism' (a wider category, including lying and secretiveness, and which can also include free-riding) and (b) a 'small numbers exchange condition', i.e., a situation in which prices may not be set efficiently because there is an insufficient range of buyers and/or sellers bidding and offering. If there is a large number of buyers and sellers, then market processes can outweigh the risks of opportunism; but when there is a small number, then controls on opportunism are insufficient and prices are false indicators. There is a time element here, too: for even where a large-numbers condition obtains at the outset of a process of contract execution, it frequently happens that the signing of an original contract means that when the contract comes up for renewal, potential bidders have dropped out (including for the sort of stochastic reasons discussed above); therefore recurrent short-term contracting can be costly.

The advantages of internal organization are summed up thus:

> Issues here are dealt with as they arise rather than in exhaustive contingent-planning fashion from the outset. The resulting adaptive, sequential decision-making process is the internal organization counterpart of short-term contracting and serves to economize on bounded rationality. Opportunism does not pose the same difficulties for such internal sequential supply relations as it does when negotiations take place across a market because (1) internal divisions do not have preemptive claims on profit streams (but more nearly joint profit maximize instead); and (2) the internal incentive and control machinery is much more extensive and refined than that which obtains in market exchanges. The firm is thereby better able to take the long view for investment purposes (and hence is more prepared to put specialized plant and equipment in place) while simultaneously adjusting to changing market conditions in an adaptive, sequential manner.[37]

A third pair of conditions derives from the combination of (a) uncertainty and (b) opportunism: this is called 'information impactedness'. In this case, information available to one party in an exchange may be unavailable to the other parties.[38] This pair, which cuts across the other two, exacerbates them both. Within an organization, information is said to be fed up and down the hierarchy more efficiently, thus avoiding the opportunities which some parties might have to keep information for themselves; of course, internal opportunism and information overload (bureaucratic paper-shuffling) are dangers too. In effect, all of these conditions can be applied to the theory of interests and political choice. Costs, once again, are even less easily quantifiable in politics – and one of the main criticisms of transaction cost theory within economics is the difficulty of identifying, much less quantifying, such costs with any precision.

If there is any one thing which it is chancy for a political scientist to attempt, it is the prediction of future events – even elections, where much 'hard' data, including previous results, cost–benefit analyses of manifestoes, opinion survey data, etc., does exist, but where educated guesses are the best that can be achieved. Uncertainty and bounded rationality make political science, as the old saying goes, a science more like meteorology than like chemistry or biology. And every school child knows that all politicians are opportunists (liars), while all group members would be free-riders if possible – as well as that information impactedness is chronic in politics.

But what is interesting here is the role of the small-numbers condition. In Olson's treatment of interest groups, the small-numbers condition is what makes groups *more*, not less, efficient (in his categories of 'privileged' and 'intermediate' groups). In Williamson's treatment of internal organization, however, *large* numbers make groups more efficient. How can we reconcile this apparent paradox? The answer takes us back to the difference between the efficiency of groups *endogenously* to control free-riding – Olson's problem – and the issue raised earlier in this chapter about the efficiency of groups in transacting business *exogenously* with other groups (and with the state), or the 'unity is strength' principle. For, in principle, the larger each group, the smaller will be the total number of groups likely to arise from a given population. Williamson is in effect saying, *pace* Michels, not that 'organization means oligarchy', or at least not in so many words, but that in a wider market context internal organization is the most effective means of controlling oligarchy and making it as efficient as possible. Given the presence (or, conversely, the absence) of these conditions, what sorts of transaction costs are relevant to determining whether transactions ought to be assigned to internal organization rather than to the market?

The list presented here is not taken directly from Williamson, but derived from what I take to be an implicit systems analogy in the way he develops his argument. Thus there can be said to be three main categories of political transaction costs: input-related costs, withinput-related costs, and output-related costs. Each of these includes aspects derived from Williamson's three pairs of conditions. Input-related costs might include, firstly, costs of gathering information about individuals' preference schedules – the raw material of groups' 'common interests'. These costs may be prohibitive if there are serious uncertainties, especially with implications for full-line supply or for a much more intractable problem – the relative intensity of preferences on a cardinal rather than an ordinal scale. However, knowledge of what actual or potential members really want may permit, for example, a form of price discrimination or market segmentation which would maximize participation; and internal organization, possibly but in no way necessarily around a 'political entrepreneur', could allow a trial and error process to occur sequentially which might even identify a 'core' of values which would be sufficiently stable to save on other costs. Similar remarks can be made about further input-related costs, such as costs of aggregating preferences, formulating demands, and mobilizing members.

Withinput-related costs might include the presentation, transmission, and formulation of demands both endogenously, within the group infrastructure and between the staff and the rank-and-file, and exogenously, to target officials or other relevant groups, as well as to the media and to the population at large. Particularly costly can be processes of negotiation and bargaining, in time, in the requirement for information, in staff skills, etc., as well as in monetary resources; this can involve both negotiation between representatives of different factions within the group, or the negotiation of deals with other groups, with policy communities, or with the state. Not only are there problems of uncertainty/bounded rationality, but also of opportunism/small-numbers bargaining (and of information impactedness too), as any study of negotiating processes will demonstrate. Following through a piece of legislation can be similarly costly, especially in the United States, given the complexity of the process. And, of course, all of this requires both strategic and tactical coordination, budgeting, maintaining morale, etc.

Output-related costs include the implementation and administration of policy outputs; this is particularly important where the group is in an ongoing collaborative relationship with other groups or with the state, for example where trade unions must enforce corporatist wage bargains on their own rank-and-file. Perhaps the most important category is one which is clearly the most difficult task for large groups to undertake in the absence of efficient organizational structures, and which includes the monitoring of performance of members, of officials, of other groups, etc.; the evaluation of such information; the use of feedback to adapt performance; and the application of sanctions to free-riders, shirkers, dissenters, etc.

It is also possible to extend the concept of transaction costs to relations between groups (and between groups and the state), such that an ongoing collaborative relationship saves on having to renegotiate compromise solutions on a recurrent basis, saves on the costs of actually *breaking* a contract (involving a loss of shared resources or the danger of retaliation), or saves on the costs of dealing with internal conflict if exogenous conditions change in such a way as to undermine the 'core' or alter the conditions of full-line supply. When trade unions go on strike, for example, they must not only take into account the costs of breaking off negotiations with employers; they must also organize the collection and distribution of money for strike pay, they must engage in internal negotiations between, e.g., soft or hard factions, and they must monitor the solidarity of the strike and apply sanctions.

But it must be re-emphasized that transaction costs are not a one-way street in favor of internal organization. There can be transaction cost diseconomies within organizations too, of course, especially if internal pricing is pitched higher than a potential market level – and therefore that alternative organizations, or no organization at all, can provide the good more cheaply.

Miscalculations can bring down organizations. Also bureaucratic overload can push transaction costs up within organizations, a feature which leads theorists to distrust highly centralized organizational forms. And if there are problems with full-line supply or the presence of an 'empty core', i.e., that members have trouble agreeing on priorities, then the sort of sanctions required for maintaining, mobilizing, and monitoring members' actions may push up private costs to the extent that centrifugal forces – exit – undermine the group itself. Such constraints on organization are even more important in collaborative relationships between groups and other groups, and/or with the state. None the less, collaborative relationships at whatever level, once institutionalized, lead to the entrenchment of presumed predictability, routine, and inertia, reducing the *perception* of uncertainty; thus it will take greater than usual momentum from endogenous conflict or exogenous shocks for structures to break down. The threshold between market and hierarchy may in fact be a very sticky one.

Semiprivate Goods
In the context of both (a) economies of scale and (b) transaction cost analysis, it has been argued that it is the presence of semiprivate goods which tips the balance of the threshold in favor of collaborative structures rather than markets. Olson in fact makes 'exclusive collective goods' the condition which makes groups work. Telser,[39] in his discussion of cartel theory, develops his own approach partly around the concept of semiprivate goods – that cartels are efficient where semiprivate goods are concerned, and that they may be particularly necessary in times of falling demand, when an empty core can lead to 'chaotic competition'. The latter is not a condition widely canvassed in neo-classical economic theory; political theory does better with chaotic versions of anarchy (as distinct from the benign version adopted by public choice theorists).

This chapter suggests further that semiprivate goods are in fact the 'stuff' of most politics most of the time. Pure public goods are few and far between. National defense may seem to be a public good to most of the public, but it is a semiprivate or private good to the constituent parts of the military–industrial complex (respectively). Welfare policy involves all three kinds of goods. Semiprivate goods are particularly significant for group activity in the industrial policy issue area; subsidies usually affect sectors or sub-sectors of industry, as do tariff and non-tariff barriers, support for research and development, regional assistance, and wage policies. They are not the only type of goods which support collaborative structures, of course, but they do have a particularly important role in the typology of allocative processes presented below.

Organizational Form and Processes of Political Allocation

So far we have argued (1) that the market analogy is more robust than any of the alternatives in terms of the empirical experience of a plural universe of groups; but (2) that the far-reaching implications of the internal logic of organization as both an economic and a political process are either defined out of or only dimly perceived in the interest group debate. In turn, organization is (a) a more ubiquitous allocative process than either pure market processes or pure authoritative processes, (b) one which is complementary to, and enhances the efficiency of, both markets and governments, and (c) characteristic of both fundamental economic phenomena (firms and cartels) and political interest groups.

Specific ways have been suggested that organization can be more efficient than pure competitive markets – achieving economies of scale and other coordination capacities, economizing on transaction costs, and pursuing a wide range of semiprivate goods as common group goals. But we also have mentioned that organizations do not always achieve such economies. Firstly, economies of scale can run out or become complex, as when minimal optimal scales are both rigid and multidimensional; also, of course, what looks like efficient production may not be appropriate to the effective demand for the product. Furthermore, the conditions for transaction cost economizing are complex, and organizations can develop high internal transaction costs if they are overly rigid or bloated. And finally, the category of semiprivate goods is not a sufficient condition for cooperation, but a facilitating condition, while, for example, the combination of a 'nonempty core' (the congruence of preferences) plus a stable or rising demand may make competition more efficient than collaboration.[40]

In this context, the approaches which have been discussed here – and some others as well, including mainstream organization theory[41] – also suggest that in a range of specific circumstances certain particular forms of market/organization mix may be more efficient than others. This is particularly true for organizations which keep going a long time, especially where there is no fixed (but at most a probabilistic) limit to the number of iterations. These conditions are generally true for the sorts of market/organization mixes we are concerned with here, whether economic firms or cartels, on the one hand, or political interests, on the other. In such circumstances, decentralized structures, such as those produced by the 'evolution of cooperation',[42] are often prone to centrifugal tendencies, especially insofar as their control and monitoring systems are not strong enough to resist the growth of internal dissent or free-riding, on the one hand, or exogenous shocks, on the other; an exception might be large, single-issue cause groups, which can be more resilient for a number of reasons.[43]

Perhaps more important, and central to traditional critiques of bureaucracy and monopoly/oligopoly power, is that highly centralized structures – such as those referred to as the 'unitary form' by Williamson – have limits to their internal expansion. Not only are there limits to material economies of scale, such that a U-shaped (or shallow W-shaped) long-run unit cost curve is generally observed as scale expands, but there are also growing managerial scale diseconomies in such organizations,[44] linked with transaction cost diseconomies.[45] Game theory also points to growing inefficiency with increasing size in centralized organizations, especially with imperfect monitoring.[46] However, these inefficiencies of both the decentralized and the centralized organizational forms are not seen as undermining the various arguments in favor of the ubiquity and robustness of internal organization presented earlier in this chapter. Rather, all of these authors see one particular sort of market/organization mix as combining the virtues of both market and organizational efficiency. This is variously called the 'multidivisional form', 'federal' or 'nested' structures, or, at inter-firm level, 'efficient cooperation'.[47]

Such structures in fact combine the benefits of small groups, as perceived by Olson, with what are essentially managerial economies of scale and/or transaction cost economizing – reducing haggling costs, pursuing semiprivate goods such as research, controlling opportunism through joint profit maximizing, developing strategic coordination at central level while decentralizing monitoring to local level where it can be carried out more cheaply, etc. 'Unity is strength', then, so long as the benefits of unity, especially *strategic* decision-making and the provision of semiprivate goods, can be separated from detailed operational decision-making, the costs of which can more easily lead to scale diseconomies and are more efficiently borne at divisional or local level. The use of the concept of 'federalism' to describe such structures, then, would seem to be quite misleading. Their strength comes not from a *division of powers* between levels, but a *division of functions* on an efficient-cost basis. The 'lessons' which have usually been drawn from the different approaches discussed in this chapter are similar in substance, too, with the current fashion in management doctrine for 'lean and mean' strategic management – combining strategic centralization at the top with tactical and operational *flexibility* at the bottom.

In recent literature, the efficiency of such management approaches is often seen to be greatly enhanced by the development of information technology and the centralization/flexibility mix characteristic of the so-called 'Third Industrial Revolution', especially at the level of the transnational firm. Indeed, there is more than a passing resemblance between such structures and the lessons said to be learned not only from General Motors, but from Japanese[48] or Austrian[49] methods of 'flexible manufacturing systems' in efficiently restructuring industry in the face of rapidly changing international competitive conditions.[50] What is interesting in some of these cases, furthermore, is that the state, too, takes on functions of superstrategic management, especially through certain *dirigiste* forms of financial control or administrative guidance, the model for which is usually taken to be Japan's Ministry of International Trade and Industry (M.I.T.I.) – or, perhaps more prosaically, Massachusetts's Lowell Plan. It is at this level that the distinction between 'market' and 'organization' also overlaps and blurs into 'government' or 'authority'. This is why, we will argue later, neo-corporatism – macro, meso, and micro – is likely to prove in the long run to be a more robust analytical framework than has been seen to be the case since the rise of pluralism has turned many analysts away during the 1980s,[51] despite the fact that some of the more rigid assumptions of earlier versions have been superseded. Corporatist allocative processes can constitute particularly strong versions of 'nested structures' in certain circumstances.

It is also why state theory bounces back, too – because states are no longer seen primarily as 'authoritative' institutions providing public goods, but rather as sets of embedded processes crossing the false (or ideological) public/private frontier. These sets of embedded processes are intricately intertwined in the state in the advanced capitalist era: public goods and authority; semiprivate goods and organization; and private goods and markets (whether setting the 'market framework' or intervening at a microeconomic level). Given the central role of interest groups in linking these three levels, e.g., through informal 'functional representation', it is they – through a fusion of powers rather than a federalist separation of powers – which are at the core of the 'nested structures' of the organized political marketplace.

It is possible, given all that has been said above, to sketch out a tentative typology of political allocative processes to replace the obsolete 'market–government' distinction and to define the different kinds of inextricably intertwined organizational mixes which the structuration process gives rise to. This typology is based on two dimensions: firstly, the nature of the *goods* being pursued by the actors concerned; and secondly, the *organizational form* which the structure of the organization takes. For each dimension there is a three-fold categorization based on the discussions earlier in the chapter. For the dimension comprising the goods being pursued by the actors involved, there are private, semiprivate, and public goods; and for the dimension covering types of organizational form, there are the decentralized market form, the multidivisional or 'nested' form, and the unitary/centralized form. Each 'box' consists of a particular type of organizational mix resulting from actor/structure interaction – or the structuration process

Table 3.1 *Political allocative processes*

Goods	Organizational form		
	Decentralized/ market	Multidivisional/ nested	Unitary/ centralized
Private	Unrestricted competition	Restricted competition/ neo-pluralism	Central planning/ state-licensed monopoly
Semiprivate	Clientelism/ 'private government'/ 'captured state'	Corporatism/ policy communities/ 'arms-length' *dirigisme*	Indicative planning/ strategic *dirigisme*
Public	Abstract public goods/rights/ regulation/ 'rule of law'	Macroeconomic fine tuning/ controlling aggregate balances	Physical public goods/pure natural monopoly

– and is referred to as a specific type of 'political allocation process'. And each of these types of political allocation process will be familiar to those who have studied particular case studies or approaches to comparative politics, public policy analysis, political economy, political sociology, and the like. Let us examine each in turn (see Table 3.1).

It should be stressed that these categories are not meant to represent whole states or countries. They represent processes, examples of each of which can be found in all countries. Even the equivalent of central planning can be found in various nooks and crannies of the economic activities of the state in the most capitalist of countries (especially in the military, for example), and it is a commonplace to note that more pluralistic processes are to be found at many levels in countries said to be 'totalitarian states'. However, of course, part of the utility of any typology is that, if cautiously used, it can lead to generalizations about specific systems. Sweden is often said to be a 'corporatist state'; what is meant by this, however, is that corporatist processes are more widespread and have more significance for our understanding of how Swedish politics works. But it would be wrong to assume that corporatist processes are the only processes that exist in Sweden, or even that they are the only significant processes. Furthermore, it may well be that certain types of issues tend to be processed in different ways, as Cawson has pointed out,[52] and in different countries there may be different issues which get relatively efficient or even privileged treatment – e.g., 'economic' rights

in more corporatist systems, personal rights in more 'pluralistic' ones.*
Nevertheless, this is not a typology of states, but of processes.

In this typology, the four 'corner' boxes represent what, we would argue, are the relatively pure – and unrealistic – allocation processes which result from applying the two basic dimensions of public choice theory: (a) a dualistic, exclusive distinction between 'market' and 'government' as allocative processes; and (b) a dualistic, exclusive distinction between public and private goods. We might assume that competition over private goods in the context of a minimal, neutral state would most resemble the model of unrestricted market competition; this, of course, does not mean that state intervention does not exist, but only that state intervention would tend to be limited to the kind of market-establishing and market-maintaining framework intervention outlined at the beginning of this chapter. The allocation of private goods in a context where major economies of scale, high transaction costs, etc., have led to the development of a centralized or unitary organizational form, would of course approximate a classical system of central planning and/or state-licensed monopolies. Public goods allocated in a minimal or decentralized organizational context would tend to be carried out through the application of general, universalizable rules, as exemplified by the broad concepts of regulation, rights, or the 'rule of law'. And public goods allocated in a centralized organizational context would generally approximate to the pure public goods model as depicted in public choice theory, with control processes minimizing free-riding.

However, for the purposes of this book, it is more realistic to look at the mixed cases represented by the middle column and the middle row of the table. Most political (and, indeed, most economic) structures in fact represent a fusion of decentralized and centralized organizational structures; while much political (as well as economic) competition concerns mixed or semiprivate goods. These are the boxes which most conform to real-world observation by comparative political analysts of the way that the plural universe of groups is actually structured and the ways in which interest intermediation works most of the time in practice. Private goods allocated in the context of multidivisional or 'nested' structures best approximate to the kind of neo-pluralism which Lindblom portrays. The allocation of public goods in the same sort of structural context involves the predominance of such processes as the manipulation of broad policy instruments, as in the archetypal manipulation of fiscal and

---

*For example, recent research of indicates that while women's economic rights are better catered for in Sweden, their gender-specific personal rights – protection against violence, etc. – are better safeguarded in the more pluralistic United States; see R. Amy Elman, 'The Sexual Politics of Swedish Neocorporatism', paper presented to the meeting of the New England Political Science Association, Cambridge, Mass., 8 April 1989.

monetary aggregates comprising macroeconomic fine tuning.

Finally, the process of allocating semiprivate goods in each of these organizational contexts approximates to the models which have dominated the study of comparative politics in the past couple of decades: (a) in the context of a decentralized organizational (or state) structure, the allocation of semiprivate goods resembles clientelism or 'private government';[53] (b) in the context of a multidivisional or 'nested' structure, in which functional deconcentration is strategically controlled from the center, one would expect to find a smaller universe of large interest groups collaborating in cartel-like fashion through corporatist structures, policy communities, 'iron triangles', and the like, in their pursuit of semiprivate goods; and (c) in unitary or centralized systems, one would tend to find such goods allocated through a more 'top-down' process such as indicative planning or strategic *dirigisme*, in which the relative unity or competition among state actors (rather than among competing interests themselves) would be the most important force shaping outcomes. In fact, this 'middle row' will be the subject of closer examination in Chapter 6.

Individual and group agents, then, far from being atomistic competitors, form ongoing organizations which are structured specifically for the purposes of entering into continuous intermediation processes and for survival, system maintenance, and goal-seeking within those processes. In this context, longer-term perceptions of the structural constraints on action – what public choice analysts call the 'shadow of the future' – is relatively very high, as it is with large firms, and this high 'discount parameter' increases the effectiveness of cooperative strategies. Groups thus develop cost/benefit thresholds which become clearer over time, other things being equal – although internal dissent and exogenous shocks are significant threats in the changing real world environment. And intraorganizational actors will monitor those thresholds in order to attempt to minimize disturbance as well as to perform their tasks in a 'satisficing', if not always an optimizing, manner. Change in the plural universe of interests and agents, then, tends to come about in the manner of a 'punctuated equilibrium' – in which structural patterns seem relatively stable over periods of time, but the sorts of meso- and micro-level changes which we described in Chapter 1 build up (in the manner of Kuhn's paradigms), leading to more fundamental change at irregular intervals or critical conjunctures – rather than in the continuous adjustment process of a competitive marketplace.

What is true of interest groups internally is also true of relationships between groups and other groups, and between groups and the state, for example in the context of ongoing corporatist relations or among policy communities. Indeed, the state itself, as we have argued earlier, is an intricately intertwined set of embedded processes – market, organizational, and authoritative – which together constitute the structured field of action within which individual and group agents devise their strategies and operate their tactics. States, incidentally, also operate as macro-level 'agents' within an international system characterized by a certain amount of 'anarchy' (in both the positive and pejorative senses of the word). Within this context, both state structures and large groups themselves, to be effective, develop multidivisional or nested structures characterized by a fusion of powers but a division of functions. Strategic tasks are most efficiently carried out at central level; tactical or operational tasks are most efficiently carried out at divisional or local level. In this context, agents are able both to utilize scale economies and to economize on transaction costs such as monitoring (thus controlling free-riding more effectively), while developing the kind of unity which gives strength in the wider structured action field – similar to the economic concept of 'joint profit maximization'. If they do not do this effectively, they do not survive. Barriers to entry are lowered, and alternative groups, parties, and even regimes arise to compete for structural power.

Both the strengths and weaknesses of 'pluralism', then, derive from the market analogy. On the one hand, there is indeed a plural universe of individual agents and groups, manifest and latent, which is not circumscribed primarily by exogenous structural factors of the orthodox kind. On the other hand, however, the operation of this plural universe fits with neither the market model of allocation nor the authority model. It fits most closely with an ongoing organizational process which provides the crucial dynamic within the wider process of structuration with which we are concerned in this book. The dynamics of agency are inextricably intertwined with the structure of games which constitutes the structured field of action of politics. In the next chapter we will look more closely at the way that the dynamics of agency and the elements of state structure interact, both in terms of different levels of the process of structuration and with regard to the internal and external structural fields which shape the 'meta-game' of the state itself.

Notes

1. Axelrod, *The Evolution of Cooperation* (New York: Basic Books, 1984).

2. Reddy, *Money and Liberty, op. cit.*

3. Lindblom, *Politics and Markets, op. cit.*;   Williamson, *Markets and Hierarchies, op. cit.*

4. A. Grant Jordan, 'Corporatism: The Unity and Utility of the Concept?', Strathclyde Papers in Government and Politics, no. 11 (1983).

5. Lindblom, *op. cit.*

6. Philippe C. Schmitter, 'Still the Century of Corporatism?', in Frederick Pike and Thomas Stritch, eds., *The New Corporatism* (Notre Dame, Ind.: Notre Dame University Press, 1974).

7. Cf. Arnold Rose, *The Power Structure* (New York: Oxford University Press, 1967),

and Peter Bachrach, *The Theory of Democratic Elitism* (Boston: Little Brown, 1967).

8. See Carnoy, *The State and Political Theory*, *op. cit.*; Jessop, *The Capitalist State*, *op. cit.*

9. See Martin A. Schain, 'Corporatism and Industrial Relations in France', in Cerny and Schain, eds., *French Politics and Public Policy* (New York and London: St Martin's Press, Methuen and Pinter, 1980), ch. 10.

10. Alan Cawson, *Corporatism and Welfare* (London: Heinemann, 1982). See also Cerny and Schain, *Socialism, the State and Public Policy in France*, *op. cit.*, Introduction, and Chapter 6, below.

11. Alan Cawson, ed., *Organized Interests and the State: Studies in Meso-Corporatism* (London: Sage, 1985), and Cawson, 'Is There a Corporatist Theory of the State?', in Graeme Duncan and Robert R. Alford, eds., *Democracy and the Capitalist State* (Cambridge: Cambridge University Press, 1987).

12. Olson, *The Logic of Collective Action*, *op. cit.*

13. See Iain McLean, *Public Choice: An Introduction* (Oxford: Basil Blackwell, 1987), and Jonathan Bendor and Dilip Mookherjee, 'Institutional Structures and the Logic of Ongoing Collective Action', *American Political Science Review*, vol. 81, no. 1 (March 1987), pp. 129–54.

14. Bendor and Mookherjee, *op cit.*, p. 130.

15. Olson, *op. cit.*, p. 132.

16. See McLean, *op. cit.*, ch. 2.

17. See Terence M. Moe, *The Organization of Interests: Incentives and the Internal Dynamics of Political Interest Groups* (Chicago, Ill.: University of Chicago Press, 1980).

18. Axelrod, *op. cit.*, and Bendor and Mookherjee, *op. cit.*

19. McLean, *op. cit.*, p. 22.

20. Jan-Erik Lane, *State and Market: The Politics of the Public and the Private* (London and Beverly Hills: Sage, 1985), p. viii.

21. Consider Olson's reference to business lobbying: *op. cit.*, p. 143.

22. Williamson, *op. cit.*, and Jackson, *The Political Economy of Bureaucracy* (London: Philip Allan, 1982).

23. See Lester G. Telser, *A Theory of Efficient Cooperation and Competition* (Cambridge: Cambridge University Press, 1987).

24. Williamson, *op. cit.*, is an excellent review of the issue.

25. Douglass C. North, 'A Neoclassical Theory of the State', in North, *Structure and Change in Economic History*, *op. cit.*, ch. 3.

26. Scherer, *Industrial Market Structure*, *op. cit.*, pp. 81–151.

27. See P.G. Cerny, 'Introduction', in Cerny, ed., *Social Movements and Protest in France* (London and New York: Pinter and St Martin's Press, 1982).

28. Moe, *op. cit.*

29. Scherer, *op. cit.*, pp. 84ff.

30. Olson, *op. cit.*, pp. 148–59.

31. See Jacques Gansler, *The Defense Industry* (Cambridge, Mass.: M.I.T. Press, 1980).

32. See Schmitter, 'Still the Century', *op. cit.*, for the distinction (and the links) between state and societal corporatism.

33. Scherer, *op. cit.*, p. 148.

34. Bendor and Mookherjee, 'Institutional Structures', *op. cit.*, p. 136.

35. Williamson, *op. cit.*

36. Williamson, *Ibid.*, p. 9.

37. *Ibid.*, pp. 9–10.

38. *Ibid.*, pp. 31ff.

39. Telser, *op. cit.*

40. *Ibid.*, pp. 2–9.

41. See Herbert A. Simon, *Administrative Behavior* (New York: Macmillan, 2nd edn 1961) and *The Sciences of the Artificial* (Cambridge, Mass.: M.I.T. Press, 1969).

42. Axelrod, *op. cit.*

43. Bendor and Mookherjee, *op. cit.*, pp. 143–4.

44. Scherer, *op. cit.*, pp. 86–7.

45. Williamson, *op. cit.*, pp. 133–6.

46. Bendor and Mookherjee, *op. cit.*, pp. 132–40.

47. Respectively by Williamson, *op. cit.*, pp. 136–55, Bendor and Mookherjee, *op. cit.*, pp. 140 ff., and Telser *op. cit.*

48. Chalmers Johnson, *M.I.T.I. and the Japanese Miracle: The Growth of Industrial Policy, 1925–1975* (Stanford, Cal.: Stanford University Press, 1982).

49. Michael J. Piore and Charles F. Sabel, *The Second Industrial Divide: Possibilities for Prosperity* (New York: Basic Books, 1984).

50. Cf. John Zysman, *Governments, Markets and Growth: Financial Systems and the Politics of Industrial Change* (Ithaca, N.Y.: Cornell University Press, 1983), and Robert B. Reich, *The Next American Frontier* (New York: Times Books, 1983).

51. E.g., Charles S. Maier, 'Preconditions for Corporatism', in John H. Goldthorpe, ed., *Order and Conflict in Contemporary Capitalism* (Oxford: Oxford University Press, 1984).

52. Cawson, *Corporatism and Welfare, op. cit.*

53. Cf. Christopher Clapham, ed., *Private Patronage and Public Power* (London: Pinter, 1983), and Grant McConnell, *Private Power and American Democracy* (New York: Knopf, 1966).

4

The Modern State at the Crossroads:
Structuring the Field of Political Action

Structures, then, are not *a priori* givens, but aggregated clusters of games (and 'meta-games'). And agents are not abstract rational actors, but real individuals and groups, circumscribed in time, space, and perception, and by organizational processes which are the accumulated outcomes of previous plays of several games – including the institutionalization of power resources which favor certain agents over others in both present and future. What gives structuration its character, then, is not any permanent functionalism or deep structural immutability. Rather, it is that structuration is essentially an historical – a diachronic – phenomenon, a phenomenon which leads to the emergence, consolidation, and development of different states, with analogous but different real-world structures. These real, historically generated state structures differ in a number of ways, ways which were explored in Chapter 2, and will be explored further in the second half of this book. But the core of these differences, taken together – the way they fuse into configurations which permit broad generalizations about the differences between countries – lies in the way that characteristic patterns of constraints and opportunities develop and are structured. Different states have different *structures of autonomy* – i.e., the elements of state structure shape, dominate, or intertwine with the actions of agents (and other structures) in ways which differ in both degree and kind.

The way that structures are structured, and that agents act, at any one point in time, is not just the consequence of the circumstances of that time. It is the way that those circumstances relate to the diachronic process of structuration, which contains the residues of previous accumulated choices and which casts a blurred but immediate shadow over the various pathways leading to the future. It is this historical reality which gives social structures and political structures their force, because it fosters both of the two competing illusions about choice and decision-making: the illusion of free will and rationality, on the one hand; and the illusion of determinism, on the other. Thus social structures in general, and state structures in particular, develop different forms of structural autonomy. This autonomy is not, however, found so much in the 'power' of the state or the capacity of state actors to compel other agents (and structures) to act; it lies in the way that state structures constitute and shape the structural field within which, and in relation to which, agents act and other structures are formed and patterned.

The significance of political structuration and of the historical development of the state is that the state is not just any social structure. However, this is not to claim that it is the kind of unique, virtually metaphysical, overarching structure which Plato sought to imagine in the *Republic* or which Hegel saw as the culmination of history. In the way that the state operates, it is in fact much like other social structures. And yet the modern state, more than the empires, city-states or clans which it has historically superseded, has developed into a sort of 'crossroads' structure, the potential autonomy of which lies in its position within the wider field of social and economic structures – and of other states. This is the case in two ways. At the crossroads of state societies, first of all, other social and economic agents and structures have regularly come to interact and interpenetrate with each other as well as with the state itself, through the optic, the prism, the filter or membrane, of state structures. When capital and labor interact, it is within the context of norms, privileges, and rights instituted and maintained through the process of state structuration; thus the state in the modern world has constituted the structured field of action within which non-state actors conflict or cooperate. When individuals and groups seek to combat a social evil, they do it through the framework or by means of the direct instruments of the state.

Secondly, and perhaps more importantly, a state's relations with other states have historically had a mutually reinforcing effect on state structures. States may be in competition and conflict with each other, but their very character as states was born out of, has been nurtured by, and is reinforced through, the fact that their external environment has been increasingly dominated by other states. Of course, the process of state structuration is essentially contingent, and therefore the origin of the modern state may be conceived of as an 'historical accident', so to speak – the outcome of critical events and the actions of critical agents at critical points in time. But the consequences of that accident have been to *reproduce* state structures at sundry levels, ranging from national consciousness itself, the core notion of social identity in the modern world, to the main building-blocks of the world system. State structures have tended to reproduce themselves – both internally and externally – and to expand their scope and range even in circumstances which might rationally have been thought to sound the death knell of the state – internal revolution and reaction, world wars, the development of a capitalist world economy, etc.

The structural autonomy of the state has been the result, then, of the interaction of these two levels of structuration, the endogenous and the exogenous. This articulation of the internal and external activities of the state through an historically developing set of institutional structures – filled by a changing population of state actors, their own perceptions of reality and conceptions of rationality molded by their structural environment – has been manifested in two particularly significant ways. The first of these consists of the many different levels at which state structures have developed and operated – the fact that the state has come to permeate so many levels of everyday life, from birth and death registration or traffic regulations and parking tickets, at one end of the scale, to living and dying 'for one's country' or establishing and monitoring the rules and procedures for launching a nuclear attack that could annihilate the planet, at the other end. States in the contemporary world have developed a high degree of interpenetration with other structures and agents, both internal and external. All of these things occur without 'the state' losing its internal organizational coherence or without undermining its intricate relational web. The second consists of the very 'centrality' or central position of the state in the wider structural field in which it is situated – both in relation to other structures 'within' the same social space, and in the transnational environment of war and peace, trade and intercourse. Interpenetration and centrality, then, make the modern state different from other social structures, and give state structures a unique potential capability for autonomy – *pouvoir* rather than *puissance*.

The state, in theory contingent and fragile, but in history, adaptable, self-reproducing, expanding, has therefore not only come to constitute the main 'political' structure in society, but has also come to be located in the site where it claims to stand, and is believed to stand, for society itself. This complex structuration has led to the development of a number of features of the state which traditional theories have been insufficiently capable of analyzing and explaining. These features are not permanent structural givens, as in orthodox structural theories, but critical regions or arenas of the structured action field – particular linked clusters of games which are disproportionately significant for the overall process of structural stasis and change, i.e., for the very process of structuration itself in the contemporary state. They delineate the parameters and game-patterns of those particular arenas of the structured action field where actors, acting strategically, have the most potential to make choices which influence the character of the structure itself; and they are also the regions where the intersection of structural elements can be most constraining for *future* patterns of structuration. For it is in these regions of the overall structured action field where future 'meta-games' take shape. Let us look first at the way in which different modes of structuration create different levels of constraint; then at the way in which the structuration of the state has come to constitute the central focus of a range of wider, internal and external, structuration processes; and finally, at the crucial arenas of state structuration which dominate the changing architecture of politics in the contemporary world.

Modes of Structuration and the Potential Autonomy of the State

The main danger of looking at the state as 'standing for society' is of course that of reification. However, the mutually reinforcing effects of state centrality and of historical unfolding do in fact give the state a none the less holistic quality. Just as 'charisma' is not a magical quality,[1] so the state is not a magical structure. However, it is endowed culturally with the trappings of magic – it appears as a 'natural', rather than as an artificial, conventional or cultural phenomenon – and is sustained partially by what Bourdieu has called 'social magic', or the investing through language of institutions and their spokespersons with authority.[2] This holism reflects the two most basic processes in the generation of knowledge and understanding: the antinomy of analysis and synthesis.

In order to explore that which is known badly or not known at all, the two most common starting points involve first, analysis, or the hypothetical postulation that a phenomenon can be broken down into more easily examinable component parts – and that understanding what those parts are and how they work will help 'explain' the way that the broader phenomenon works – and secondly, synthesis, or the hypothetical postulation that when a series of phenomena are put together, they will build into a broader phenomenon which will be different, and work differently, from its component parts taken separately. In this second sense, then, it is fundamental to both practical and intellectual knowledge to hypothesize that we can gain vital insights by taking the view that, to use the old phrase, 'the whole is greater than the sum of its parts', and then to go on to test that hypothesis, both by looking at its logical implications and plausibility, and by testing it empirically. Boudon's and Blau's various categories of structural theories represent stages of such processes.[3]

Our own hypothesis, again, is that social structures are not immanent, but contingent/historical/accidental in terms of first causes; however, out of a combination of their range, scope, centrality, and durability, some structures (in this case state structures) may come in a *de facto* fashion to develop the capacity to coordinate and even dominate other structures in a quasi-self-perpetuating way. They come to represent and to manifest accepted ways of 'doing things', reinforced by the well-known postulate that the potential costs of change are normally seen to be greater than the costs of inertia; this is reflected in everyday fear of unanticipated consequences, the maxim 'better the devil you know than the devil you don't', etc. Indeed, what are sometimes seen as 'psychological' dimensions of the process of choice can be interpreted as the cultural products of such background structures – risk aversion, the *a priori* assumption by an agent that other people are likely to think in the same way as does the agent in question, and the like.[4] Structures which shape behavior become powerful factors in themselves and are likely to resist extreme or frequent changes, although they will necessarily change incrementally, adapt, and decay.

Of course, in critical phases or crises, they may change abruptly. Indeed, as Alvin Tofler has argued, change may actually be a necessary condition of stability in complex structures, as people have to 'run in order to stand still', so to speak, in a context of rapid economic and technological change; inability to change rapidly enough in the contemporary world may lay the groundwork for more disruptive changes.[5] Abrupt change can be the result of one of two developments: either the effects of the decay of the structure itself, or its inadequacy to deal with changing tasks and activities; or the emergence of a sufficiently widespread alternative perspective – a belief or awareness that potential benefits will outweigh potential costs, whether in conscious ideology or simply in practical consciousness (even unacknowledged) – which provides the lever for broader change. Such change can then transcend mere dysfunctions, inefficiencies, or the like, especially in the hands of significant actors not wedded to existing structures and capable of significant strategic and tactical action within the interstitial gaps, exploiting the tensions characteristic of the structure. That capacity for strategic and tactical action on the part of significant – strategically well-placed – actors derives from the fact that structures provide a range of *opportunities for action*, as well as the better-known and perhaps more obvious constraints on action.

Structures are, as we have argued before, not just 'constraint structures', but also 'opportunity structures'. Those opportunities can be analyzed by separating out the different modes according to which structure and action interact, i.e., the different ways in practice that opportunities and constraints combine, in the process of structuration. In each mode, the dynamics of structuration reflect not only different possibilities for agents to influence the balance between stasis and change in the wider structure, but also different types of structural autonomy. Here we will identify and examine three such modes of structuration. The first mode consists of the more observable and measurable components of structure, or what we will call 'simple structure'.* This involves the relatively static pattern of constraints and opportunities present at the beginning of a 'play of

---

*This might in some ways be called 'objective structure', or structures as relatively observable empirical phenomena ('objects' or 'facts'), but we do not wish to imply that this 'mode' is more 'objective', in the philosophical sense, than the other two structural modes. What we mean is simply that this mode appears to concern more concrete, *a priori* factors, as set out below.

the game' (or a series of such plays), and determines in a probabilistic fashion the parameters of the cost–benefit analysis framework which an agent would apply in making his or her choices. The second mode comprises the dynamic possibilities inherent in the wider 'structured field of action', or the ways that uncertainties and structural indeterminacies combine to make actual outcomes contingent for significant categories of action. The third mode concerns the way in which structures come to appear to possess a capacity for action in themselves, to seem to take on a holistic, subject-like quality; this we call 'structures as apparent wholes', and it is here that language and history have most often led to reification. Let us look at each mode of structuration in turn.

Simple Structures

In the first place, structures are interlinked collections of *rules and resources*, as Giddens puts it.[6] They represent (a) a particular distribution of material and non-material resources, and (b) a set of rules as to how those resources can and cannot be used. Thus they embody and manifest fundamental, *a priori* inequalities between the possibilities that different individual and group agents have for taking action at any point in time; but at the same time they also involve a range of potential ways in which those fundamental inequalities can come into dynamic relation with each other in real action situations. They represent the structure of probabilities on the basis of which rational agents may attempt to construct cost–benefit frameworks to orient their actions, but they do not determine actual, real-world outcomes any more than the probabilities involved in tossing a coin determine whether 'heads' or 'tails' will come up on any one play.

One can conceptualize this by looking at the game of football (or any other sport) at the outset of the game or match: the rule book and the contractual arrangements linking teams in a league with common norms; the teams, with their existing sets of players, administrative structures and administrators, salaries and expenses, physical attributes such as stadia, etc.; the home towns, with their potential for audiences and reservoirs of loyal followers and the like. This is not the game as action (what the British call 'the match'), but the bricks and mortar, flesh and bones, cash and credit, and formal and informal 'rules of the game'. This is the basic institutional framework, the underlying conditions, the fundamental 'givens', or the 'simple structure' (despite its obvious empirical complexity). Outcomes of action involving this 'simple structure', whether within the structure (endogenous action) or outside it (exogenous action), can only be predicted on the basis of statistical probabilities – or educated guesses. And given the problematic nature of adequately measuring relative resources and subjecting them to testing according to hypotheses derived from the rules (which is the aim of formal game theory), educated guesses and 'rules of thumb' may not only be more frequently resorted to, but may also be more accurate, especially if based on an agent's (or an analyst's) long and intimate 'experience' with the operation of the structure in question.

The relative stability and durability of 'structures as objects' – a major facilitating condition for their endogenous autonomy – is reinforced (but not totally ensured) so long as resources are distributed in favor of actors supportive of the structure, and so long as rules are clear and likely to be followed. Thus simple structures have a certain endogenous autonomy. Such structures can also be autonomous on an exogenous level, insofar as their internal resources and rules are sufficiently strong and mutually reinforcing – and sufficiently mobilizable – to ensure their survival in the face of external competition from other structures and agents. Such autonomy, however, while real in the concrete, synchronic sense, takes on a different character in an active, diachronic situation, when the structure becomes a field of action.

Structures as Fields of Action

In the real world, then, such structures become fields in which complex and interlocking 'plays' of the game take place. At any one point in time, they reflect inequalities between the actors and also the ways, in a perfect and rational world without uncertainties, in which those inequalities interact. But they then become, in Crozier and Friedberg's phrase, 'structured fields of action' – i.e., the stakes and rules in the light of which agents, thinking and operating strategically and tactically, translate potential into action. As Crozier and Friedberg have pointed out, no actor is entirely devoid of choices of action in this context, but each has a repertoire of possible choices. These choices are bounded by the simple structure at one level, but at another level the range of outcomes is contingent upon a number of factors. The first of these factors is the perception of potential courses of action by the actors themselves, and this perception can, crudely speaking, come into play in various ways.

Firstly, of course, perception can come into play through conscious goal-oriented behavior and systematically rational choice, occasionally permitting the perception of potential 'winning' strategies which are not immediately obvious but which can occasionally go so far as to alter the original 'givens' of the simple structure itself. In the second place, there are structure-bound, conservative forms of perception, which take for granted a range of perceived limitations but permit agents to pursue shrewd strategies of survival, the maintenance of one's position in the structure, incremental change, outsmarting one's rivals in roughly similar positions in the structure, moving up and down a recognized hierarchy or pecking order in orthodox steps, rule-bound cooperation, etc. And finally, perception can be primarily reactive, responding to the actions of others at a level of practical consciousness – an approach which can range from instinctive self-defense to apathy. Beyond these three relatively structure-bound forms of choice, of course, there lies the option of attempting not just to break or bend, but to transcend, the rules and the existing distribution of resources in a more radical way.

The outcomes of these courses of action will not, however, vary simply with the choices of the agent who is the primary focus of the analysis. In the first place, uncertainty about the conditions of the game – about the real and complex nature of the 'simple structure', its rules and resources, constraints and opportunities – will always be present to some extent, and often to a great extent. Unanticipated consequences and opportunity costs are not only present, but can dominate the 'plays of the game' and overshadow intentions. ('The best laid schemes o' mice an' men gang aft a-gley' – Robert Burns.) For instance, Douglass North's analysis of the emergence and role of the state is based on the hypothesis that 'perfect competition' in markets is so rare that a non-market structure, the state, emerges out of the market process itself and comes to dominate that process in the search for elements of structured certainty – this being indeed the rule rather than the exception. This is analogous to Williamson's argument about the origins of hierarchy.[7] In the second place, however, other actors (including other structures, from interest groups to latent social categories) are also acting strategically and tactically within the same game, with perhaps different levels of perception of the game, different uncertainties, and, of course, different goals. Persuasion, bluff, cunning, and the like represent aspects of the dynamic ebb and flow of action.

Thus the translation of rules and resources into outcomes ranges from the sort of statistical probability represented by 'simple structure' to occasional results which are entirely unpredictable, *even where agents are acting conservatively and indeed wholly reactively*. Both agent and structure have a certain fluidity of action within this context. Relative stability in these continual and complex interactions promotes institutionalization; the other side of the coin is found in processes of decay or collapse, in various types of 'de-institutionalization'. Whether institutionalization or de-institutionalization actually occurs in regular, patterned ways has long been a central focus of political and social theorists, and analogies with biology abound (equilibrium, evolution, and, as recently applied to the state [and taken up earlier in this book], 'punctuated equilibrium', which is currently fashionable among certain quasi- or post-Darwinist revisionists).[8] But whether the intended and unin-tended consequences of such actions reinforce existing structural forms and practices, or undermine them, they can only be studied historically, *a posteriori*; they cannot be predicted, except as pleading, polemic, or luck. For example, the Toynbeean decline of contemporary 'civilization' can only be 'predicted with hindsight' . . . Stasis and change must therefore be carefully traced back, in ways which will necessarily simplify and in part distort. But to the extent that agents must take structural fields into account in their strategic action, and that outcomes are to some extent independent of the sum of the intentions of agents, then those structures have an autonomous impact on those actors and on that action.

Structures as Apparent Wholes
This is the most problematic level of the 'opportunity structure' and of the potential of structures themselves to have an autonomous impact. It is at once the most important mode of structuration and yet in most danger of leading to reification – the 'fallacy of the organism'. At the level of the state, it is represented in the notion of *'raison d'État'*. It can be seen to manifest itself along two dimensions. In the first place, it occurs when agents within a structure on the one hand internalize the rules, values, and goals, and on the other implicitly accept the naturalness of the distribution of resources, which are embedded in the simple structure – i.e., when they operate strategically *within* the structured field of action. In this way, their agency is in effect delegated to the structure, leading to the structure having an indirect but apparently real capacity for action – virtually an agency of its own – with regard to its endogenous operation. Actors see themselves as acting not only within the norms of, but actually on behalf of, their abstract image of the 'state' or 'nation' (or, in other structural contexts, church, family, class, etc.). In an analogy with Marx's analysis of class consciousness and struggle, a latent structure becomes a structure 'in itself', and then a structure 'for itself' – although here (a) this is characteristic of all social structures, not just class structures, and (b) for reasons which will be discussed at greater length later in this chapter, the 'centrality' of the state makes it a more potent structure in its capacity for potential action than class. The most extreme case of structures acting as 'apparent wholes' is, of course, in times of war.

In the second place, however, the structure can be seen to be endowed with a more direct form of apparent agency insofar as it interacts with other analogous structures in a wider, exogenous structured field of action. This at first seems easier to accept for primary groups with biological ties such as the family than it is for secondary groups like political associations, and yet we have been more or less taking for granted that interest groups, for example, can constitute collective 'agents'. The leap to seeing the state as agent in the transnational field is perhaps not so great as it might at first appear. Indeed, such collective agency in an exogenous field reaches to the core of the identification of individuals, subgroups, etc., with the structure itself (in this case, the state); this emerges most clearly when structures come into contact in such a wider field with other structures which individual and group agents recognize as similar or analogous to their own structural 'unit'.

To the extent that family or kinship structures are virtually universal in society (as anthropologists recognize by treating them not only as the central object of their enquiries much of the time but also as 'natural' structures), then they will have the capacity to act as virtual agents in their interactions with each other. In an analogous line of reasoning, to the extent that states have come to constitute the norm of 'international society' – especially where not only are they generally seen as coterminous with 'domestic' society (the image of home and family) but where the world itself has also come more and more to be characterized by state formation as the normal cleavage *between* societies – then states will operate as virtual agents in their relations with each other. For example, in his Inaugural Address, President Bush harked back to the time 'when our fathers were young . . . [and] our differences stopped at the water's edge';[9] such images have been fundamental to perceptions of the state throughout its history, and are powerful molders of behavior.[10] These images provide the most powerful cultural cement enabling the state virtually to act as an apparent whole.

Let us consider in a schematic way how structures can become apparent subjects. First, it is necessary to assume the presence of a simple structure of rules and resources; in this case, the 'state', with the component elements outlined above in Chapter 2, must be seen to be a real historical phenomenon. Such a structure might be envisioned, hypothetically, to have arisen in a wholly non-teleological fashion, either by some sort of 'pristine accident', or as the outcome of previous processes of structuration (which may or may not have been predictable, i.e., the structure may have been the consequence either of a process of institutional conservation or of one of radical and critical change). This simple structure is also then a structured field of action, with constraints and opportunities ranging from discourse, rhetoric, and culture, on the one hand, to coercive sanction, on the other. It is peopled by a set of actors whose understandings and expectations (perceptions, norms, goals) are set and shaped by their relationships with the structure.

These relationships comprise a complex series of dimensions ranging from a core – the perceptions, norms, and goals embedded in which are dominated by a direct relation with the structure, presumably involving actors invested with authority within the structure itself ('state actors') – through a series of concentric circles, to the mass public – for whom a *key* set of perceptions, norms, and goals, operative at significant times but still vitally important when latent (from traffic rules to the national self-identity), are set at the level of the structure, in relation to which such agents are relatively powerless.[11] Therefore, unevenly skewed patterns of action occur, actions carried out within and through skewed structures and manifested in processes shaped by the intersection of structure and conjuncture, pattern and event – structuration, *bricolage*, critical phases, crises, conjunctures, institutionalization, punctuated equilibrium, incremental changes, and the like.

These patterns of quasi-constrained, quasi-independent action, in turn, can have an impact not only on the structure itself, but also on shaping interactions with other structures, both endogenous and exogenous. In this way, the structure plays an indirect role as agent within specific conjunctures. But this is an historical, diachronic, iterated set of games. Therefore, once this indirect role has been played in a specific conjuncture, it tends to repeat itself, both through embedded perceptions, norms, and goals, and through expectations of other structures and structural actors. Axelrod observed, for example, that the most important factor determining a player's choice of move in an iterated game was his or her perception of the other player's *previous* move.[12] This gives the structure the capacity to 'act' as a subject in a succession of such specific conjunctures, with each conjuncture either reinforcing or undermining the original structure's capacity to act. If the tendency is toward reinforcement rather than undermining, then patterns of future expectations with regard to action become further entrenched.

Within such a context, the structure itself will develop an identity and virtual self-image, with its sub-agents and constituent structures using that image in a feedback sense to orient their own actions. In this way, the structure more or less comes to shape itself, both in channeling the actions of its constituent elements – even altering its own rules and resources – and in creating a pattern of interaction with other exogenous structures. Thus the process of structuration itself eventually comes to be made up of structures which in turn act in significant ways as if they constituted autonomous agents. Of course, this does not wipe out the capacity of constituent elements – sub-agents and substructures – to act as independent agents too, depending on the constraints and opportunities embedded in the evolving structured action field; nor does it completely 'free' a structure to act without constraint, as it is always acting in a wider structured field populated with other exogenous structures and agents. Nevertheless, its virtual subjectivity is as clear as is that of its own constituent 'collective agents'.

The whole, then, becomes greater than the sum of its parts in an historical process of structuration. Thus particular structures can potentially develop a wide-ranging autonomy in terms of the way that the actions of agents and of other structures are shaped – whether as simple structures, as structured fields of action, or as apparent wholes. But we are talking about a *potential* here. Whether or not structures actually do operate in this way is not given, but contingent. In terms of the state, this potential has been realized historically through the development of the centrality of state structures, not only mediating but also determining – not completely, but to a greater extent than any other structural form – both the patterns of interaction and development of other endogenous structures and the exogenous formation of the 'states system' at the international level. The modern state, therefore, has become, through its admixture of simple structure, capacity to shape the actions of others through the structured action field, and quasi-holistic collective quality, a different sort of structure from the others, located at the 'crossroads' of modern society and connecting internally different state societies with each other in a process of mutual reinforcement.

The Density and Centrality of the State

In the long time-span of history, even modern history, states have only been one of the competing and cooperating structures within society, interacting in a multitude of ways with kinship, other forms of ethnicity, religion, class, etc., and adapting to that situation in various ways. Prior to the ascendancy of the modern state, and during much of the modern era too, the most common form of intersection of these structures has been found in empires, in which an umbrella-like political structure (usually based on state-like structures in a central territorial or ethnic core) engages in certain essential common activities like military defense on behalf of other structures which retain a wide degree of autonomy, whether local structures or wider religious, ethnic, or other bonds and institutions. Where the state or proto-state has been the channel for the organization of a wider range of common activities, as in hydraulic societies (irrigation works) or certain agricultural bureaucracies, it has sometimes taken on a denser and more concentrated form and has been dominant over a wider range of other structures. On the other hand, the structure of the state itself, especially the early state, has often been diffuse, dominated by other structures.

Historical change has usually involved the shift of the state from being a rambling and diffuse structure – not clearly delineated, and permeated by other structures – to being a more dense structure, clearly differentiated from other structures and therefore developing its own logic and autonomy in the ways hypothesized above. When this happens, the state develops a wider appearance of being holistic, a whole greater than the sum of its parts, and therefore comes to stand for society itself, although this has not been (and never could be) actually realized in any ideal-type sense. However, political structures also decay, as we have pointed out earlier. Perhaps more important, however, is that as state structures become more dense, they also become more complex. And as they also come to interact in more and more complex ways with other states and transnational structures in the international context, the very development of density comes not to embody any simple hierarchical centralization of the state, but rather a more extensive and intricate set of dynamic structural relationships – less an imposing edifice of power, and more a spider's web to catch social, economic and political flies. Thus the autonomy of the modern state is not manifested in its closed and unitary nature, as the 'billiard-ball school' of hard-nosed *Realpolitik* in international relations would have it, but in the density, resilience, and effectiveness of its web in dealing with the complex issues of advanced capitalist society in a relatively open world political economy.

In the development of the modern state, a process the early stages of which are usually roughly located in the sixteenth and seventeenth centuries, however, a number of features of the state, first taking shape in Europe, have reinforced each other to give the state in the twentieth century a predominance and an autonomy which it had not previously possessed. Whereas previous states or state-like political forms, especially traditional empires, had mainly existed in a context in which their environment was primarily composed of non-state structures – the conflicts between ancient and early modern empires being a kind of intermediate stage between family, tribe, and clan, on the one hand, and modern states, on the other – states in recent centuries have found themselves confronted with other states in an expanding and mutually reinforcing process. The breakdown of the ideological and structural dominance of the Roman Catholic Church in post-medieval Western and Central Europe; technological developments which spread communications and economic linkages through the formation of urban centers, markets, and production systems which cut across the system of feudal landholding and other relations; and the manipulation of regional, linguistic, and ethnic loyalties by competing dynastic families claiming to be invested with the traditional authority deriving from each of these other structures in flux – a familiar enough story – provided the raw material for the formation over recent centuries of the kind of 'nation-states' which we now take for granted and think of as almost natural political units at certain levels.[13]

Endogenously, the formation of these seemingly holistic nation-states has always had elements of the artificial about it, as other agents and structures have competed for power and influence within them. And exogenously, too, transnational linkages have remained crucial to the development of Europe, and, through European expansion – both direct colonial expansion by conquest, and cultural diffusion of European ideas and ways of doing things – to that of the rest of the world. The process which was the fundamental catalyst for the precipitation of nation-states was, of course, the long series of wars between emerging post-feudal proto-states, and the gradual appearance of more rigid territorial boundaries with rights of exclusivity and attempts to impose greater social homogeneity: the institutionalization of nationally-based religions (or of increasingly national branches of religions such as Roman

Catholicism with more state control, as with French Gallicanism); the integration of national markets; the crystallization of nationally-based systems of social stratification (as elites became less cosmopolitan and more consciously indigenous, and mass publics less provincial and more consciously national); the nationalization of linguistic and ethnic identity (usually from the top down, as with the artificial imposition of French, English, Italian, and other languages on peripheral groups); and the search for *new* national cultures. All of these elements of the inextricably intertwined 'nationalization' and '*étatisation*' processes received critical reinforcement as the result of wars between competing dynasties with their proto-state structural foundations and their need for a social and economic base of support – legitimacy, personnel, and taxes.

Revolutionary attempts to transcend these multi-dimensional barriers of exclusivity were torn between their pretensions to universality and ubiquitous applicability, on the one hand, and the need both to utilize existing state structures and to appeal for their authority to already crystallized national identities.[14] Both the French and Russian Revolutions were universal in their claims and mainly national in their direct impacts. Indeed, it was the rejection of both of these revolutions on the grounds that they violated the barriers of national exclusivity which led to the most significant resistance to their claims – not only from competing dynasties and governments, but also from the populations in territories outside their national bases. And for the bearers of revolution themselves, national chauvinism often negated the universal appeal of their messages when carried abroad (witness Napoleon and Stalin). When these new nation-states, then, each of which retained certain imperial pretensions from their earlier histories and from the ideological appeal to the traditional legitimacies of the Roman and Holy Roman Empires, carried their expansionary dynamism abroad – whether for religious, economic, political, or other reasons – they carried the ideological and exemplary seeds of nationalism along with them. They planted these seeds through their imperial conquests and settlements in the Americas, Africa, and even Asia (where they found a different pre-existing state tradition, along with quasi-national social identities, especially in Japan) and they prepared the ground there, usually forcibly, for nation-state formation in crucial periods to come.

Thus although the state is an historically specific and contingent structure, its strategic position with regard to other structures both endogenously and exogenously has proved to be self-reinforcing and self-reproducing, both in the capacity of different particular state structures to reproduce themselves, and in their capacity to force or catalyze the formation of other state structures in an active and expansive fashion. Within this process, some state structures are strong, not in the sense that they are necessarily authoritarian or centralized, but in the sense that they can act as apparent subjects or wholes both internally – in standing for society and acting for that society to the extent that other endogenous structures act through the structured field of the state – and externally – in organizing and acting in relationships with other states and trans-national structures. In this way, even a so-called 'non-state society' like the United States is actually a strong state society,[15] although the internal principle upon which the American state is constructed is a decentralized one which does not give precedence to the *potestas* of the unitary state.

On the other hand, some state structures are weak not in the sense that they are decentralized or based on a common-law-type 'bottom-up' (rather than top-down) structural principle, but in the sense that they cannot act as subjects in either of the ways we have outlined.[16] The ongoing, multi-dimensional civil war in Lebanon, or the politics of famine relief in Ethiopia, are only two of the most salient examples of recent years. Given that strong state structures have become the norm, if not the whole reality, of the contemporary world – the standard by which political units are judged in practice and in theory – then we must evaluate their autonomy and structural power in terms of their political effectiveness not only in acting within their endogenous and exogenous environments, but also in mediating between the two and autonomously shaping both at the same time.

The state has come to be the main structure the strategic position of which not only stems from its capacity to, but also requires it to, mediate between what can schematically be called activities of war and peace, on the one hand, and activities of political market maintenance and coordination, on the other. In the former case, we find externally directed activities of interaction with other analogous structures identified as 'foreign', 'other', 'them', 'assumed hostile until proven otherwise', etc. In the latter case, we have internally directed activities of interaction within a state-defined group where others are identified as 'domestic' (the analogy of the house or family), 'the same', 'us', or 'assumed to be cooperative until proven otherwise' – at least within the bounds of recognized rules and the existing (unequal) distribution of resources. The state is a structure of assumptions about the activities and intentions of others, based on historical *bricolage*, social imitation, and structuration. The modern state has become pre-dominant – again, in being presumed to stand for society – (a) because it emerged by accident in historical circumstances where it adapted to, and was able to channel, shape, and control, material and social circum-stances more effectively than any other social structure; (b) because it adapted to and provided means of successfully controlling (or at least limiting the effects of) a variety of new circumstances and condi-tions (especially industrialization, class struggle, international economic expansion/interpenetration, and the technology and ambitions of modern warfare) better than other structures; and (c) was able thus to increase in turn its structural capacities and legitimation. State structuration, in effect, was characterized by the maintenance of a 'virtuous circle' from the post-feudal period to the middle of the twentieth century.

This virtuous circle, however, must not be mistaken for inevitability. The state is neither universal nor a higher stage of some sort of teleological evolutionary process. Should other structures, larger, smaller, or more complex in different ways (the standard range runs from extreme decentralization, which would be the ultimate objective of anarchy or true communism, to world government) prove superior in structural capacity in a phase of stress and change, *and* prove capable of acquiring sufficient legitimation, i.e., have its perceptions, norms, and goals assimilated into the strategic and tactical activity of its constituent individual and group agents, then the virtuous circle could conceivably be broken and the modern state superseded. But this would, obviously, require more than the weakness of the state; it would require superior competitive structural capacity – infrastructural strength and autonomy – on the part of *other* structures.

Nevertheless, should the state not be superseded in this way by other structures, then it will continue to exist as a working structure, shaping the 'meta-game' of political structuration. This working structure can be situated on a matrix based on two dimensions: the first of these stretches from states which are internally autonomous and robust (strong) to those which are internally bounded, penetrated, and controlled by non-state structures (weak); the second dimension stretches from states which are externally independent and autonomous to those which are relatively more subject to external pressures and demands. As Table 4.1 indicates, the spread of the state system and the overall 'virtuous circle' of state development does not mean that all states possess the same degree and kind of autonomy. The apparent robustness of the state in the twentieth century does tend to obscure the fact that some of the features of the state have become not stronger but weaker, as internal conflicts spread, class inequalities expand more and more through the capitalist world system, transnational structures evolve or are constructed to deal with problems that states cannot solve, and world markets become more and more integrated and interdependent. Yet at the same time, a larger number of activities of society *qua* society – the relationship of the individual with the public sphere, the clash of national identity with transnational activities (i.e., the consumer's desire for cheaper and/or better quality imports from abroad when national industries are in danger from foreign competition), etc. – are carried on under the assumption that the state either does or ought to play the crucial mediating role.

Table 4.1 *Types of state autonomy*

	Externally autonomous	Externally dependent
Internally strong	Autonomous	Satellite
Internally vulnerable	Private/instrumental	Penetrated/diffuse

Furthermore, the state structure effectively becomes the main broker between public and private goods in the economy, so that when an economic activity is 'decommodified' (i.e., taken out of the market), or, indeed, 'recommodified', it is the state which is expected to make, or to constitute the structured field for the making of, the normative decision. 'Economic' actors are presumed to be concerned only with their own utilities (self-interest), while the utility of society is a matter for the state in default of the alternatives. And yet the state is not always in a 'strong' position to control such decisions. The state is also the privileged focus of activities concerned with public participation. Voting, democratic parliamentary institutions, civil rights, protest, pressure group activities, indeed the very identity of the individual in a society based on the notion of individual liberty, are all processes structured by, through, or in relation to the state.

One can go further, and say that the state is the focus of morality and of the social bond itself, as religious or other forms of morality address themselves to state regulation, whether in regard to direct church/state relations, in debate on the rules of life and death (the death penalty, etc.), in the conflict between 'pro-life' and 'pro-choice' positions on the abortion issue, in discussions on whether the welfare state erodes or protects the family and/or the individual's capacity for moral behavior, and on all of the other moral concerns which are embedded in debate and legislation at all times. Outside the state, preaching is basically to the converted or the convertable; when morality is thought to require extension beyond this circle, it is a matter for the state. And finally, of course, once the society is defined as coterminous with the state, then the survival of society comes to be seen as identical with the survival of the state; defense becomes the ostensibly self-evident bottom line of the state's functions.

Therefore, although the state is by no means the only significant social structure, and although it has serious weaknesses as well as strengths in dealing with other social structures, both endogenous and exogenous, it does have *de facto* centrality. Other structures either pass through the state or are defined (or define themselves) in relation to the state. This centrality is, then, the key feature which differentiates the state from other structures and gives it capacity to adapt, assimilate, endure, and expand, rather than decay or collapse in critical conjunctures. Where centrality is weak or undermined, then decay or collapse is more likely. Even here, however, the structure of the international system, based as it is on the formal if artificial equality of state sovereignty, can provide crucial resources to state actors in order to maintain state structures – aid, foreign intervention, legal resources, the legitimacy which comes from outside recognition, and the like. The very range, scope, and number of other structures and activities which take the state as their reference point – which pass through the 'crossroads' of the state in the ever-increasing traffic flow of contemporary society – is what gives the state its distinctive role.

The strong state no longer merely claims jurisdiction and sovereignty or forces people into state-defined societies; it has become the central field of social *praxis*. But what is the significance, and what will be the impact, of the continual crises of weak states, especially in some parts of the Third World? The most important factor may well be that predominant elites in such weak states more often than not seek to reinforce their own power by emulating the statist norm originally imposed by the developed world and embedded in the system of state sovereignty – and that mass movements and opposition groups generally seek not to destroy the state *per se*, but to control it (or to participate in controlling it). If this continues to be the case within weak states, given also the international reinforcements available, then it looks as if weak states are more likely to approach the norm over time than to falsify it (though, as we have said, it can be falsified).[17] As a result, the state takes on an aura, represented by legitimacy, as well as the feel (through social activities which revolve around it), of being the core institutional structure of society *per se*.

At the most basic level, then, the state is not so much different from other social structures in terms of substance or essence, but rather in its strategic position and reach, which have developed in a contingent but self-reinforcing fashion. And the most important infrastructural characteristic of the state is its relation to the development and maintenance of the collective identity and consciousness of its constituent agents and substructures, both endogenously (in their relationship with each other) and in their common identity in contradistinction to other state societies. The state, where developed in its autonomy and structural power, is the primary influence on the process of coding and decoding messages – from the flow of sounds (Boudon) to the investing of authority in the linguistic marketplace (Bourdieu). The sense of being 'British', or 'American', or 'French', etc., and the ways in which this sense provides the foundation of social identity in the contemporary world over and above ties of kinship ('amoral familism'[18] has come to be seen as *deviant* behavior), class (in the transnational sense of 'workers of the world uniting'), etc., gives the state a privileged position in the contemporary flow of events, conjunctures, critical phases, and the like. It becomes the very condition of 'practical consciousness', rivalled only by that more insidious, equally ubiquitous but less emotive, less holistically visible and less linguistically salient structural formation, the market.

Of course, the main danger to this pre-eminence of the state in the contemporary world is the increasing integration of the world market-place, an issue which we will deal with at greater length in Chapter 8. But the responses to this parallel development have paradoxically tended to reinforce the state in a wide range of ways. Thus although the phenomenon of national identity is not given but problematic, its adaptability and tenacity have predominated despite recent challenges. In this linguistic sense, then, the state and the sense of national identity which the state has both imposed and nurtured, seem to 'make sense' of an unequalled range of social phenomena. Thus the state constitutes the main channel which shapes the learning process in the life-long interaction between the individual-as-member-of-the-primary-group (the complex of relations between the individual and his or her primary identity) and the wider society. Indeed, given that the nature of the individual/primary group complex is itself not given but problematic, when stresses occur in kinship structures, families, friendship networks, etc., those stresses tend to 'let the state in' – to cause constituents of the primary complex to look to the state to regulate and hopefully to alleviate those stresses.

The state, of course, is likewise looked to in order to regulate and hopefully alleviate stresses from both the marketplace and the international environment, thus expanding its role and presence internally and externally. And once the state is 'let in', given its pre-existing centrality, other structures tend to be at least partially assimilated to the state's logic and exposed (if not fully subjected) to the state's structural power. In this way, the state is continually being reconstituted (through structuration) at all levels of society, as has been argued by Michel Foucault, on the microscopic levels at which he sees the operation of 'circuits of power' in the activities of surveillance and punishment which permeate modern state societies and which constitute the 'underside' of the *praxis* of the state – the coercive, all-seeing and brutal face of social solidarity and national identity. In this way, the state is 'naturalized' not only through language, but through the body. Punishment is the internal substitute for war in the 'corporal naturalization' of the state,[19] an essential element which Bourdieu, too, emphasizes in stressing the importance of painful initiation rites as the most effective method of naturalizing the investment of authority.[20] The role of national sport – the increasing nationalization of the Olympic Games, for instance – is one element in this process.

This also paradoxically helps to explain the disorientation caused to American society by the Vietnam War, in which the supreme corporal initiation rite, war, led not to the reinforcement of identity and authority, but to their de-legitimation and existential questioning. This is an experience which all major colonial and imperial powers have been through since World War II. The centrality of the state as structure was seriously challenged by the American defeat, but no visible alternative emerged to provide a new focus for national identity – the failure of the 'counterculture' of the 1960s being patent. Whereas Britain and France have found new post-imperial roles, the United States has not. After the period of *malaise* which was so painfully reflected in the public image of the Carter Administration, the American state, with the leading role taken by President Reagan, quickly sought to reassert its *symbolic* unity and strength at this level of corporal naturalization – in new symbolic confrontations with the Soviet Union and the more real (or 'media-real') re-initiations of the Iranian and Lebanese hostage crises since 1980, intervention in the Lebanon and the various aerial confrontations with Libya, the invasion of Grenada, or the Los Angeles Olympic Games, all of which contributed to the 'feel-good' 'new patriotism' of the mid-1980s, which reached its height in the 1986 Statue of Liberty Centennial celebrations. Only when this re-initiation had been successful in symbolic terms – and in spite of setbacks like the Iran-Contra scandal – was it possible for the Reagan Administration to begin to grapple with the harder issues of international affairs and move away from 'unilateralism' to a foreign policy based more on interdependence.[21]

The Critical Arenas of the Contemporary Structured Action Field

The centrality of the state, that characteristic which is so crucial to the reproduction of social relations and to the self-reproduction of the state itself, is, as will be clear from the analysis above, itself in a continual process of stasis and change, of interaction of structures and agents, of meta-games in a dynamic interface with micro-games. These sets of critical relationships do not stand still. The contemporary state, on the surface, may look like the evolutionary product of the history of the modern state, which from one perspective it is; but this product has not been one of smooth evolution. Rather, it has been the product of circumscribed conjunctures in which different kinds of alternative possibilities have generated both different kinds of states, and different kinds of processes which remain in tension, characterized by interstitial gaps, and thus open to significant potential for change, in spite of the general historical predominance of the reinforcing structural processes discussed above. What possibilities exist in the contemporary world? What kind of interstitial gaps and tensions lead not only to the possibility of, but also to the *necessity for*, change? Structuration means that structures must change in order to stand still (as well as to change!);

the question is, which changes are most critical to the future patterns of state – and societal – development?

The most paradoxical aspect of the historical development of the state lies at the heart of the 'political process', as outlined in Chapter 2. This is the fact that the predominant focus of politics, in terms of both culture and action, has been on the way that political officials are chosen and how they conduct themselves in office: how mass publics influence (in 'democratic' regimes) or do not influence (in 'authoritarian' regimes) the choice of legislative and executive officeholders, and how various forms of accountability and responsibility work (or do not work); how election systems, political parties, pressure groups, and the like, channel and organize these choices and forms of conduct; how 'political power' is structured in terms of the social composition of elite strata and the political and ideological motivations of individual leaders and groups; and how executive and legislative 'decision-making processes' both reflect and distort the demands and the ideological and/or personal preferences of 'the people' and their 'representatives'. That the 'political process' has been the most salient aspect of politics is easily understood. It is the most public arena of politics, that aspect of politics which claims to embody both the principal forms of legitimacy of modern politics – the inclusion of mass publics in the 'body politic', on the one hand, and the efficient control of decision-making and policy-making processes (ensuring that 'inputs' are converted faithfully into 'outputs'), on the other. When one says 'politics', this is the image one sees.

Political scientists, too, spend much time examining these processes. Key characteristics of modern politics are said to be the spread of liberal democracy (and therefore the power of a greater number of people to influence what the state does), or the growth of interest groups and parties and their competition for influence or for office, or the focus of politics on individual politicians and leaders (especially through the images transmitted by the mass media). And yet, at the same time, critical analyses – usually analyses rooted in political theory, political sociology, and political economy – continually warn about the limits of this sort of political power. Elections may lead to some shift in the center of gravity of political power and policy-making, but, as Joseph Schumpeter argued, this is usually little more than the competition of elites for the people's vote[22] – a competition which creates distant and ephemeral ties between electors and representatives, ties of little consequence compared to the ongoing, everyday, lifetime links (economic, social, organizational, personal) between elites who know how to toe the bottom line of system stability and network solidarity. Elections in this context often become mere rituals, actually symbolizing the ongoing deference and subservience of mass publics to their so-called 'representatives', giving elites crucial legitimacy, and allowing them to mobilize mass publics to support their policy preferences rather than the other way around.[23]

There exist both benign and malign versions of this approach. The benign version is found in the tradition, rooted in the observations of Aristotle or of de Tocqueville, that democracy cannot exist unless it is stable – that it is not prone to be overturned by demagogues, or undermined by class or group conflict. Stability thus becomes the *a priori* value, which must be assured before democracy can be; therefore every democracy, to be democratic even in a limited way, must be 'tempered' by a high-minded aristocracy committed to the common good (Aristotle), or linked together by intermediary strata with an interest in maintaining the system (de Tocqueville),[24] or fused with 'authority structures' which paradoxically do not lead retrogressively back to authoritarianism but which give democratic processes greater cohesion and security.[25] Pluralism, too, usually embraces a benign variant of this perspective; organized interest groups, with their internal authority structures, are seen to give democratic interest competition an effectiveness which individual political action cannot.[26] The malign version comes in many forms, from the elitist theories of Mosca, Pareto, and Michels (and their many predecessors and successors) to the class analyses of Marx and others. After all, it was Lenin who argued that liberal democracy constituted the 'best shell' for capitalism because it reduced to a minimum the need for direct physical control of the proletariat by giving them an apparent, if misleading, active role in the system – maximizing 'false consciousness'. In between the benign and malign versions are the theories of Max Weber and others who argue that modernization requires organization and bureaucracy, which leads to either (or both) rational efficiency and/or Kafka-esque repressiveness.[27]

But the limits on political power are much more complex than either the benign or the malign version of authority theory, elite theory, or class theory. They involve the structural constraints built into the interstices of the architecture of the state. The clusters of games which make up the political structured action field provide *differential* interstitial spaces and opportunities for agents to make strategic decisions which do more than just confirm the routine reproduction of the structure. Political movements, political groups, political parties, and political leaders are *relatively weak agents* in the 'meta-games' of state structuration. They change too often; they are based on relatively ephemeral outside support; they are concerned with processes such as passing laws or making general policy decisions, activities which often bear little relationship to how state activities are carried out in practice; and they often do not have the specialist competence or expertise to engage in day-to-day supervision of the bureaucracy, or in the ongoing bargaining process between state officials and 'interests', or in the economic and social activities of the state, or in the way that welfare rules, tax structures, spending policies, and the like, affect different groups and individuals in society on an unremitting basis. The web of the state prevails and reproduces itself most of the time.

Only two kinds of political groups or leaders can make a major structural impact: firstly, those who have sufficient outside support or political momentum to transform the system exogenously by attacking it head on and cracking it apart by opening up the interstitial spaces and exacerbating the tensions of the structure, and, most important of all, by replacing old practices with new; or secondly, those who are most like permanent bureaucratic officeholders – long-serving incumbents, effective managers, committee specialists, and the like – who have some kind of endogenous vision of change and who can manipulate the available levers in the structure through the steady application of a long-term vision. But even the combination of both of these characteristics is often not enough to do more than just maintain or improve on existing patterns;[28] and even the most successful revolutionaries become enmeshed in the micro-games of the state structure.

The paradox of the development of the modern state, then, is that the most salient and striking focus of political culture, the primary source of legitimacy, loyalty, and identity in modern society, even the *raison d'être* of 'modern politics', is situated within that particular arena of state structuration which is often the most limited and constraining in its practical impact on the way that the state really works – on the 'withinputs', structural biases, and clusters of games which determine policy outputs and political outcomes. Political actors do not, in the main – *with occasional significant exceptions in particularly 'permissive' structural and conjunctural settings* – determine such major structural issues as (a) whether a state is externally autonomous or externally dependent, or whether it is internally strong or internally vulnerable, (b) whether state actors can or cannot enforce particular long-term settlements *vis-à-vis* major interest groups and social categories, (c) whether and how far the state affects and interacts with social activities and the way people live in a changing society, or (d) broad patterns of state intervention in the economy. The academic debate in Britain today about the meaning of 'Thatcherism', for example, seems to indicate that political leaders can have a significant long-term impact; however, the structural tensions in the British polity and economy, the structural character of the British political and administrative system, and the problematic role of Britain in the world economy, created in the late 1970s and early 1980s a rare and critical set of structural gaps, an unusual range of structural opportunities, which Margaret Thatcher was able skillfully to exploit.

Political opportunities are situational, although the capacity to grasp those opportunities varies with the rational choices of the actors involved. In order to explain conjunctural successes, one must first explain the structure of opportunities and constraints within which agents act. In the rest of this book we will look at a range of major arenas of state structuration: the ways that structural fields constrain political leaders and political party systems; the ways that state structures shape patterns of interest intermediation and processes of political allocation; the ways that the state gets 'let in' (or 'sucked in') to a range of social activities and practices (differentiation and 'de-differentiation'); and the way that changing patterns of economic exchange and international interpenetration are interacting with the process of state structuration as the twenty-first century approaches, creating fundamental changes in forms of state economic intervention – the contemporary 'competition state'. In covering these key arenas of state structuration, we hope not only to elaborate the theory of structuration, but also to extrapolate recent and current structural trends into some broad predictions about the future of the state and the forms of politics which are increasingly likely to characterize the world as we enter the next century.

Conclusions

The ability of the American state to reconstitute itself in the wake of the most destabilizing and traumatizing set of events since the Great Depression is testimony to the structural robustness and autonomy of the state, its capacity to manipulate rules and marshal resources, in its role as a central structured action field through which other structures are channeled and shaped. This renewal also points to the state's continuing capacity for collective agency, its effective role as an apparent whole, through a variety of significant conjunctures, making those conjunctures more significant than they might otherwise be by imposing new conditions endogenously and jockeying with rival states exogenously. However, the challenges faced by the American state are rather different in the 1990s than they were in the 1970s. Rather than a crisis of identity, the United States is faced with a crisis of economic competitiveness and possible long-term relative decline.[29] Other First World states, also strong and autonomous, in addition possess structural capabilities which are altering the basic equation of state power and state economic intervention in the contemporary world. Communist states, facing their most serious crisis of post-revolutionary stagnation in a rapidly changing world, are undergoing radical change. Third World states are sometimes finding the road to state consolidation and maintenance rockier than ever before, not just because of outside conquest or domestic violence, but because of transnational economic vicious circles, especially the debt crisis.

The structuration of the state is becoming more complex in today's world marketplace, and the structural changes which states and state actors are involved in today may take a significantly different configuration in the future. This does not mean that the state will be superseded. What it does mean is that the state may have to change more than ever before in order to convert its capabilities to the problems which are increasingly being faced in the world economy if it is to maintain some kind of virtuous circle of structuration. The state as we know it is giving way to a much more complex form – less like an extended family, more like a firm. However, in order to maintain support and legitimacy, it must continue to *appear* to be like a family. The domestic requirements of loyalty and of economic performance may come into greater conflict and tension, creating new interstitial gaps and logics and new opportunity structures. The state today is therefore at the crossroads in more ways than one. In addition to its structural autonomy and centrality – its developed capacity to structure social action – it must operate in a world environment in which new kinds of structural responses, new kinds of structured 'meta-games', are likely to be more efficient than the old. In Part II of this book we will look at some of the specific ways in which the architecture of politics has been changing, and try to discern where it is going.

Notes

1. See the discussion of charisma in P.G. Cerny, 'Foreign Policy Leadership and National Integration', *British Journal of International Studies*, vol. 5, no. 2 (April 1979), pp. 55–89.

2. Pierre Bourdieu, *Ce que parler veut dire: l'économie des échanges linguistiques* (Paris: Fayard, 1982).

3. Cf. Boudon, *Uses of Structuralism, op. cit.*, and Blau, *Study of Social Structure, op. cit.*

4. Such psychological factors – which we argue are generated by the process of structuration – are examined in George A. Quattrone and Amos Tversky, 'Contrasting Rational and Psychological Analyses of Political Choice', *American Political Science Review*, vol. 82, no. 3 (September 1988), pp. 719–36.

5. Alvin Tofler, *Future Shock* (New York: Random House, 1970).

6. Giddens, *Central Problems, op. cit.*

7. North, *Structure and Change, op. cit.*

8. See Stephen Krasner, 'Approaches to the State: Alternative Conceptions and Historical Dynamics', review article, *Comparative Politics*, vol. 16, no. 2 (January 1984), pp. 223–46.

9. 20 January 1989.

10. Cerny, *The Politics of Grandeur, op. cit.*, especially ch. 5.

11. See Gaventa, *Power and Powerlessness, op. cit.*

12. Axelrod, *Evolution of Cooperation, op. cit.*

13. Cf. Perry Anderson, *Lineages, op. cit.*, and Charles Tilly, ed., *The Formation of National States in Western Europe* (Princeton, N.J.: Princeton University Press, 1975).

14. See Skocpol, *States and Social Revolutions, op. cit.*

15. In contrast to the claims of, e.g., Dyson, *The State Tradition*, *op. cit.*, and Badie and Birnbaum, *Sociology of the State*, *op. cit.*

16. For a recent argument along these lines, see Joel S. Migdal, *Strong Societies and Weak States: State–Society Relations and State Capabilities in the Third World* (Princeton, N.J.: Princeton University Press, 1988).

17. Krasner, *Structural Conflict*, *op. cit.*

18. Edward Banfield, *The Moral Basis of a Backward Society* (New York: Free Press, 1958).

19. Foucault, *Power/Knowledge*, *op. cit.*

20. Bourdieu, *op. cit.*, pp. 129–30.

21. See Kenneth Oye, Robert J. Lieber and David Rothchild, eds., *Eagle Resurgent: American Foreign Policy in the Reagan Era* (London: Longman, 1987).

22. Joseph Schumpeter, *Capitalism, Socialism and Democracy* (London: Allen and Unwin, 1943).

23. J. Peter Nettl, *Political Mobilization* (London: Faber and Faber, 1968).

24. Alexis de Tocqueville, *The Ancien Regime and the French Revolution* (Glasgow: Collins, 1969; originally published 1851).

25. The best-known contemporary version of this argument is found in Harry Eckstein, 'A Theory of Stable Democracy' (Princeton, N.J.: Princeton Center for International Studies, 1961).

26. Rose, *The Power Structure*, *op. cit.*

27. Dahrendorf, *Class and Class Conflict*, *op. cit.*

28. P.G. Cerny, 'The Process of Personal Leadership: The Case of de Gaulle', *International Political Science Review*, vol. 9, no. 2 (April 1988), pp. 131–42.

29. Cerny, 'Political Entropy and American Decline', *op. cit.*

PART II

CHANGING PATTERNS OF POLITICAL STRUCTURATION AND THE FUTURE OF THE STATE

5

The Limits of Political Power:
Personal Leadership and Party Systems

The future of the state lies in the way that the structuration process develops during the coming generation. The state, as we have said, is at a crossroads, historically as well as analytically. In the past few centuries of state development, the emergence, formation, and consolidation of the state as a 'meta-game' – shaping the key conditions of political and social choice and action – has centered upon its location, its *site*, at the crossroads of endogenous social formation, political allocation, and economic development, on the one hand, and exogenous political interaction, military rivalry, and economic competition, on the other. This location has been crucial to the form of action taken by other social and economic actors and forces – in other words, the state, both in terms of the actions of state actors and the institutional biases built into state structures, has been in a unique position to fashion the contours of the overall structured field of action of the modern world. Because of its unique location, the structure of the state has been the one most important factor conditioning the parameters of strategic political action during the construction of society as we know it today. And for this reason, in spite of a wide range of developments and trends which might, in another strategic context, have weakened the state – the development of *both* capitalism and socialism, in particular – state structuration, all in all, has been characterized by a 'virtuous circle' of development.

The structural capacity of the state to continue to 'hold the ring' of social, economic and political development in the twenty-first century – just like the structural capacity of the state to deal with the development of industrial society in the nineteenth and twentieth centuries – is not self-evident, but problematic. The existence of a virtuous circle will once again be challenged by both internal and external changes, changes which will alter the 'givens' of political life. Externally, the main action context which nurtured the development of the state – war – is perceived as having higher and higher costs and fewer and fewer benefits than ever before; this outlook is becoming more and more widespread, whether one is considering nuclear war, the conquest of peripheral territories (as in the Iran–Iraq War which dragged on through most of the 1980s), or the effective control of far-flung formal or informal empires. International relations are coming more to reflect the economic realities of an interdependent and interpenetrated world production system, financial system, and marketplace, with the alternatives of both protectionism and isolation, on the one hand, and war and forced compliance, on the other hand, becoming less strategically and tactically viable. Furthermore, increasingly global environmental questions such as the 'greenhouse effect' or the depletion of the ozone layer make some sorts of direct multilateral action appear more necessary even to those countries which have most benefited from transnational free-riding in the past.

Internally, the main action context which nurtured the development of the state – the nationalization of political unity, social identity, and economic activity – is still vibrant and alive at certain levels, but problematic at others. The impact of the changing international context has been critical here too. The nationalization of social identity and political unity has been shown to be crucial for the political direction of Britain by the tremendous impact of the Falklands War of 1982; for the United States, as we argued in the last chapter, such events as the invasion of Grenada had a similar impact in the shadow of the post-Vietnam identity crisis. But for the Soviet Union, with its non-Russian ethnic majority; for China, with its huge geographical differences of economic structure and its centuries-old tradition of regional autonomy; for many Third World countries such as the Lebanon, Ethiopia, Peru, Afghanistan, or Angola; and even for First World countries such as Britain with its unsolved relationship with Northern Ireland, or Germany with its division into East and West: the nation-state framework has continued to prove problematic. And when it comes to economic activities – production, finance, and market exchange – the limits of the national framework and of state action are testimony to the failure of centralized economic planning in the Communist countries, the mixed record of state-driven development policies in the Third World, and experiences of stagflation and recession in the First World in the 1970s and early 1980s.

The appearance of Reaganomics and Thatcherism in the West, of *perestroika* in the East, and of a new pragmatism in the Third World, all reflect the fact that the conditions which constitute the internal/external structural axis have changed. Internally, for example, this means not just that local or regional (geographically sub-national) ties are being reasserted (which they are, however unevenly), but also that socio-cultural trends, especially consumerism, and sectoral economic activities, such as the development of the service sector or the requirements of different industries both old and new for competitiveness on the world marketplace, make the conditions not only for state action (the decisions of state actors), but also for the process of state structuration, very different along certain dimensions from the conditions which prevailed previously.

The state still occupies a key strategic location at the crossroads of contemporary politics, but significant changes in the structural working of the state – changes which significantly affect its potential 'decisional capacity' – are already in progress. In the first place, the kinds of activities which the state undertakes have already been shifting, and will continue to shift. And in the second place, whether the state continues to maintain a virtuous circle of structuration – holding the ring of socio-economic development – will depend both on institutional developments and on a range of strategic choices, made by state and non-state actors alike, which shape those institutional developments.

The changing environment of state structuration, however, will not 'determine' the future of the state in the twenty-first century, any more than it has in the past. Internal and external changes constitute necessary conditions for change, not sufficient conditions. The key to change lies in the ways that such changes interact with the existing structural logic or opportunity structure of the state – its structural constraints, on the one hand, and its interstitial gaps and tensions, on the other. The problematic issues thrown up by the new challenges which we have outlined will continue to be processed, for some time at least, by the same kinds of state actors, and through existing state institutional processes. Thus the crucial independent variable will be the way that such new problematic issues are processed by those actors and through those institutions. Therefore it is necessary to look more closely at the way that those issues are likely to be processed, given the existing condition of the state structuration process. There are several possible alternative outcomes, which can for the sake of argument be reduced to three broad paths of development: (a) either state structures will process these new issues in a relatively stable way, with the state's existing decisional capacity making it possible for effective and dynamic 'solutions' to be reached; or (b), at the other end of the scale, states will be unable to process these new issues in significant ways, leading either to a decay or a transformation of the state form altogether, as has so often been predicted in earlier epochs of change; or (c) the state will not collapse, nor will it deal with these new problems effectively, but there will be a long period of 'muddling through', in which different states will act in increasingly different ways, rivalry and conflict will grow, but not so far as to undermine the international system, and tremendous ongoing efforts will have to be made by state actors just to keep the system going and to keep conflict within bounds – a kind of *entropy.**

Although all modern states have certain structural features in common, as we argued in Chapter 2, and although agents tend to make rational choices in terms of structured fusions of the decisional principles of

---

*'Entropy' is defined in the *Concise Oxford Dictionary* as a 'measure [from physics] of the unavailability of a system's thermal energy for conversion into mechanical work'.

market and hierarchy, different states have different structural configurations. Therefore structuration processes in changing environmental conditions will take somewhat different forms; they will not be the same in different countries. But neither will those structuration processes present simple patterns of across-the-board 'national' divergence; differences will cut across state structures unevenly. Consequently, the presentation of a range of nationally-derived state models, such as the American model or the Japanese model, is an insufficient analytical basis for examining and understanding the current dilemmas of state actors and the future directions which the structuration process is likely to take. Rather, it will be necessary to identify what we have called the key structural arenas or regions within which state structuration – the interaction of structure and agency – takes place in contemporary politics, and to show the parameters of potential stasis and change in each of those arenas. For reasons which will become clearer as the next four chapters progress, the key arenas on which this book will focus are 'political' power (in the narrow sense of the term, as discussed toward the end of Chapter 4), structured collaboration between the state and major organized interests (the intermediate cases of 'political allocation', as discussed in Chapter 3), the processes by which the boundaries between the 'state' and 'society' change (the 'differentiation' and 'de-differentiation' of state structures), and the forms of 'state intervention' in the economy which are coming to characterize states and economic actors in the increasingly interpenetrated world marketplace.

These arenas cut across the 'elements of structure' outlined in Chapter 2; each arena involves the interaction of state actors and institutional factors in ways which reflect the intersection of elements of structure, on the one hand, and the nature of issues facing the state, on the other. The first arena, political power, involves not just the 'political process', but the capacity of political officeholders to react to, to cope with and to control effectively the factors which constitute the key issues which affect and influence state structuration. To what extent are *politicians* in a position actually to resolve the major issues facing the state as we approach the twenty-first century? The second arena, that of interest intermediation, involves not just whether interests are catered for or controlled by state actors, but how the process of interaction between state actors and interest agents constrains or opens up the range of possible outcomes. To what extent does interest intermediation shape state structuration – and/or to what extent, looking at the other side of the coin, does state structuration shape interest intermediation?

The third arena, that of differentiation and de-differentiation, involves not just the apparatuses of the state and state intervention, but a wide range of questions about the possibility that there might exist a coherent and autonomous 'civil society' – nationally or transnationally – the key actors in which can take the lead in fostering change; or whether that 'civil society' will still remain dependent on state structuration for its very composition and character. And finally, the interaction of state and economy – involving politicians, state apparatuses, and state economic activities, again on both national and transnational levels – raises the most important question: how the interaction of states themselves will force those which are less economically competitive to structure their institutional instruments and patterns of state intervention in the economy in order to react to (and actively to exploit) the competitive challenges of other states, and how this will impact on the other three arenas. Ultimately, the future of state structuration will depend on changes which cut across these different arenas and their different constitutive games.

In this chapter we will look more closely at the structural constraints and opportunities which set the parameters of political power and the games which political leaders and party politicians play. With regard to their structural capacity to make the kind of key strategic choices which will shape the state structuration process in the future, we will argue, classic 'political elites' – elected officials, party leaders, members of legislative bodies, leading national politicians, and the like – are relatively highly circumscribed and constrained in terms of the limited alternatives which are structurally open to them *in comparison to the nature of the most pressing problems* which the state faces. The structural requirements confronting individual 'personal leaders' who want to 'get something done' are severe and intense; it is much easier for them to have a limited impact upon a particular policy sector or specific issue, although even here the mobilization of opposition generally makes compromise and muddling through the most practical option. For political parties and party politicians, the structural requirements of coalition-building among social categories and interest groups, among intra-party factions and personalities, and between what we will call 'coalition arenas' – between organizational levels and within different institutional sub-structures with distinct structural logics – makes party an unreliable and ineffective source of structural change.[1]

Limits and Possibilities of the Leadership Process

The study of personal leadership – leadership exercised by a single individual – confronts the analyst with one of the most fundamental dilemmas in social science.[2] Like the historian's grappling with the relationship between 'event history' and the *longue durée*, or the theorist's vacillation between between philosophical analysis and the history of ideas, the political scientist's search for regularities and structural explanations often meshes poorly in practice with his or her pragmatic perception of the idiosyncratic influence of individuals on politics. The 'great man' (or woman) approach to political stasis and change has been rightly excoriated for its misleading oversimplifications, and yet it seems blindingly obvious that personalities do matter: that the relationship between individual psychologies, social structures, and political/historical conjunctures can vary dramatically and unpredictably; that political outcomes depend upon a complex conjunctural nexus in which 'leadership' can be both a crucial and a relatively independent variable; and that even political structures can undergo incremental change – or, more significantly (if only very rarely), paradigmatic change – as the result of individual interventions.

The aim of this section is to outline a fairly simple framework for the analysis of personal leadership as part of the process of political structuration, and to inquire as to what the impact of leadership is likely to be as the state heads into the twenty-first century. We will first suggest what might be some of the dimensions of such a process, the ways in which individual leaders interact with wider political structures and processes; we will then consider four of the more salient 'styles' of personal leadership which emerge from the interaction of these dimensions; and, finally, we will comment on how recent experiences in several countries illustrate and highlight the problematic nature of leadership in the contemporary state.

Personal leadership is not a holistic phenomenon which can be reduced to primary properties such as authority or charisma. As useful as these can be for locating certain characteristics of leadership, they are themselves complex effects of a variety of interacting causes, and therefore frequently raise more questions – often *hidden* questions, occasionally concealing a hidden agenda – than they can answer. Rather, leadership is situational, not only the complex confluence of a variety of different processes with different dynamics, but also the contingent consequence of circumstance. Normative attempts to routinize 'strong' or 'effective' leadership in institutional formulas usually produce paradoxical results: at best they create a *potential* which may be realized only when contingent factors converge, as in Neustadt's notion that the American President's only real source of power is his 'power to persuade';[3] at worst, they can lead to debilitation, as with the dissolute descendants of declining dynasties, or to perversion, as argued in the classical analysis of tyranny, the condemnation of Machiavelli, or the critique of modern authoritarianism; but most of the time they just bend to the winds of wider political, social, and economic constraints. Political processes, *pace* Plato, cannot be made to produce philosopher-kings. Personal leadership, then, must be studied in a way which is susceptible to both historical and comparative analysis.

The study of political processes generally privileges two complex clusters of factors in the generation of political outcomes: the 'body politic' or the socio-economic environment and its inputs and constraints; and the state. In this analysis we will combine these two with a further cluster, the 'personal equation' (for want of a better term) of the leader/political actor in question. The various forms which personal leadership can take, and the potential for effective leadership, derive from the process of interaction of these three sets of factors in specific conjunctural circumstances. Each of these clusters is also a set of complex but not incompatible relationships between the various component factors, and therefore needs to be conflated into a scaled dimension, although for the sake of simplicity we employ contrasting modal pairs of characteristics to represent each scale. By combining these modal characteristics, one can construct a partial typology of styles of personal leadership (identifying only the most salient among a wider range of possible types) and thereby generate hypotheses both about the way in which the leadership process itself works in practice and about the impact which that process may have on society and the state synchronically and diachronically. Let us begin by sketching in the three main factors.

Three Factors Affecting the Leadership Process

The Personal Equation. Far from representing a psychologically-defined notion of innate personality or a set of normatively defined 'leadership qualities', the personal equation dimension reflects the contingent confluence – the coincidence – of several factors. Different aspects of the personal equation will condition the individual actor's *potential* effectiveness in different leadership situations, although they will affect the dynamics of those situations only insofar as opportunities for action are appropriately structured. Individuals with a variety of psychological 'personality types' – from an aggressive sense of command to a reluctant or low-profile shouldering of burdens – may act 'effectively' in different situations. At the same time, the conscious or rational intention to act in a leaderlike fashion can lead either to a more effective, thought-through approach to situations, or to a level of aspirations out of proportion with the possibilities. Furthermore, a tendency toward tactical thinking, on the one hand, or strategic thinking, on the other, may be more or less appropriate according to the conditions structuring each situation. And the association of action with a complex and abstract personal political philosophy either may make leaders more effective for having a longer-term and more comprehensive view of situations, or, on the contrary, may ossify their thought processes or blind them to real constraints.

It is necessary, however, to conflate these various factors into a single dimension for the purposes of the wider analysis. We believe that it is possible to construct such a scale without doing too much injustice to the variety of factors subsumed under it. The poles of such a scale might be labeled 'passive/reactive' on the one hand, and 'active/anticipatory' on the other. In the former case, the individual concerned might be more passive in terms of personality, with little conscious intention to play a leadership role, a tendency to deal with specific conjunctural problems in an essentially short-term fashion (rather than necessarily 'solving' problems over the longer term), and a distrust of theorizing. In the latter case, an assertive personality, a conscious willingness to and readiness to play a leadership role, a strategic approach to problems, and a developed philosophy relating means to ends, might combine to comprise the potential for what is often thought in everyday language to be the stuff of 'leadership'. Of course, a 'passive/reactive' personal equation does not necessarily mean that the individual is *not* providing leadership, especially in appropriate situations (see below) – but is merely providing leadership of a very different kind.

The Individual and the 'Body Politic'. The second dimension concerns the relationships which exist between the individual actor and the 'body politic' or 'political nation', i.e., those socio-economic groups and categories which play a role in or have an impact on the political process generally (including their leaders and representatives). Most contemporary approaches to political sociology, including pluralist group theory, elite theory, and Marxist class analysis, are what have been called 'society-centered' theories; such approaches depend for their underlying structural plausibility and dynamic explanatory capacity upon the assumption that political and bureaucratic actors in fact express, and act on behalf of, wider social forces, by either consciously representing or unconsciously reflecting the subjective and/or objective 'interests' embodied in the socio-economic positions, systemic roles, and actual activities of those groups and categories. Now Nordlinger has shown in great theoretical detail how state actors may in fact act autonomously from such wider social forces;[4] and his analysis implies that what state actors can do as a collectivity, individual actors can do personally. In the case of personal leaders, they can act in ways which go against the 'interests' of the groups of which they are or have been members, they can undermine the power of the elite strata or networks into which they have been born or socialized, and they can betray their class.

Relating this *potential* capacity to the process of leadership in particular situations, again, is critical to an understanding of whether, and how, the action of individual leaders affects the interplay of forces in particular conjunctures – or, more importantly, whether the individual leader can initiate and pursue, in an autonomous and personal manner, action which modifies or transforms the structural pattern of the political process itself. Whether an individual is able to act (and indeed does act) autonomously of his or her social position, then, is a key aspect in any analysis of personal leadership. This capacity may result, in philosophical terms, either from an innate 'free will', or from such social-structural causes as a 'contradictory class location',[5] or from structural factors specifically characteristic of the state itself. But for the sake of this analysis, these factors can again be conflated into a single scale, the poles of which are labeled 'representative' and 'autonomous'. (In doing so, we are also ignoring the fact that these poles, and the scale itself, have certain sub-modes: that a 'representative' individual may represent a section or faction, or might, in contrast, represent a consensus; and that an 'autonomous' actor may express that autonomy by attempting to *impose* his or her 'will' – or, in contrast, might be seen as a 'trustee', having attained a quasi-Burkean latitude to use his or her own judgment.)

The Individual Leader and the State. This dimension aggregates a variety of factors which are directly relevant to the organizational form of the state. First, it is important to know what position the individual holds in the formal hierarchy of state offices, and what the legal and conventional characteristics of that hierarchy permit such an officeholder to do or restrict him or her from doing. Thus the pre-existing parameters, built up over time and in codes, of such notions as 'the powers (or limits) of the presidency', are crucial to the leader's *potential* for personal action. Then there is the question of the leader's social position within the group of 'state actors'; greater or lesser deference and prestige, whatever the leader's *formal* position, comprise another key element in assessing the potential range and scope of his or her actions in a variety of situations. Furthermore, as we have argued elsewhere,[6] a key element, both material and symbolic, can be the position of the individual *and of the state as a whole* in external relations with other states and with international structures. A leader who can effectively marshal the material capacities of the state in the outside world, or who can at least create the *impression* of being able to do so, will have a rather different potential for 'leadership' in the domestic arena – as well as the international arena – from one who cannot do so. And finally, linked with all of the factors already mentioned, is the relationship which the individual actor already has, or can forge, with the ideological aspects of the state – its pattern of legitimacy, its cultural image and structure, its myths. A leader who can manipulate myths – who can deconstruct and reconstruct the culture of the nation-state itself – is in a very different position from one who is restricted to conforming to the text and playing out the script.

Again, this analysis requires a conflation of these factors into a single dimension: in this case, the two poles can be labeled 'state-bound' and 'authoritative/exempt'. The former is straightforward enough; the latter implies that (a) the individual's authority is to a significant extent derived from his or her personal position, and (b) that authority is great enough to allow the leader to go beyond the norms and constraints of the state structure. For the 'state-bound' actor, the potential for personal leadership is restricted to system maintenance and system adaptation; for the 'authoritative/exempt' leader, he or she has a more or less far-reaching capacity to transcend the limitations of 'normal' behavior and to affect the working of the state as a whole. A restricted hierarchical position, a lack of personal credibility with other state actors, a limited and essentially domestic horizon, along with a predilection to comply with existing cultural norms, would combine in clear contrast with a singular (in some cases unique) hierarchical position with wide discretionary influence, deference, and prestige among colleagues and/or subordinates, 'clout' abroad, and a special cultural position – an ability to manipulate symbols and images of identity and national interest.

Four Leadership Styles

By combining the various modal characteristics of each of the three dimensions elaborated above, it is possible to construct a typology of leadership styles. A full typology would be too complex for an exercise such as this, however; therefore we will deal with only four of the more salient styles: two polar cases and two mixed cases.

Routine Leadership. The routine style of leadership[7] combines (a) a *passive/reactive* personal equation; (b) a *representative* relationship with public opinion, pressure groups, elites, and the like; and (c) a *state-bound* position. An individual who manifests such a style can, of course, still be engaged in 'leadership' in the wider analytical sense, although it might not be recognized in everyday normative language as 'real' or 'effective' leadership. Nevertheless, in a range of specific situations characterized by ongoing, non-crisis problem-solving, either a dormant or a fragile public opinion, and a state with clear constraints on its internal cohesion or social authority, routine leadership may in fact be the most effective kind for dealing with day-to-day decision-making without disrupting or undermining the fabric of the political process itself. This point has been made not only about France,[8] especially under the Third and Fourth Republics, but has also often been taken to be the traditional 'strict constructionist' interpretation of the American presidency (with 'great Presidents' like Lincoln or the two Roosevelts seen as exceptional). Indeed, for Max Weber, the 'routinization' of exceptional or charismatic leadership was seen as a sign of the diachronic normalization and institutionalization of leadership, thus making it more effective in future situations.[9]

Integrative Leadership. An 'integrative' style of leadership would combine (a) an *active/anticipatory* personal equation with (b) a *representative* relationship with the 'body politic' and (c) a *state-bound* structural context. Such a leader would still be concerned primarily with reflecting the interests and concerns of society and the public, and would not seek to go beyond the limits of the existing state structure and of his position within it. Nevertheless, with an 'active/anticipatory' way of thinking about and trying to solve problems, an integrative leader would consciously seek to harmonize, stabilize, and mold the political process around a fairly well-developed conception about what decisions need to be made, what their outcomes should be, and how they would fit into a broader vision of the direction in which society is or ought to be heading. The integrative leader is often seen to be the ideal for a liberal democracy, except possibly in wartime, combining the modesty of a *primus inter pares* – the 'first among equals' with a quiet rather than an assertive authority – with a capacity to persuade and convince colleagues of the necessity of certain forms of action, rather than to rock the boat. This is not limited to liberal democracies, however; similar comments were made in the 1960s and 1970s about the concept of how 'collective leadership' was supposed to work in the Soviet Union.

Catalytic Leadership. A 'catalytic' leader combines (a) an *active/antici-patory* personal equation and (b) an *autonomous* stance *vis-à-vis* opinions and interests, but is still (c) *state-bound* in terms of powers and norms. The sociological autonomy characteristic of this style of leadership per-mits the individual leader to take more unusual, more comprehensive, and perhaps even bold initiatives stemming from an active and anticipatory perception of and approach to problems. These will either be imposed upon the body politic, or be acquiesced to by it in an *ex post facto* fashion. However, the catalytic leader cannot go so far as to confront the norms and usages of the state itself. The greatest potential for effective innovation engendered by this style is limited to initiatives and courses of action which either (i) pave the way for the consolidation and further development of a range of pre-existing trends toward change, increasing the momentum and impact of change, or (ii) spark off a range of new changes, the potential for which simply needs catalyzing and setting in train. The system may change by itself in the last analysis, but the action of the catalytic leader provides the impetus and helps shape and channel the direction and form of change. Obviously the success of this style is dependent upon the underlying conditions of the socio-economic context and of the state structure; should these be either too ossified or too volatile, then the catalytic leader may either fail, or be found to be outrun by events and conflicts beyond his or her control.

Transformative Leadership. The transformative style of leadership com-bines (a) an *active/anticipatory* personal equation, (b) the *autonomy* of the leader with respect to socio-economic forces, and (c) an *authorita-tive/exempt* relationship with the state. This is the other polar type, at the opposite end of the scale from routine leadership. We prefer not to label it 'crisis leadership' or 'heroic leadership', as Hoffmann or Crozier would, because it does not necessarily depend on the presence of a specific crisis – although a crisis would be an obvious situation where such leadership might be especially effective – nor is the leader necessarily 'heroic', a quality too limited in conception to the 'personal equation' dimension (although heroes might in some circumstances be well fitted for the role and might find it easier to obtain acquiescence). Rather, transformative leadership is distinct from the other types, and most significantly from catalytic leadership, in its ability to transform the norms and structures of the state itself – to autonomously influence the process of state structuration.

Leadership and State Structuration

Personal leadership is perhaps the most potentially significant – as well as the most salient – form of individual agency in political life. Leaders can cut across the logistic barriers which detach political agents from ordinary people in society. They can personalize and embody issues, problems, and conflicts in such a way as to make them understandable and assimilable to ordinary people. In the contemporary world, the focus of broadcast media has multiplied this potential immensely. Impressions made by presidents, prime ministers, and opposition leaders dominate the process of political socialization even more in the television age. When they hold offices with strategically significant political powers and resources, when they can manipulate not only their own images but also images of social cohesion (or conflict) and of the 'national interest', and when they can devise and organize their own actions strategically and tactically, they have unequalled capacity to influence and shape the process of political structuration. And yet, the complex cluster of games in which they are enmeshed – involving their own 'personal equation', their relationship to public opinion, social categories and interests, and their structural position within the state – entwine them in structurally constraining situations in which this potential is not only rarely realized, but often seems just to be a mirage when faced with the 'realities' of 'practical politics'. We choose leaders (or have them chosen for us) in order for them to do things which they most often cannot hope to achieve.

An understanding of when political leadership *does* work therefore requires an analysis of the structural conditions – the opportunity structure of interstitial gaps and tensions – which makes effective agency by personal leaders possible; it requires an analysis of political structuration. Former United States President Ronald Reagan is often seen as an example of an effective programmatic leader, whose policies of tax reduction and deregulation brought in a new era in American politics. And yet Reagan's most insightful critics are not those who oppose his programs *per se*; nor are they those who focus on his personal peccadilloes, such as his short attention span and lack of understanding of detail. Rather they are those who perceive the structural constraints built into the American system of government, when 'checks and balances' become manifested in the fragmentation of the policy-making process, where log-rolling-type 'distributional policy' predominates which depends on there being payoffs for everyone,[10] and when key issues such as economic and budgetary policy result in an ongoing stalemate dangerous to the maintenance of the system itself – structural constraints which in a very different political context were seen to lead to a 'deadlock of democracy'[11] and which remain central to the processing of the very kinds of issues which state structures must deal with in the twenty-first century.[12]

To these critics, the very success of certain early Reagan policies – policies the distributional nature of which permitted supportive coalitions to form rather than provoking the mobilization of veto or blocking coalitions, especially the 1981 tax cuts or the invasion of Grenada – highlights the incapacity of the President to deal with the opportunity costs, the negative side-effects and after-effects, which those policies generated. Reagan's personal leadership represents the clearest example of the paradox discussed earlier – how the outward appearance of strong leadership (reinforced by his uncanny ability to foster the image of strength and effectiveness despite, for example, ethics scandals or the Iran-Contra Affair) not only distorts, but may actually hide or mask, the structural incapacity of any President of the United States to do much more than 'muddle through'. In an era when patterns of state structuration are changing transnationally as well as domestically 'from the welfare state to the competition state', the paradoxical reliance of the American system on presidential leadership for its innovatory thrust, while presidents are at the same time confronted by such complex structural constraints, does not bode well for the processing of the main issues which will confront the American state in the twenty-first century.

Relatively strong personal leaders such as General de Gaulle or Margaret Thatcher have owed their positions more to the existence of complex structural conditions with significant interstitial gaps, tensions, and changing patterns of constraints – especially the decay of certain pre-existing constraints, and the opportunity to act strategically to shape new ones. 'Permissive' conditions have thus been present. In the case of de Gaulle, many of the structural resources which he could call upon to strengthen his position and to support a wide range of his policies (including major constitutional changes) were either already part of the French state tradition, for example, the presence of a strong civil service with an elitist ethos, or were the product of rapid socio-economic change in France in the postwar period well prior to de Gaulle's return to power in 1958, such as economic growth and a wave of industrialization, or reflected the combination of both. De Gaulle's success was not only the result of his ability to manipulate significant gaps and tensions in the state structure, especially those reflected in the chronic weaknesses of previous constitutional regimes, but also depended on the pre-existence of significant structural resources the absence of which would have undermined his position. The dynamic economy of France and the improvement of its competitive position in the 1960s and early 1970s – before the international oil crisis – testified to the 'fit' between Gaullist leadership and wider transnational trends, too, although his successors in the late 1970s and 1980s have found more recent domestic and international economic issues far less tractable, even given the structural resources available to political leaders in the Fifth Republic.[13]

As we have already pointed out, the success of British Prime Minister Margaret Thatcher has been the result of the conjunction of several factors. The industrial crisis of the 1970s had already made solutions of the kind which had previously prevailed[14] considerably less viable in changing international competitive conditions. The British electoral system and parliamentary structure allowed the Conservative Party to win large majorities of seats on minority votes, enhancing the pre-existing fusion of legislative and executive powers. The credibility of the civil service had been undermined by its lack of economic (as distinct from financial) expertise and by attacks from both the Right and the Left. And not only have the opposition parties been in internal disarray, but the Conservative Party too has been in internal transition from the postwar hegemony of supporters of Disraelian 'one-nation' ideology to representatives of a more fundamentalist neo-classical capitalism (a transition which began in the late 1960s). Thus, like de Gaulle, Mrs Thatcher has been in a structural situation which had already generated significant opportunities which a leader, especially one with an 'active/anticipatory' personal equation, could effectively exploit and manipulate. She did not even have to undertake major constitutional change, because she was able to employ the pre-existing structural resources of the British state, which give the Prime Minister, in certain conditions, a wide scope of control over parliament and over the state apparatuses; thus she was able, in particular, to dominate the policy-making process sufficiently to alter some of the basic conditions governing state economic and social activities – i.e., by utilizing the potential decisional capacity of the British system.* The major catalytic factor, however, was not so much Mrs Thatcher's leadership *per se*, but the extent of Britain's structural economic crisis.

---

*That such structural potential exists in the British state does not, however, mean that it can be used or exploited under more 'constraining' structural and environmental conditions; see pp. 216–29 below.

History is littered, however, with political actors who aspire to be transformative or catalytic leaders but who are confronted by less exploitable structural conditions. This can either lead to their defeat and even send them into oblivion, in spite of their apparent skill, character, or vision, or effectively compel them to learn new skills and to operate as routine, or, at best, integrative leaders. Mao Tse-tung led one of the most important revolutions in modern times, and was widely seen as a transformative leader in various ways. However, as political structures crystallized in the decade-and-a-half following the Chinese Revolution, he saw the kind of change which he had struggled for endangered by a new structuration process which, in his view, could only lead to the recrudescence of the very combination of deadening bureaucratization at the center and local recalcitrance at the periphery which his revolution had been aimed at overturning – trapping the mass of people in a new web too much like the old.

The Cultural Revolution which he helped unleash in 1966, based on an attempt to institutionalize a 'permanent revolution' in which leaders would be periodically swept away and replaced, was itself a truly revolutionary idea, because it would have transcended the principal confines of the structuration process itself. In the event, however, the result was the breakdown of central control, widespread violence, and economic disorder. Since Mao's death in 1976, the process has been reversed and the thrust of structuration re-oriented in an attempt to maintain the trappings of the revolutionary order while undertaking Western-style economic modernization. Ironically, Mao's eventual successor, Deng Xiao-ping, who had been purged in the Cultural Revolution, has been able to exploit the opportunities created by the decay of the Maoist system, while at the same time maintaining a relatively low-profile image, more like that of a routine or integrative leader. Despite the promise that the Chinese Revolution might provide a model for a process of change which would transcend at least some of the constraints which state structures and traditions had imposed upon the French and Russian Revolutions,[15] a subsequent process of structuration has been creating a very different pattern of constraints and opportunities, not just resurrecting previous state structures but also reflecting the changes wrought by internal upheavals and the conditions prevailing in the outside world. In particular, the economic isolation – or world-wide revolution – needed for the success of the Maoist experiment in an increasingly interpenetrated capitalist world was not achievable, and his successors have chosen to attempt to exploit and manipulate external opportunities rather than to insulate China from them – or to try to overthrow them.

Whereas Mao Tse-tung was unable to orchestrate a radical deconstruction of the state itself and Ronald Reagan found his more modest project of rolling back the state enmeshed in the complexities of the

Madisonian system, leaders like General de Gaulle and Margaret Thatcher were able both to exploit manageable structural gaps and to pull on a wide range of potential structural levers in marshaling their resources more effectively. In all of these cases, both constraints and opportunities are fairly simple to identify. Most structural situations are far messier, of course. The influence of a variety of factors is highly ambivalent. A structure which is more stable may have both more constraints and more opportunities: the leverage which needs to be applied in order effectively to exploit interstitial gaps and tensions may have to be greater, as the thrust of active leadership comes up against the inertia of existing habits and relationships; but at the same time, the levers which can be pulled may be more effective and credible in appropriate circumstances. An unstable structure may provide more apparent opportunities for action, but less secure structural levers, leading to greater risk of failure and the possible lack of safety nets to offset that risk – as many Third World leaders have found.

Similar comments can be made about, for example, the depth and intensity of cleavage and tension within a structure, or the broad direction of historical trends toward structural expansion or decay. Tensions may increase the range of possibilities for manipulation, but also create *positions acquises* and vested interests which reduce the scope for coordination. And if, for example, what Huntington calls the 'amount of government' is low, it may constrain leaders, who have to marshal complex supports from outside the state; on the other hand, however, it may also give them the opportunity to control and shape the structuration process itself. In this context, of course, state structuration may come to revolve disproportionately around an influential leader or set of leaders, and this itself can become a major issue, especially if opposition to a personal leader comes to be equated with opposition to the structure in general. It is rare in such cases that the structuration process can be strengthened by increasing the power and influence, even if ostensibly institutionalized, of the leader himself or herself; institutionalization, in contrast, usually involves the routinization of the tasks of leadership and legitimated arrangements for succession and for the interaction of different leadership positions.

On the other hand, decay, as well as constraining leaders in many circumstances by limiting the potential scope of their effective action, may in other conditions also be a necessary condition for the bypassing of constraints, by creating structural gaps and tensions which can be exploited. This has been the case for Soviet leader Mikhail Gorbachev, whose room for maneuver has greatly depended on the prior atrophy of the Soviet Communist Party and the economic planning system, especially in the Brezhnev era – although he has also used the authoritarian structures of the party, paradoxically, to strengthen his own position *vis-à-vis* party *cadres*. The jury will be out for a long time in this case, and Gorbachev's goals will require something approaching transformative change. Nevertheless, he has both been able to use the strong position of the leader of the Soviet Communist Party and to exploit the decay of other structural features of the Soviet system. Again, the problem here will not simply be initiating change, but also maintaining change and institutionalizing it throughout not only the state, but also the society and the economy. It is quite possible that the mobilization of opposition to change in the Soviet Union may limit its range and scope, and even lead to significant reversals. *Perestroika*, 'restructuring', is by definition a form of transformative change; its success will not be found in the maintenance of Gorbachev's leadership *per se*, but in the institutionalization of new clusters of games. Ultimately, a leader's ability to cope with and exploit the pressures of both domestic and transnational issues – relative economic stagnation, the 'technology gap', growing consumer demands, the costliness of the 'arms race', etc. – will depend on his or her capacity to transform the processing of those issues into manageable *tasks*, tasks which can be institutionalized and thus be less dependent on personal leadership *per se*. Effective leadership, paradoxically, creates its own constraints.

On the whole, the complexity of these kinds of situational factors – and the relationships between such factors – significantly increases the probability that personal leaders, whatever their 'personal equation', will have only limited scope for action. Indeed, the more preeminent the leader, the higher his or her position in a hierarchical structural context, the more limited will his or her scope for action be in key ways. For example, the higher the position, the greater the number of games which the leader must be playing at the same time; a position of influence in one game context is unlikely to be matched by similar advantages in other contexts at the same time. Few leaders will benefit from being able to exploit the weaknesses of other actors and structures across a range of games in the way that de Gaulle or Thatcher were able to. Victories are rarely transferable from arena to arena, depending on the nature of the structure itself in different cases, depending upon the capacity of opposition to mobilize veto power or initiate autonomous actions which could lead to alternative outcomes, and, of course, depending upon the 'fit' between leader and structural situation. Even strong leaders are usually limited to tactical maneuvering rather than strategic action. And the position of the state at the crossroads of domestic and transnational processes of structuration raises issues which both raise the profile of personal leaders and build a more and more complex pattern of constraints into the structured field of action in which they must navigate.

Coalition Arenas and the Limits of Party Politics

The same questions must be raised about political parties, which not long ago were regarded by a wide range of political and social scientists to be the quintessential organizational feature of modern polities, both democratic and authoritarian. While this section will concentrate on competitive party systems,[16] some comments will also be made on non-competitive systems. In competitive political systems where access to formal office is determined by voting, political parties, in the widest sense of the term,[17] become the privileged vehicles for many of the most salient forms of strategic political action. Their character as organizations allows the mobilization of resources over time which personal leaders cannot hope to achieve alone. This is not to say that other organized vehicles – e.g., interest groups – are not also crucial (the 'secondary circuit of representation'); indeed, we will argue in the next chapter that they are becoming more crucial for processing the most important issues facing the contemporary state. However, their relationship with voting is, at best, indirect (they are not accountable), and they do not participate directly in office-seeking and office-holding. Thus parties have become the carriers of political legitimacy, and have often been said to be the crucial structural elements which articulate social, economic, and political demands – the contemporary version of the 'will of the people' – with the structural necessities of 'governing'. The capacity of parties to create organizational channels and 'transmission belts' which can effectively link the body politic and the decision-making process is a key problematic of contemporary politics. But we will argue here that parties, like leaders, become enmeshed in structural games which are more likely to constrain their capacity to process key issues rather than to enhance their ability to innovate or to control outcomes.

Party Systems, Access and Control

Although interest groups and other linkage structures of course have a central role to play in the contemporary state, parties have a more central *normative* role and are more salient participants in the 'political process', with its logics of inclusion and control. And parties operate within a structured action field, usually referred to as a 'party system'. However, the concept of a party system has been applied in a very circumscribed manner in political science. On the one hand, the distinction between 'two-party systems' and 'multiparty systems' still dominates the literature,[18] and recent attempts to modify that distinction, for example by references to the degree of 'polarization',[19] have done little more than attempt to shift the boundaries, or to explain some of the counter-intuitive effects, of the analysis. On the other hand, parties and party systems have to some extent been incorporated into the literature on interest groups and interest intermediation through such concepts as 'consociationalism'[20] and certain kinds of neo-corporatism, as we shall also see in Chapter 6; these developments are very significant, but tend to concern particular political parties – especially social democratic parties – rather than party systems. Here we argue that the concept of the party system itself needs to be redefined in order to integrate the elements of the structured field within which political parties, in the plural, interact strategically in their quest for access and control. Party systems are shaped by a range of interactive games which limit the effectiveness of parties as decisional agents.

In doing this, we will argue that political parties are doubly constrained in terms of their capacity to shape political outcomes: on the one hand, they are of course constrained by the resources which they can mobilize from the wider society, resources involving people, such as votes (and voters), rank-and-file loyalists and activists, *cadres* and leaders, and material resources such as finance, office space, media attention, and the like; on the other hand, they are constrained by specific key features of the structure of the state. In the latter sense they are constrained by the rules of the game and the structure of games which make up the state. But not only are they caught between these two forms of structural logic and material necessity; they are also caught up in an intermediating structured field of games which relate parties to each other – party systems. Thus parties and party systems link environmental givens – the distribution of resources among groups and individuals in society, cultural factors such as rituals and images, and the multifarious objectives of political actors – with the constraints and opportunities embodied in the formal structure of political institutions (or the 'political process' in the sense employed in Chapter 2 above); but they also constitute an intervening set of structured games.

This third, intermediate structural level of constraint and opportunity (games within games) operates in two somewhat contrasting but closely linked ways. In the first place, political parties, as formal organizations, develop the characteristics of organizations – in particular, a vested interest in organizational persistence, and an internal division of labor or hierarchy which leads to the development of a range of different but linked internal vested interests. In the second place, party systems, in a much less formal (but no less rigorous) fashion, develop patterns of competition and coalition – seen here as two sides of the same coin – which may also persist over time by controlling uncertainty. Within the parameters of these various 'natural' and 'artificial' sets of constraints, parties-in-party-systems act to transform the raw material of environmental resources into the finished product of collective decision-making within a given institutional structure. Let us look more closely at how this transformation process works.

Firstly, then, the formal structure of political institutions constitutes a crucial set of constraints and opportunities. Of course, not all institutional rules are equally significant in shaping the transformation process. Certain activities are by their very nature reductionist, and have the effect of *condensing* inputs into forms which are relevant to the process – i.e., forms which are recognizable to and seen to be manageable by the actors who populate the institutional structure, and which are more readily processed through established channels with their inbuilt structural biases. The rules governing these particular 'condensation' activities are of an importance disproportionate to their place in the formal-legal corpus. Two of these sorts of activities are especially important for the structuring of the party system: voting, and the institutional decision-making process. Both of these activities can be more or less complex. Not only do electoral systems differ, but the number of different types of officeholders who are elected (often at different times) may vary greatly from system to system. Thus the structures of *access to elective office* will vary greatly, and this variety will be directly related to the formal rules governing elections. Furthermore, *decision-making processes* involve a number of concrete stages (initiation, debate, voting, possibly the repetition of these stages in another house of the legislature, approval and implementation by the executive, possibly later legitimation, e.g., by a Supreme Court, etc.) within the so-called 'legislative process' alone, not to mention the broader questions of executive–legislative relations, center–periphery relations, and the like. Once again, the formal rules governing the control of the decision-making process will vary widely and will directly constrain the way that that control is gained and exercised in practice. Access and control, then, are the necessary means to the achieving of goals within the system, and structures of access and control fix crucial sets of parameters for strategic action.

In the second place, the structured field of action is constructed within an environment which is characterized by what could be broadly labeled a 'relation of forces'. Individual or group actors with long-range goals, shorter-term objectives, and more or less specific or diffuse value preferences will participate in the game. These actors will possess – i.e., will, in various circumstances, be able to mobilize – a range of resources.[21] The purpose of the actors' strategies will necessarily be to mobilize the *relevant* resources to attain the objectives which they might reasonably anticipate to be potentially obtainable within the structure of the game as a whole. But resources held *a priori* do not automatically convert into game-winning trump cards. The possession of capital, or of mass support, or of charismatic personal leadership, and so on, are crucial resources for parties as organized actors; however, their effective utilization depends upon their mobilization and upon the actors' capacity to maneuver these resources in competition with other actors possessing, possibly, different resources – or even the same sorts of resources in differing amounts or with different qualitative characteristics.[22] Thus the raw material of resource distribution and value preferences in society must be transformed into goals and mobilizable resources which are relevant to the range of anticipated outcomes permitted by the various constraints and opportunities built into the structured action field. This *transformation* process passes *via* the condensation activities regulating access and control discussed above.

Within a political system where access to formal office within the decision-making process is open and competitive, and where control of that process is dominated by those officeholders,[23] the privileged vehicles for this transformation process will be the political parties. The 'bottom line' of the operation of parties within this structured action field is found at the level of access; indeed, this is the lowest common denominator of the very concept of party.[24] The American party system is organized almost entirely in terms of controlling access.[25] However, in many party systems, party organization is also intended to control the day-to-day working of the decision-making process as well.[26] But parties, as more or less formal organizations,[27] interact strategically with each other in structured ways. They compete with each other and form coalitions with each other. And this process, while much less formal than intra-party organization, may be even *more* constraining. For example, the heterogeneity of American parties internally is legendary; but the many obstacles in the path of a third party attempting to join or replace the Republican or Democratic parties at national level over time are equally so. Indeed, the two characteristics are often seen as complementary, with the systemic constraints on 'entry' *enabling* the fragmented internal structure of American parties to continue without collapsing.

Institutional Topography and Coalition Arenas
It is this mutual interdependence of parties upon party systems, and party systems upon parties, which is at the core of this analysis. The structure of competition/coalition which constitutes a party system, it is argued, will be strategically determined (*ceteris paribus* – within the limits of parties' rational game-strategic behavior) (a) by the formal requirements of access and control, and (b) by the capacity of parties as actors to adapt to and to manipulate these formal requirements in pursuit of their goals through the mobilization of relevant resources. Thus the morphology of a party system begins with two sets of independent variables. The first, deriving from history, economy, and society, is the *environment* – the raw material of social structure, goals, and demands, and the possession of potentially mobilizable resources. The second is an *institutional topography* which isolates the relevant rules of the game which shape the parameters of strategic action by increasing the possible payoffs for certain forms of strategic behavior and penalizing other forms.

This approach can be particularly significant, for example, when attempting to explain change in a party system. In the case of advanced capitalist societies, analysts are divided over the true impact of the various changes which have taken place since World War II. A range of explanations have been proposed by political scientists for party system change in France since the advent of the Fifth Republic in 1958. Economic growth, modernization, *embourgeoisement*, political stability, presidential supremacy, and the like, have all provided themes for analysis.[28] And there is no doubt, for example, that environmental changes have been particularly far-reaching in altering many of the conditions which have been seen to underlie the 'stalemate society'. However, the consequences of those changes have been interpreted in diametrically opposed ways by, say, pluralists and Marxists. In any case, such explanations are very broad and generalized, and can be applied, in various ways, to a wide variety of advanced industrial societies, including Britain and the United States, where little system change has occurred.

But they are of very little use in attempting to explain differences between party systems, for they miss out the crucial dimension – the structure of constraints and opportunities, as perceived and experienced by the actors themselves. They do not accurately reflect the dilemmas of strategic action, because they define all game-rational action as either good (pluralists) or bad (Marxists) and therefore regard the more specific choices made by actors as relevant only in terms of either system maintenance or the struggle for socialism. Now these wider theoretical perspectives are essential in the sense that actors must be responsible for the normative implications and consequences of their actions. None the less, party actors also operate *within* the system, and this means that their actions are shaped by the possibilities of 'legitimate' success within its structure. Given the uncertainties built into the interstitial gaps and tensions built into the structure, then, the structured field constitutes a set of significant conditions which gives their action a clear – and replicable – rationality and helps to make sense of a morally complex and often confusing world.

Game-strategic behavior, then, while controlling some important areas of uncertainty, does still involve what actors perceive as significant margins of freedom of action, of choice of goals, and of the wider credibility and legitimacy of outcomes to justify their choice of playing the game. And, in contrast to theories built around the justification of game-playing *per se*, theories built around the infrastructure of the game itself focus upon a wide range of large and small strategic and tactical decisions which, taken cumulatively, actually constitute the building-blocks of collective action. Such theories are more appropriate for explaining *specific* decisions and patterns of behavior. However, such patterns are easy to take for granted in political systems which are long established and in which structures of action may be more or less hidden by custom, habit, or ideology. They can sometimes more easily be pinpointed and examined in situations where change takes place, and, in particular, where relevant changes in the rules of the game occur, requiring strategic adjustments.

It is necessary, if we are to explain changes in a party system, not only to look at 'environmental' changes, but also to ask whether and how the institutional topography has altered, and whether the new topography demands different forms of strategic action. If this is true, then it must be determined whether environmental conditions will provide an obstacle to such new forms of action, or whether 'permissive conditions' exist.[29] If the consequences of a particular configuration of environmental conditions are not massive and self-evident – for example, if party conflict does not simply *mirror* class, ethnic, religious or other conflict – then the control of uncertainty will depend more and more upon the intermediary constructs which characterize the structured action field. And to the extent that party actors within that field act in a strategic fashion, they they will be constrained to engage in a process of institutional learning.

This process may be more or less lengthy; sometimes it is not completed before the system itself collapses because of environmental constraints, as in the German Weimar Republic in the 1920s and 1930s. It may be more or less even; sometimes particular parties, unable or unwilling to adjust, will block development or look outside the system for support (e.g., Stalinist Communist parties outside the Soviet Union, or right-wing parties seeking military support). And it may be more or less successful; sometimes parties with strong organizational resilience and resources can resist integration into a new and still weak institutional system and force pragmatic modifications of the rules of the game. Indeed, all institutional learning is characterized by accommodation, pragmatic adjustment, and the establishment of conventions and practices. Only in this way do the rules of the game, formal and more or less precise, become transformed into elements of the structured action field. The institutional topography of a state shapes the structured action field of the party system in three ways: by defining the stakes of the game (the characteristics and the divisibility of the payoffs); by determining the different fields on which the different 'plays' of the game take place and the advantages of success in each play (the relationship between the separate battles and the winning of the war); and by orienting the internal organizational structure and make-up of the actors (the parties) toward an efficient coordination of strategy and tactics within this wider structure of the game.

The first and last of these sets of influences have, in rather different ways, been the subject of treatment in the political science literature. With regard to the basic characteristics of strategic attempts to win certain payoffs, the literature on the theory of political coalitions has formulated several propositions, the best known of which is the assertion that, from a rational perspective, actors will attempt to form 'minimum winning coalitions'; coalitions must be 'winning' (at least potentially), but coalitions which are too large are unwieldy and a waste of resources.[30] To some extent, the application of this theory to empirical evidence, and the various modifications which it has undergone, have partially undermined its primary analytical value – its generality and its predictive quality.[31] One of its early formal adherents came to the conclusion, following extensive testing, that no such *a priori* rationalistic theory was generally applicable, and substituted an incremental conception of coalition-building.[32] In our view, however, the problem with applying such a theory lies not in its formal presuppositions, but in its method. Coalitions in the real world are built in circumstances which are never entirely replicable and are not subject to control; and the intersection of a range of different games, with their interstitial gaps and tensions, is, as we have pointed out earlier in this book, characterized by complex regions of indeterminacy. Riker's main *caveat* – that actors have to deal with more or less 'imperfect information' about the state of play in each game (and across multiple games) – always substantially applies.

But Riker's notion of the 'minimum winning coalition' as a principle of rational choice cannot be disproved as such, and indeed is quite useful as a rule of thumb, *ceteris paribus*. That argument revolves around a central assumption. This assumption is that the rational choices involved in coalition-building will vary directly with the nature of the payoff. If that payoff is indivisible – or is perceived as such – and cannot be shared between winners and losers, then the constraints imposing game-strategic rationality upon those actors will be at their maximum strength, and the pressures to adopt a minimum winning coalition strategy will be the greatest. As with the concept of indivisibility in 'public goods', the strength of this assumption lies in its logical plausibility, not in its operationalizability for quantitative testing.* However, the inference remains that *zero-sum games over indivisible stakes constrain players in ways that positive-sum games do not.* Thus the rules of the game are crucial in that they define the very meaning of 'winning' and therefore either permit or constrain the range of coalition strategies open to actors. But some sets of rules are more permissive, and some more constraining, than others. This point is made by Sartori about electoral

---

*Its susceptibility to formal mathematical modeling is, of course, a matter of some dispute between formal game theorists and more empirical and/or discursive political scientists. The author of this book is generally an advocate of comparative case study methods rather than formal modeling, although the latter is certainly a useful tool for generating complex hypotheses for empirical and historical testing.

systems, which he classifies as 'weak' (proportional representation) or 'strong' ('first-past-the-post', or single-ballot, single-candidate, simple-majority systems); the former merely mirrors certain of the environmental resources of the actors – votes – while the second penalizes certain actors and rewards others systematically in a zero-sum fashion.[33] The maximization of the effective use of resources involves fitting them into the pattern of interstitial gaps and tensions generated by the rules of access and control.

Next, with regard to the internal organizational structure of the political parties themselves, organization theory suggests that strategic considerations frequently predominate over both goals and resources as the source of hierarchy and behavior. Michels's 'iron law of oligarchy' was a reaction to the downgrading of both ideological objectives and the mass base of the German Social Democratic Party simultaneously in the late nineteenth century; however, his explanation, in terms of elitist theory – more or less a version of Lord Acton's dictum that 'power corrupts' – is less plausible than an explanation in terms of middle-range strategic objectives. Joseph Schlesinger argues that the crucial determinant of party organizational structure is what he calls the 'structure of opportunities' presented by the system of formal officeholding characteristic of a particular set of political institutions.

This structure of opportunities is constituted by (a) a set of basic constituencies or districts with particular features – size and social composition of each constituency, coexistence of different types of constituencies and the relative importance of each type, frequency of elections, etc. – and (b) a hierarchy of offices, not so much in terms of formal powers as of career ladders, both in the structure of ambitions among politicians and as reflected in the wider political culture. The basic unit of party organization, then, is the 'nucleus' – the organizational structure necessary for the capture of one office – and the party organization as a whole can be seen as the articulation of a network of relations among the nuclei.[34] Schlesinger, writing about American parties, describes a fairly loose form of articulation, although different political systems might require tighter hierarchies where there are tighter hierarchies of offices.[35] Indeed, most systems do. Thus the institutional topography impacts directly upon the form of party organization.

Now we come to the third way (in our original enumeration, the intermediate way) in which the institutional topography constrains the party system: the system of coalition arenas. These are the different fields in which the different 'plays' of the overall political party game take place. The political science literature here is much less satisfactory. Constitutional literature on federalism and the separation of powers can be a useful starting point, but its legalism is often a barrier to its application as a means of explaining strategic behavior. Economic theory can help, too, but the links between macroeconomics and microeconomics are the weakest part of economic thought (an gap which institutional economics is attempting to fill). On a commonsense level, political commentators and analysts do, in fact, focus on just this problem – relations between the British cabinet and the majority parliamentary party, relations between the American President and the committees of Congress, relations between the president and the majority party or parties in a semi-presidential regime such as that of France or Finland.[36] But systematic comparative analysis is rare and theory rudimentary.

Coalition arenas are identifiable because they possess distinct structures of access and control. Each is composed of individual officeholders chosen at elections which differ from elections to other coalition arenas in one or more of the following ways: rules of candidate eligibility; number of constituencies; timing of elections; length of tenure of office; institutional nomenclature ('National Assembly', 'Senate', 'Presidency', and so on); and, frequently, electoral system. Each has a set of formal powers and a distinct role, *de jure* or *de facto*, in the decision-making process – a role which, at the very minimum, permits that body collectively to block or delay decisions. In military terms, each is a distinct 'theater' in which battles are fought, and which together comprise the war. The point about coalition arenas is that *each* arena contains the necessary elements for the formation of a distinct system of coalition and competition. Any party system, then, is itself a congeries or cluster of such coalition structures.

But a number of factors, both endogenous and exogenous to the party system *per se*, intervene to structure and constrain the articulation of relations between such 'compartments' of the overall process: the *sequence* of elections to different arenas; the existence of issues which cut across arenas; the perception of politics on the part of the mass public in relatively holistic terms (whether in the language of ideology or of power), frequently heightened by the mass communications media; the ongoing demands of organizational coherence (parties are themselves organizations with their own internal structures); specific powers and procedures (veto, dissolution, chains of events in the normal process of legislation and/or parliamentary control, specific linkage mechanisms such as joint committees, etc.); and the personal and social networks which develop around faction leaders or around common ideological, class, educational, or other ties.

Institutional systems can be classified according to the systems of coalition arenas which characterize them. A familiar criterion for such classification is the *number* of such arenas, which can be seen, for example, in the classification of parliaments into unicameral and bicameral. But a further, and crucial, criterion is that of the *relative equality or inequality* of arenas in terms of the collective influence of the members of each arena upon the state and the political process as a whole – inputs, withinputs, and outcomes. And a third criterion is the *polarity* between arenas, or the substantive differences between their respective game structures (rules, resources, players, substantive issues routinely dealt with, etc.). A number of hypotheses can be developed about the relationship of various coalition arena systems to the the performance of the state in general, hypotheses analogous to those developed elsewhere about social cleavages or about multiparty systems.

These hypotheses derive from a complex central proposition about the impact of the particular system of coalition arenas in question. This proposition is that: (a) the greater the number of arenas, (b) the more equal their weight, and (c) the greater the polarization between the members of each; then the lower will be the innovative capacity of the party system *per se*, i.e., the less will the parties have the potential to play an organizationally coherent role – whether in setting the political agenda, in formulating and/or implementing policy, in determining outcomes, or in autonomously shaping the structuration process itself. The reverse, however, does not necessarily hold, because of the greater role of environmental factors. Insofar as the impact of the structure of coalition arenas on the party system *per se* is concerned, however, a more limited hypothesis would suggest that the greater the number of arenas, the more equal their weight in the decision-making process, and the greater the polarity between them, the less coherent and unified will *party organization* be, and, consequently, the more will coalition-building be an *ad hoc* process dependent upon the simultaneous maintenance of a variety of different (and sometimes conflicting) strategies for use in more or less widely differing circumstances (e.g., the need to promise different things to different people).

This is not to say that the centralization of a party system around one balanced and predominant arena automatically increases the state's decisional capacity, for there are other crucial variables to consider. Just as Sartori argued that proportional representation electoral systems were 'weak' because they merely reflected the 'raw material' of votes without providing for effective structural control of the decision-making process, while 'first-past-the-post' systems were strong in that they distorted and molded those raw materials in ways which supposedly made it easier to govern, so coalition arena systems can be 'permissive' or 'constraining'.*

*In looking at coalition arenas, the words 'weak' and 'strong' are misleading. 'Weak', in Sartori's sense, means 'permissive'. A 'weak' structural environment is one in which the conditions of the game – and the outcomes – are more directly determined by the *a priori* configuration of party resources rather than by the institutional rules of the game, and *vice versa* for a 'strong' structural environment. Parties and party systems may, of course, be classified as 'weak' or 'strong' along very different dimensions.

'Strong', for Sartori, means that the rules are strong, forcing the parties to play a particular set of games, whatever they may be; the structure in this case is more 'constraining'. In this sense, a fractionalized multiple-arena system is, paradoxically, likely to be highly constraining – inducing parties to mold their activities to complex structural constraints; but this means that the parties themselves are likely to be 'weak', as energies are absorbed and deflected in the attempt to overcome and bypass structural hurdles. On the one hand, then, a single-arena system such as a parliamentary system is likely to be permissive; here, however, the parties themselves may be *either* 'weak' or 'strong', depending on a combination of (a) the rules of access to the various arenas (the electoral system, in particular) and (b) the distribution of the 'raw materials' of social structure, political conflict, and economic competition. Thus a single-arena system is more 'permissive', and a wide range of party systems may result.

On the other hand, the absence of a centralized, single-arena system, unless compensated by centralizing factors, will be likely to lead to systemic stalemate or immobilism, as the number and significance of opportunities for potential 'veto centers' and 'blocking minorities' to exploit gaps and spaces in the system increase. The existence of a multiple-arena system thus limits the influence of party organization upon political decision-making and privileges alternative channels of political communication and pressure – personal networks, iron triangles, etc. – in the generation of decisions and outputs.[*]

Coalition Arenas and Party Systems

This takes us back to the problem of the party system, for the classic interpretation of the operation of parties in the United States was to argue that in an institutional environment of 'checks and balances', political parties in effect had come, at least in the twentieth century (and especially since the presidency of Franklin D. Roosevelt in the 1930s and 1940s) to

---

[*]A further consequence of the differentiation of coalition arenas can, of course, be the privileging of certain types of *decision* or substantive issue content in each different arena. This is the core of Lowi's contention that in the United States, Congress seems to be the source of 'distributive' decisions (patronage, log-rolling, and other positive-sum games in which all, or at least most, actors can share in a divisible payoff), whereas the presidency is the source of 'regulatory' and 'redistributive' decisions, in which either actors have to be coerced to act in certain ways or resources are redistributed in a zero-sum or near zero-sum fashion. For Congress to reach a decision, because of its rules of access and control, almost everyone has to be a winner; the executive branch has both crucially different rules and different sorts of both institutional and material resources to deal with losers. Theodore J. Lowi, 'American Business, Public Policy, Case Studies, and Political Theory', *World Politics*, vol. 16, no. 4 (July 1964), pp. 677–715.

constitute the 'sinews' of the system, the real organizational infrastructure holding the otherwise crumbling eighteenth-century edifice together. But parties have themselves retreated in the United States, their coherence undermined by the incremental and fragmented character of the primary election system, the impact of Vietnam, Watergate and the institutional failures of the Carter and Reagan years, the atrophy of once-crucial state party organizations, and the focus of the media on personalities, at the local as well as the national level. The differences between Republicans and Democrats are real, of course, insofar as the 'center of gravity' of each party reflects different outlooks and cultures – among both mass publics and party elites – on real issues of substance such as the nature of the welfare state.

Nevertheless, where actual decision-making processes are concerned, many variables affect the ways that games are played, and outcomes are generally the result of factors other than the party identification of officeholders. Divided sovereignty has thus produced a potential for entropy in the American state in general. But what is important for this argument about parties is that the structure of constraints and opportunities in the American state has been a key factor in generating a party system in which American parties tend to represent a cluster of veto groups and blocking minorities rather than to work as agents of innovation or effectiveness. It must be made clear, of course, that there is no easy 'solution' to this predicament. Obviously even a fundamental constitutional shift to a parliamentary system, as proposed by political scientists in the 'responsible government' debates in the 1950s and 1960s or most recently by former Senator J. William Fulbright – in order to strengthen the coherence of foreign policy-making in particular[37] – would be highly problematic, for it might just as likely lead to the instability of multi-party politics, given existing social, economic, and political cleavages and conflicts. A parliamentary system, being relatively 'permissive', might be less successful at consensus-building. Of course, however, given the pride of place given to the United States Constitution in American life and culture, such sweeping constitutional change would be unlikely to achieve the momentum necessary to overcome the many structural hurdles erected by the existing system. It is not easy to rewrite history.

At the same time, parliamentary systems do not, of course, automatically lead to the development of party systems with greater innovative capacity. Britain has been the most notable example of a parliamentary state with a strong, centralized party system, and historical explanations are many and varied. But most explanations see the emergence of hierarchical, disciplined parties – focused on a zero-sum, single-arena, coalition game – as the key structural factor contributing to the development of the state itself in the nineteenth and twentieth centuries. The robustness of the British party system – whether it derives historically from the 'class alliance' which blocked absolutism and supported parliamentary supremacy in the seventeenth century, from the process of democratization in the nineteenth century, or from the 'incorporation' of the industrial working class *via* the Labour Party in the twentieth century – was certainly reinforced and entrenched by the overrepresentation of the 'winning' party in the House of Commons as the result of the 'first-past-the-post' electoral system. In Britain it *has* been the parties which have provided the 'sinews' of the political process; the electoral system has allowed the parties to control the 'nuclei' at the constituency level, overrepresentation has enabled the party leadership to control a majority in the House of Commons, and the control mechanisms of the legislative process have made the leader of the majority party – the Prime Minister – into the institutional fulcrum of power. Even here, of course, there are significant limits. Given the character of the British civil service and of the interest intermediation system – caught up in a consensual 'logic of negotiation' – British parties and party leaders, with the partial exception of the Thatcher Government, have been very poor at dealing with the main challenging issue of contemporary British political life, i.e., long-term economic decline.[38]

Thus Britain, at the level of the 'political process', at least, is an exception to the general run of parliamentary systems. In twentieth-century history the great majority of party systems in single-arena parliamentary contexts have been fragmented, whether because they reflected deeply-rooted patterns of social conflict and the resulting complex problems of transforming and mobilizing social and economic resources in the 'political process', or because of the conflict-reinforcing results of proportional representation, or a complex combination of factors. This has often been blamed on the destabilizing operation of multi-party systems, but that is usually a complicating symptom rather than a cause.[39] The result has sometimes been institutional failure, as with the Weimar Republic, Third and Fourth Republic France, or a large number of cases in the Third World, where post-colonial competitive party systems and weak state structures proved fragile in the face of conflicts. Widespread experiments with single-party systems have proved no more hardy. However, either the lack of deep social conflict (as in Scandinavia or Australia), or the presence of a closely-knit social hierarchy or 'elite cartel' (as in the Netherlands or Japan, in very different ways), along with rising prosperity through much of the postwar period, have changed that situation in Western Europe and some parts of Asia, although fragmentation remains the rule in Latin America, Africa, and many other parts of Asia. In most of these countries, however, it has not been the strength of the party system which has been the cause of stability; indeed, either institutional factors have played a large role or other political allocation processes have predominated – or both, as in the case of the Federal Republic of Germany.

Political parties and party systems, then, have not lived up to their promise as the key organizing structures of twentieth-century politics. In fact, they have been strongly constrained by structural fields of action constituted by a combination of their socio-economic environments and the institutional settings in which they operate. Strong competitive party systems with a high innovative capacity are rare – and the strongest of the single-party systems, in the Soviet Union, Eastern Europe, and China, have come under increasing pressure both from outside the party and from within. The salience of parties, for example at election time, often merely underscores in a paradoxical way their weakness in terms of policy-making and even representation, when 'real' decisions are made in more complex arenas cutting across political officeholders, bureaucracies, and a range of interests coming together in regular circuits – or are not made at all. The rhetoric of party politics is no longer the language of state structuration in the world – if, as some would argue, it ever was. And the gap between the body politic and the state which parties and party systems were meant to fill – a gap of legitimacy and communication – remains problematically wide, even if the rituals of electoral politics and the facade of formal accountability are still key elements in the symbolic manipulation of ostensible consensus. Thus the 'track record' of parties and party systems does not bode well for their future capacity to process the most challenging issues facing the state or for their potential to shape the political structuration process itself.

Conclusions

The limits on the power of political officeholders in the contemporary state are highly significant for an understanding of the political structuration process and the direction which it is taking. Personal leaders represent one of the core paradoxes of the state, especially its liberal democratic variant. Democracy is meant to restrain the power of leaders, but the structural complexities which actually constitute the real constraints on the influence of personal leaders also create a felt need for leadership itself. Leadership is demanded, both for the creation of comprehensible images of political processes, as manifested in the personification of political life which symbolic leadership generates, and in order to transcend structural constraints and create opportunities, thereby enhancing the decisional capacity of the state itself. But it is at the same time highly constrained, depending upon the conjunctural coincidence of appropriate leadership skills and the existence of permissive situations. Parties, too, represent a major paradox – that what were supposed to constitute the main 'transmission belt' for demands from the people (or for revolutionary change) are neither efficient articulators and aggregators of demands, on the one hand, nor effective agents of top-down change (whether authoritarian or democratic), on the other, but have become, with some exceptions, relatively epiphenomenal and often feeble elements in the sideshow which is electoral politics.

These limits, of course, are circumstantial; war, crisis, extreme personal popularity, a vacuum of power, or a major electoral victory may create conditions in which leaders and, to a lesser extent, parties, can exploit larger interstitial gaps and greater structural tensions, transcend constraints, control indeterminate outcomes, and even overhaul the structure of games – the meta-game – itself. Even in these circumstances, however, the possibilities are limited. And in the circumstances of the 1990s, as transnational interpenetration of structures and the refocusing of the state along lines of international economic competition come to channel and even drive the dynamics of political agency along new lines, the opportunities for political officeholders at the nation-state level to fulfill the expectations which voters, in particular, are supposed to have of them are likely to shrink further. As we will argue in the next three chapters, political outcomes in the twenty-first century will come more and more to be determined in other 'regions' of the state structure, whether it be in complex processes of political allocation involving collaboration between state actors and major interests, in the growing interpenetration of the state and the everyday life of civil society, or in the shift of state economic intervention to the pursuit of competitiveness in an open international marketplace.

The capacity of state actors and state structures – at the crossroads of a changing world – to 'hold the ring' of political structuration in terms of the vast range of policy and operational decisions which confront them will depend less on leaders and parties. Nevertheless, the spread of popular expectations and of formal liberal democratic structures, to which at least lip service is paid everywhere, is likely to *increase* the symbolic significance of leaders and parties in the rituals of contemporary political life, for without the feelings of legitimacy, representation, personification, and potential clout which they ostensibly embody, the roots of the contemporary state in society would be likely to wither. Thus the main paradox of 'political' power in the contemporary state is that as it becomes less and less relevant to actual decisional outcomes, it becomes more and more 'functional' in terms of justifying the nation-state bond and legitimating the state itself.

Notes

1. Hence our fundamental disagreement with writers like Huntington, *Political Order*, *op. cit.*

2. The following section is partly based on Cerny, 'The Process of Personal Leadership: The Case of de Gaulle', *International Political Science Review*, vol. 9, no. 2 (April 1988), pp. 131–6.

3. R.E. Neustadt, *Presidential Power* (New York: Wiley, 1976).

4. Nordlinger, *Autonomy*, *op. cit.*

5. Poulantzas, *Classes in Capitalist Society*, *op. cit.*

6. Cerny, *The Politics of Grandeur*, *op. cit.*

7. Cf. Michel Crozier, *The Bureaucratic Phenomenon*, *op. cit.*; and Stanley Hoffmann, 'Heroic Leadership: The Case of Modern France', in Lewis J. Edinger, ed., *Political Leadership in Industrialized Societies* (New York: Wiley, 1967).

8. Hoffmann, 'Heroic Leadership', *op. cit.*, and Hoffmann, 'Paradoxes of the French Political Community', in Hoffmann *et al.*, *In Search of France* (Cambridge, Mass.: Harvard University Press, 1963).

9. Max Weber, 'The Routinization of Charisma', in Amitai and Eva Etzioni, eds., *Social Change* (New York: Basic Books, 1964).

10. Theodore J. Lowi, *The End of Liberalism: Ideology, Polity, and the Crisis of Public Authority* (New York: Norton, 1969).

11. James MacGregor Burns, *The Deadlock of Democracy: Four-Party Politics in America* (Englewood Cliffs, N.J.: Prentice-Hall, 1963). Cf. Cerny, 'Political Entropy and American Decline', *op. cit.*; Stockman, *The Triumph of Politics*, *op. cit.*; Godfrey Hodgson, *All Things to All Men: The False Promise of the American Presidency* (Harmondsworth, Mddx: Penguin, 2nd edn 1984); Hugh Heclo and Lester M. Salamon, eds., *The Illusion of Presidential Government* (Boulder, Colo.: Westview, 1981); Hedrick Smith, *The Power Game: How Washington Works* (New York: Random House, 1988); etc.

12. For example, see Clyde H. Farnsworth, 'Why Trade Remains a Jumble', *The New York Times* (Business Section), 29 January 1989.

13. See Cerny and Schain, eds., *French Politics and Public Policy*, *op. cit.*, and *Socialism, the State and Public Policy in France*, *op. cit.*

14. See Keith Middlemas, *The Politics of Industrial Society: The British Experience since 1911* (London: André Deutsch, 1979).

15. This possibility was left open, for example, by Theda Skocpol, in her comparative study *States and Social Revolutions*, *op. cit.*

16. A condensed version of this section appeared as an analytical introduction to P.G. Cerny, 'The New Rules of the Game in France', in Cerny and Schain, eds., *French Politics and Public Policy*, *op. cit.*, ch. 2.

17. Not here distinguishing between parties and factions, as does Giovanni Sartori in his *Parties and Party Systems*, *op. cit.*, ch. 1.

18. With its roots in Maurice Duverger's classic *Political Parties: Their Organization and Activity in the Modern State* (London: Methuen, 1954), part II.

19. Sartori, *op. cit.*, part II.

20. Arend Lijphart, 'Typologies of Democratic Systems' (Berkeley, Cal.: Institute of International Studies, 1968), and 'Consociational Democracy', *World Politics*, vol. 21, no. 2 (January 1969), pp. 207–25.

21. See Nettl, *Political Mobilization*.

22. For a study of the manner in which the possessors of capital in France are said to employ reproduction and 'reconversion' strategies to perpetuate their social hegemony,

see Jane Marceau, *Class and Status in France: Economic Change and Social Immobility, 1945–1975* (Oxford: Oxford University Press, 1977); for the United States, see G. William Domhoff, *The Higher Circles, op. cit.*; cf. Miliband, *The State in Capitalist Society, op. cit.*

23. Of course, analogous processes can be discerned in political systems to which access is closed, but where organized factions, elites, 'apparats', etc., compete for control. Cf. Ionescu, *The Politics of the European Communist States, op. cit.*

24. Indeed, minimal definitions of what constitutes a political party focus on their role of nominating candidates; Sartori, *op. cit.*, pp. 58–64.

25. See Frank J. Sorauf, *Party Politics in America* (Boston: Little, Brown, 2nd edn 1972).

26. With more or less success. With regard to Britain, see A.H. Birch, *Representative and Responsible Government* (London: Allen and Unwin, 1964).

27. On the variety of formal organization of parties, see Duverger, *Political Parties, op. cit.* part I.

28. See P.G. Cerny, 'Social Change and Politics in France', review essay, *Scottish Journal of Sociology*, vol. 3, no. 2 (April 1979), pp. 253–62.

29. The argument that the early development of the party system of the Fifth Republic in France was made possible by permissive environmental conditions is made in P.G. Cerny, 'Cleavage, Aggregation, and Change in French Politics', *British Journal of Political Science*, vol. 2, no. 4 (October 1972), pp. 443–55.

30. William H. Riker, *The Theory of Political Coalitions* (New Haven: Yale University Press, 1962).

31. Cf. Sven Groennings, E.W. Kelley, and Michael Leiserson, eds., *The Study of Coalition Behavior: Theoretical Perspectives and Cases from Four Continents* (New York: Holt, Rinehart and Winston, 1970); and Lawrence C. Dodd, *Coalitions in Parliamentary Government* (Princeton, N.J.: Princeton University Press, 1976).

32. Abram de Swaan, *Coalition Theories and Cabinet Formations: A Study of Formal Theories of Coalition Formation Applied to Nine European Parliaments After 1918* (Amsterdam: Elsevier, 1973).

33. Giovanni Sartori, 'European Political Parties: The Case of Polarized Pluralism', in Joseph LaPalombara and Myron Weiner, eds., *Political Parties and Political Development* (Princeton, N.J.: Princeton University Press, 1966), pp. 137–76.

34. Joseph A. Schlesinger, 'Political Party Organization', in James G. March, ed., *Handbook of Organizations* (Chicago, Ill.: Rand McNally, 1965), pp. 764–801.

35. As argued in J. Roland Pennock's classic article '"Responsible Government"', Separated Powers, and Special Interests: Agricultural Subsidies in Britain and America', *American Political Science Review*, vol. 56, no. 3 (September 1962).

36. On semi-presidential systems, see Maurice Duverger, *Échec au roi* (Paris: Albin Michel, 1978), part I.

37. J. William Fulbright with Seth P. Tillman, *The Price of Empire* (New York: Pantheon Books, 1989).

38. Cf. A. Grant Jordan and Jeremy Richardson, 'The British Policy Style or the Logic of Negotiation?', in Richardson, *Policy Styles in Western Europe, op. cit.*, pp. 80–110; Hall, *Governing the Economy, op. cit.*; and Middlemas, *op. cit.*

39. The two-party system of interwar Austria is also a classic example; see Alfred Diamant, *Austrian Catholics and the First Republic: Democracy, Capitalism, and the Social Order, 1918–1934* (Princeton, N.J.: Princeton University Press, 1960).

6

The State and Interest Intermediation: Patterns of Collaborative Behavior

The second complex arena through which contemporary issues are processed is the interest intermediation system. Political scientists, political sociologists, and political economists have long been aware of the limitations on the capabilities of political officeholders to determine political outcomes, and much emphasis has been put on the competition or struggle between groups or categories derived from systems of social stratification and/or positions in the economic structure, usually expressed in terms – with varied definitions and consequences in different philosophical systems – of 'interests' and 'classes'. These interpretations have in common that, in one way or another, they give primacy in terms of explaining political action and interaction to motivations and sources of behavior which are derived from and embedded in the distribution of socio-economic resources and the dynamics of economic interaction. They are rooted in 'society-centered' theories of politics – in the 'raw material' of resources and conflicts lying outside the state *per se*, to use the terminology employed in the previous chapter in our discussion of political parties. These groups or categories which reflect, represent, or embody underlying socio-economic structures can in theory, of course (as discussed earlier, especially in Chapters 1 and 3), either 'peacefully coexist' in a political marketplace, or engage in ongoing patterns of class domination and struggle, in both of which the state is seen as an important intervening, but less than fully independent, variable.

In fact, as we have argued in Chapter 3, explaining the operation and impact of 'interests' requires an understanding of the ways that processes of 'political allocation' are structured – not only by the underlying pattern of resource distribution, socio-economic stratification, or mode of production, but also by the nature of the goods which are to be allocated and the organizational form of the structure within which they are allocated. In short, we have to look at the structuration of the allocation process, the interaction of agents and structures in those complex clusters of games which constitute the state. In this context, political science has in recent years come a long way from both the oversimplified pressure group models of pluralistic competition, on the one hand, and the oversimplified elite and class models of domination, on the other. Indeed, the development of 'neo-corporatist', 'neo-pluralist' and neo-Marxist state theory in the 1970s and early 1980s was taken by many political scientists to point to a certain fragile, uncertain, yet embryonic common ground among competing paradigms. Perhaps the most important attempt to build an analytical approach exploring this common ground in a systematic way has been 'neo-corporatism'.

Neo-corporatism began as an alternative perspective to pluralism for the study of Latin American and southern European countries. Its relation to class theory was always problematic, and it has been claimed by both neo-Weberians and neo-Marxists as their own. Its empirical focus migrated northwards in the late 1970s, in terms of countries considered to be characteristically 'neo-corporatist', to Austria, West Germany, and Scandinavia; countries such as France and Britain came to be seen as characterized by a partial corporatism, respectively excluding a major 'interest' (trade unions) and vacillating between a 'corporate bias' and a more pluralistic backlash. The framework was also applied to a variety of other countries in the First, Second and Third Worlds, whether seeing neo-corporatism as a general or partial attribute of interest intermediation systems in those countries, or identifying it as a developmental trend in industrializing and advanced industrial societies. However, neo-corporatism was not seen simply as an attribute of particular countries or as a general trend; it was also seen as characteristic of particular organizations or sectors which play a central role in political allocation processes, as we will set out in more detail later on. And it was also seen as characteristic of states. In other words, neo-corporatism represented a set of regularized, organized *interfaces*, systematically linking the raw material of socio-economic 'interests', on the one hand, and the internal structures of the state, on the other.

Thus neo-corporatism seemed to provide an analytical framework which could identify and elaborate the operational principles of a structured field of action systematically linking interests and state structures – a theory, if in many ways only a partial theory, of political structuration. However, in the seminal formulation which became the dominant mode of setting out the neo-corporatist problematic,[1] the source of neo-corporatism was seen not so much to be in the structures of the state, but rather in the tendencies of modern interests and modern interest organizations to take on particular forms, forms which were peculiarly appropriate to generating and maintaining organized interface structures with the state. Thus neo-corporatism was also a 'society-centered' theoretical project, although it gave a much larger, more systematic and more independent role to the state and state actors than did pluralism. For only a particular kind of state structure could accurately reflect and efficiently respond to the challenges of policy-making in a socio-economic environment composed of a particular type of interest formation and organization.

As Schmitter wrote, pluralism and corporatism shared certain basic assumptions:

(1) the growing importance of formal associational units of representation; (2) the persistence and expansion of functionally differentiated and potentially conflicting interests; (3) the burgeoning role of permanent administrative staffs, of specialized information, of technical expertise and, consequently, of entrenched oligarchy; (4) the decline in the importance of territorial and partisan representation; and (5) the secular trend toward expansion in the scope of public policy and interpenetration of private and public decision arenas.[2]

Within this context, however, he saw fundamental differences between the pluralist and the corporatist conceptions of how these underlying trends and relationships would work out in practice. On the one hand,

Pluralism can be defined as a system of interest representation in which the constituent units are organized into an unspecified number of multiple, voluntary, competitive, nonhierarchically ordered and self-determined (as to type or scope of interest) categories which are not specially licensed, recognized, subsidized, created or otherwise controlled in leadership selection or interest articulation by the state and which do not exercise a monopoly of representational activity within their respective categories.[3]

Corporatism, on the other hand,

can be defined as a system of interest representation in which the constituent units are organized into a limited number of singular, compulsory, noncompetitive, hierarchically ordered and functionally differentiated categories, recognized or licensed (if not created) by the state and granted a deliberate representational monopoly within their respective categories in exchange for observing certain controls on their selection of leaders and articulation of demands and supports.[4]

In 'neo-corporatism', however, in contrast to earlier forms of corporatism which were imposed by the state more or less unsuccessfully (as in the case of Italian Fascism), the basis for such arrangements was seen to lie not so much in trends within the state (although the increasing differentiation and expansion of the state are secular organizational trends also), but in trends in the organization of interests themselves – a move towards 'societal corporatism', based on Weberian organizational tendencies associated with industrialization and advanced capitalism. Societal or 'liberal' corporatism, in a manner analogous to theories of 'democratic elitism' and to the looser variant of 'neo-pluralism', saw the state as legitimizer, regulator, arbitrator, and occasionally shaper of a process of bargaining which, while highly circumscribed at some levels, was still somewhat open and competitive at others, if only because outcomes were still indeterminate in crucial ways. In other words, *because of the limited number and oligopolistic nature of interests themselves*, bargaining could take place only within a relatively restricted arena of 'interest intermediation', as we will show in more detail below. Thus neo-corporatism claimed to identify, locate, and specify a range of games which not only were highly significant for analyzing and explaining existing processes of political structuration in advanced industrial societies, but which would also become increasingly central to the processing of new issues – especially in the rapidly-changing economic conditions following the end of the so-called 'long boom' which had lasted from the early 1950s to the oil crisis of 1973–74.

The concept of neo-corporatism has seemed in recent years to have reached an impasse. Having emerged in the 1970s, it was at one time seen as one possible basis for a paradigmatic shift in the discipline of political science away from pluralism. Pluralism was seen to have been compromised by the recrudescence of social conflict in the 1960s and 1970s, by an awareness of the structural stickiness of economic inequalities in the recession of the 1970s and early 1980s, and by growing academic critiques, especially outside the United States, of the bases of pluralist theory and of the functionalist assumptions with which it had long been associated. Thus despite pejorative assumptions remaining from corporatism's abortive association with Fascism and Nazism in the 1920s and 1930s, Schmitter argued, the twentieth century was at least in some ways 'still the century of corporatism'.

And yet the term corporatism has been either abandoned in practice by many of its proponents, or relegated to specific and somewhat limited cases at one end of a 'pluralism–corporatism' scale. Rather than representing a new structural convergence among advanced industrial societies, it is often now seen as evidence of a greater divergence – a divergence resulting from different national cultural styles – in the common attempt to stabilize conflict, deal with often intractable inequalities, and promote economic recovery.[5] The very clout which it ascribes to organizations of capital and labor can undermine these attempts in some countries, while aiding them in others. Like the Westminster model of parliamentary government in the 1960s, then, corporatism is no longer regarded as transplantable. But this does not mean that it does not reflect deeper underlying characteristics of contemporary social structures. In this chapter we will look at the core features of the concept of corporatism, and its recent neo-corporatist variant, with the intention of showing that it is still in many ways a highly relevant concept. However, we will go on to suggest that the main problem with corporatism, especially neo-corporatism, is that it has not been situated within the context of political structuration.

This is true both at the level of structure and at the level of agency. At the level of structure, corporatism and neo-corporatism conceptualize the state in terms of power or force *per se* as an attribute of states, while the main 'new corporations' of advanced capitalist society are perceived as deriving from the deeply-rooted structural characteristics of capitalist society. In other words, both the state and the main economic forces in conditions of advanced capitalism are seen as the primary contemporary manifestations of what we earlier called 'orthodox structures'. In this chapter, taking the wider definition of state structuration used in this book, we will argue that a structural analysis of the state yields historically grounded patterns of rewards and penalties which shape the strategies of agents, including state actors and those societal actors represented by the corporative bodies which are the subject of neo-corporatist analyses. Thus if we want to understand how different types and patterns of corporatism develop and operate, and how relevant they will be for processing the main issues challenging the state at the beginning of the twenty-first century, we must first study state structuration. We will do this by expanding the notion of the 'organizational form' of the state as outlined in Chapters 2–4.

At the same time, we will elaborate upon the conception of agency which was developed earlier, especially in Chapter 3, expanding the notion of 'interest intermediation' to include a much wider variety of patterns than was prevalent in most neo-corporatist analyses before about 1982.* In effect, we will attempt systematically to locate several varieties of neo-corporatism within a wider set of categories characterizable as ongoing, regularized, structural 'interfaces' between the state and state actors, on the one hand, and interests – both interest groups and other agents representative of, or directly constituting, particular socio-economic interests – on the other. As we pointed out in Chapter 3 (and will develop in a somewhat different direction in Chapter 8), the structural games played in the middle column and middle row of Table 3.1, involving nested structures and/or semiprivate goods, are the predominant games of the state at the crossroads; a typology of how this works, derived partly from Table 3.1 but elaborating on the analysis of organizational form, will be offered toward the end of this chapter.

The games which both of these sets of actors (state actors and interests) play, and the choices which they have to make within the structured field of action referred to as the 'system of interest intermediation', locate this particular complex arena at an especially significant site in the processing of contemporary issues. This ensures that some of those issues, in some economic sectors and in some countries more than in others, will be processed in identifiable and analyzable ways, shaping not only the strategies of the actors but also the broad pattern of outcomes. Although we will argue later in this book that the interest intermediation 'arena' also

---

*Although the concept of neo-corporatism has itself been expanded significantly since that time, as we will argue below, with some significant loss of analytical coherence.

is structurally circumscribed within the political structuration process as a whole (a structurally 'bounded' set of games), it is a far more significant focus than the 'political process' for locating and understanding how a range of critical political outcomes will be shaped in tomorrow's political world.

Strengths and Weaknesses of Corporatism as a Prospective Paradigm

The more traditional notion of corporatism, from which Schmitter's neo-corporatism was derived, stems from the assumption common to many cultures – and prominent in feudal Europe – that 'societies' (or 'society') are *not* composed primarily of individuals or groups in open, market-like relationships with each other, a point discussed in somewhat different terms in Chapters 2 and 3 above. An explicit contrast is drawn with a notion of society as based on social contract, in which the contractual parties can be seen to hold procedurally equal values or preferences which are legitimately substitutable for each other in terms of outcomes (as most individual-based democratic theory, pluralist group theory, or public choice theory would posit). Instead, societies are seen to be composed of bodies of people – usually expressed by the French word *corps*, as characterized in, e.g., the notion of *esprit de corps* – which, because their members share distinct characteristics such as socio-economic, religious, or socio-political tasks, roles, and activities, possess a *natural* (rather than just cultural), *gemeinschaftlich* internal solidarity and even organic unity which is somehow more fundamental to the social being of associated individuals and groups than is membership of either the overarching state or the market system.

Instead of *Gemeinschaft* in this context being primarily a local phenomenon, however, as it is often assumed to be in social theory, its functionalist character allows the notion to be expanded to cover the whole geographical spread of the wider society. Thus the wider society cannot be constituted simply of a monopoly of *gesellschaftlich* bonds over the extent of the territory – or even of an organic, natural *Gemeinschaft* at the macro-societal level. Society's own existence depends upon an intricate imbrication of *Gesellschaft* and *Gemeinschaft* cutting across the social 'base'. To a certain extent, nation-states deal with this problematic by the ideological construction of nationalistic cultures merging endogenous and exogenous factors.[6] But beyond this, in the interstices of the social formation, emerging state structures would themselves form and develop around a primary structural field the infrastructure of which would be constituted precisely of and by the various *corps* and their pattern of interaction. Historically, of course, such bodies develop in a contingent fashion, and patterns therefore vary considerably.

But two broader questions obviously pose themselves. On the one hand, the development of such patterns, when seen to be present in one form or another in political systems generally, usually implies the presence of some sort of *hierarchy*. Estates, *Stände*, castes, etc., are usually not of equal rank, although there may be some claim of moral equality embedded in cultural justifications for such a system, e.g., in myths about system origin or eschatology.[7] Hierarchy usually operates within the *corps*, too. On the other hand, there is the question of how the different *corps* interact. Most normative theories which posit the naturalness of such categories also assume – or prescribe – some sort of *functional complementarity* both in the way that each *corps* organizes its members endogenously and in the way that different *corps* interact with each other exogenously (but still within the wider plane of the society/state). This complementarity may operate at different levels: on a macro-level, producing or reproducing a functionalist and almost metaphysical kind of social harmony; or, on a micro-level, merely limiting the disadvantages of Hobbesian competition and providing a deeper social substructure for an economic division of labor. Corporatism has therefore appeared as a *theory of social stability* through 'natural' hierarchy and harmony.

But despite this theorized complementarity, of course, corporatism in the real world has limited neither inequality nor conflict in practice, and is often seen to have reinforced both. Most modern social theorists, whether liberal or Marxist, have therefore usually tended to relegate this sort of *gemeinschaftlich* corporatism to the realms of historical curiosity, 'primitive' societies, false consciousness, or the non-rational elements of culture which permeate, for example, the British class system, the underlying causes of which are seen to lie elsewhere. These reactions were greatly reinforced after corporatist ideas were integrated into conservative Catholicism in the late nineteenth and early twentieth centuries, and later into Fascist and Nazi doctrine. In contrast, however, it is important to stress that the centrality of certain corporatist notions to liberal Social Catholic views of Christian Democracy and the welfare state in Europe after World War II was crucial to political, social, and economic stabilization there.

In this broad context, then, the success with which Schmitter and others have managed to rehabilitate the concept of corporatism over the past decade and a half is quite remarkable. This is due in part to the reaction of social scientists concerned with European politics – although analogous tendencies can be seen in some aspects of social science concerned with the Third World, especially Latin America – against what is often seen as the overdependence of the discipline in general on notions which are culturally biased, i.e., the view that the pluralist paradigm is essentially rooted in American ideology and American political experiences. The liberal, Madisonian tradition of American political culture is explicitly pluralist, and the assumptions built into it, based as they were on the rejection of European conceptions of democracy (as well as other European political perspectives), are often seen, in turn, to be less applicable in the European setting. The British tradition is perhaps more of a hybrid. In contrast, the ancient and medieval origins of the notion of corporatism rest on a conception of justice and order which is inherently social, rather than individualistic, and the class basis of politics is more clearly rooted and reflected in European culture than it is in the American 'liberal' tradition.[8] But it is also the result of the tendency of political science itself to continually look for alternative paradigms to pluralism.

The strength of neo-corporatism has been its ability to reach across these boundaries. It has seemed to restore the critical element to the study of elites, as it asserts that some elites are more equal than others – and that the elite levels of the organizations of capital and labor, along with those of the state apparatuses, are the real power nexus of advanced capitalist society – while at the same time clearly locating the parameters and dynamics of their competition. It also has a quasi-Marxist variant, in which corporatist intermediation can be seen as a way of ensuring that the interests of capital are met while simultaneously ensuring cross-class compliance with the outcome, even if workers' living standards are reduced and/or jobs lost in bad times (in a neo-corporatist trade-off for union 'incorporation'). Furthermore, it has a Weberian element, as the three main forms of organization maintain their clout by asserting their authority not only over their rank-and-file (in the political arena, not only over the voters but often over party leaders as well) but also, collectively, over the main decisions affecting society as a whole. And it has normative significance, in that it claims to stabilize society and to reconcile conflicting demands in a way that neither political authoritarianism nor liberal democracy can do.

Neo-corporatism is essentially assumed to work because *gemeinschaftlich* values are seen to be operative and effective both at the level of the solidarity of the respective organizations and at the level of their collective position within society as a whole. And, of course, it reflects a major way in which political and economic markets work 'imperfectly', depending upon 'political' processes to settle, e.g., the price of labor or the pace and direction of industrial restructuring – the latter being a crucial variable in an economic context in which macroeconomic policy has come under severe pressure.[9] The paradigmatic promise of corporatism, then, has resulted from its ability to span most of the major critiques of pluralism and to appear to focus on an empirical phenomenon of central concern in a wide range of societies at a quite recent, and therefore relevant and topical, stage of their development.

The Impasse of Corporatism?

The difficulty with the neo-corporatist approach has been in its attempt to locate and to specify either the 'bodies' (*corps*) which are the main components of any corporatist analysis, or their precise mode of interaction, which, taken together, as we have pointed out earlier, constitute the infrastructure of corporatism as a potential paradigm. This problem has led to the claim that corporatism has, like other alternatives discussed earlier, become indistinct from certain varieties of pluralism and cannot be taken seriously in terms of any implicit or explicit paradigmatic claims.[10] In the first place, then, there has been the problem of specifying exactly what are the new corporative bodies of advanced industrial society. The first of these, in the neo-corporatist literature, is of course capital. Therefore a major focus for a time was on employers' organizations, recognizing the significance of the role which these have come to play in a variety of policy-making processes, especially in negotiating national-level wage agreements. Capital has been seen not simply as composed of market-rational actors, but rather as a complex social organization with a lowest common denominator of solidaristic behavior, reflected in recurring cartel-like tendencies toward market domination or market-sharing rather than market-clearing. This is not new in that it reflects elitist, Marxist, Weberian, etc., critiques. However, it avoids both the emotive notion of monopoly and the more formal economic pathology of oligopoly. And it moves away from trust-like conspiracy to an open tendency toward organization and regularized negotiation.

Labor movements, the second of the new *corps*, have of course been more classically seen in this light anyhow, whether favorably or pejoratively. After all, it has always been one of the goals of trade unions to act as 'virtual' representatives of the working class as well as actual representatives of their members – whether for non-revolutionary unions, which seek to represent all workers in a bargaining context, or for revolutionary ones, which seek to unite the working class to overthrow capitalism. For the former, it has been a long-standing objective to establish parity not only with capital but also with the state in a wider social bargaining process in which unions represent 'ordinary people' *vis-à-vis* the forces of money and power. And indeed, neo-corporatist theory posits a long-term drift of labor organizations away from confrontation and toward collaboration and negotiation, too, especially as they develop organizational apparatuses with Michelsian vested interests and as they recognize the need, in advanced capitalist/industrial society, for the maintenance of the profitability and competitiveness of their own firms and of capital in general.

And the role of the state apparatus, the third 'corporation', provides the setting and the explicit harmonizing rationale for the bargaining process. Schmitter and others argue that the success of the state in this venture – in the fostering of 'societal' corporatism – comes not so much from its commanding role but rather from its *legitimizing* role; both roles are, of course, features of the Weberian conception of authority. The excessive presence of the former in Fascist-type corporatism – which Schmitter labels 'state corporatism' – is seen as the reason for the failure of such versions. Of course, the new societal or liberal corporatism needs the state as legitimator, regulator, arbitrator, and source of a certain amount of 'authoritative allocation' of material resources as well as values – whether in terms of macroeconomic management or of microeconomic intervention – and it therefore also requires the state apparatus and state actors to be relatively independent from too-narrow outside political, social, and economic pressures and influences. But the state itself in this perspective is primarily and essentially a part of the wider corporative structure and process, not truly autonomous or 'above' that process. Thus state actors in advanced industrial states find the source and rationale for their own priorities in forms of organizational behavior which are functional to the maintenance of an ongoing *collaborative process* in the form of neo-corporatism.

Unlike pluralist group theory, then, neo-corporatism asserts that two fundamental principles are inextricably intertwined. In the first place, the central roles of capital, labor, and the state apparatus in the functioning (system maintenance and change) of advanced industrial society make them, *de facto*, more significant than other 'publics, opinions, and pressure groups' – a view which would be shared by neo-pluralists like Lindblom (as well as, in their different ways, elitists and Marxists). And in the second place, it is their particular form of organizational behavior – their socio-political (solidaristic or authoritative/hierarchical) rather than market-rational character – which enables them to constitute a privileged circuit of power as the 'new *corps*' of advanced capitalism. The problem here is not with the state, which is usually assumed to conform to this model of behavior – at least in its bureaucratic manifestations if not always in the more competitive sectors of the 'democratic process'. The dimension of the triad represented by capital, however, is more complex, as neo-corporatism asserts that business will put stability, corporate control, and market-sharing before risk, competition, and market-clearing. This is consonant with twentieth-century analyses of business corporations as bureaucratic organizations or as part of a wider 'technostructure', but is at considerable variance with mainstream economic theory. The position of labor is even more complex, for trade unions are traditionally torn both between goals of confrontation and goals of negotiation, on the one hand, and between hierarchical organizational forms and rank-and-file input and spontaneity, on the other.

Therefore whether capital, labor, or even the democratic state will be characterized by this sort of collaborative behavior – rather than various forms of competitive or conflictual behavior – is the central problematic of the notion of neo-corporatism. Their interaction must be primarily peaceful, and must be seen to lead more and more, as capitalist industrial society advances, to some sort of accommodation – although the use of limited conflict is normal if power relations between the three legs of the neo-corporatist stool become too unbalanced – over the terms on which the requirements of *Gesellschaft* and *Gemeinschaft* are reconciled, i.e., the classical conundrum of medieval and post-feudal forms of corporatism. The ideal-type structure and process of neo-corporatism is thus *tripartism*, the 'success' of which in reaching accommodations in turn further consecrates the hierarchical position of the primary *corps* in the overall socio-political field of action. In doing so, it also further reinforces their internal authority over their members and emphasizes functional complementarity in the key tasks of harmonizing and stabilizing the socio-economic order of advanced capitalist societies – a virtuous circle. But the problem with the tripartite model is that it rarely exists in pure form; thus the debate is engaged over whether the phenomenon being analyzed is really neo-corporatism or just another skewed and imperfect variety of pluralism (such as neo-pluralism).

Corporatist or partially corporatist processes have been observed in a wide variety of countries, but the application of the overarching label has led to interminable debate. Of course, one of the directions in which that debate leads is toward attributing different forms of interest intermediation along a pluralism–corporatism scale to the existence of differing political cultures. We do not have the space here to deal with this development, except to say that it not only suffers from the many problems besetting analyses based on political culture* but also undermines any paradigmatic claims which neo-corporatism might make with regard to political science in general.[11] Perhaps more damaging has been that neo-corporatism has appeared to be quite vulnerable to recent political, social, and economic changes. If it is to be seen as so deeply rooted and widely representative as to constitute a potential paradigm, then how are we to evaluate the partial correlation of its incidence with the

---

*Criticisms of political culture as an analytical approach come in many varieties, but two which are especially relevant are that it tends to fall back upon the sort of reified generalizations characteristic of earlier notions of 'national character' and that it emphasizes cultural structures which are consensual rather than those which embody symbolic or material 'resistance' to the cultural hegemony of dominant groups, classes, or the state.

power in political office of social democratic parties in a period when such parties have otherwise been electorally vulnerable, whether in Sweden, Britain, France, or Germany in the 1970s and 1980s? If capital is also such an essential organizational ingredient, then why do different firms, different types of firms, and different types or 'fractions' of capital (e.g., financial and industrial, or national and multinational) conflict as well as compete in recessionary times in a manner more red in tooth and claw than during the previous period of the 'managerial revolution' – as witnessed by an increasing resort to bankruptcy and takeovers? If labor movements have become mature, *corps*-like organizations, why do strikes still bring down governments, and why is both union-busting on the Right and a new skepticism about unions on the Left so characteristic of the 1980s? And why is the state turning to Reaganomics, Thatcherism, deregulation, and the like?

The response of neo-corporatist theorists has been complex. First, they have retreated from paradigmatic claims and argue that while corporatism is one essential element of advanced industrial society, it must still be reconciled with *gesellschaftlich* elements. Therefore neo-corporatism is no longer seen to be applicable as a generalized label for a type of state or society, but merely as one end of a scale running from an ideal-type model of perfect group competition at one pole to ideal-type corporatism, essentially tripartite collaboration, at the other pole, with real-world societies comprising an uneven mixture. Identifying and structuring the in-between points of the scale, however, becomes rather more complicated, and this process has led in three further directions. The first has been to look to the neo-Marxist conception of 'the relative autonomy of the state' in order to differentiate corporatist and pluralist processes according to the different *functions* which the state fulfills in capitalist society.

In this context, in addition to 'legitimation functions', which all states carry out, the advanced capitalist state has certain specific functions stemming from the class nature of the mode of production. The two main functions specified are (a) 'production functions', which means that the state must by its very nature as a *capitalist* state act to develop, maintain, and increase the capacity of the economy and society to produce material goods (sometimes also known as 'supply-side' functions), and (b) 'consumption functions', which means that the state, because of both its capitalist character and its very nature as a state or *political* unit, must respond to extensive demands stemming from specific groups which consume both material commodities and socio-political outputs. The latter usually includes also the 'demand management' activities of the Keynesian welfare state, although these to some extent cut across the two categories through government attempts to 'fine tune' overall economic growth and activity.

To quote one set of conclusions,

we may distinguish in ideal-typical terms between (a)
a sphere of the politics of production . . .
in which capital and labor are directly represented as classes . . .
which negotiate with the state in a relatively exclusive corporate sector of the
polity . . .
which is located mainly at central and regional government levels . . .
and whose prevailing ideological principle is that of private property and the
importance of maintaining private sector profitability;
and (b)
a sphere of the politics of consumption . . .
in which a plurality of consumption sectors mobilize as non-class-based
interest groups . . .
which battle with each other over specific issues in a competitive sector of
the polity . . .
which can be found at central and local (though not regional) levels of
government but most crucially at the relatively accessible local level . . .
where the prevailing ideological principle is that of citizenship rights and the
importance of alleviating social need.[12]

Thus there may be a critical *dualism* between the production and consumption functions of the state reflected in different forms of state activity
and interest intermediation.

However, this does not deal with a second level of differentiation
within neo-corporatism, that *within* the 'production function' sphere.
For example, we have already mentioned conflicts of interest between
'fractions of capital' such as the financial community and industry, or
between business concerns which depend upon an essentially nationally-
based production and market system and those which are transnational or
multinational in their operations; a related distinction is that between big
business and small business. Each of these potential lines of conflict may
undermine the attempt to construct frameworks sufficiently cohesive to
negotiate and to collaborate in a corporatist manner with labor and the
state. Indeed, certain firms may operate in a corporatist fashion and
intersect with the state without effective reference to the rest of 'capital'
(whether peak organizations or informal networks) at all. The same can
be said for labor, where not only competition between different unions,
especially in an organizationally divided system such as that in Britain
or a politically divided one such as those in France or Italy, but also
competition between different levels of organization, e.g., craft-based
unions *versus* industry-wide unions (a form of conflict found almost
everywhere), is endemic. And the same is usually said of the state,
too, where partisan battles, pressure-group competition, 'turf battles'
between bureaucratic agencies, and competition between 'iron triangles'
and policy networks make 'the state' less a coherent functionalist unit than
a structured set of various clusters of games.

Thus our second further direction of change in neo-corporatist analysis
is the shift toward differentiating corporatism by sectors and levels.

'Sectoral corporatism' is quite straightforward. It suggests that for a number of reasons, some of which may be historically contingent, corporatist processes develop with regard to specific economic sectors.[13] Two of these have been particularly fundamental to state formation and maintenance and thus are partially a legacy of the past and partially a reflection of the vulnerability of the territorial state in international relations: agriculture[14] and defense.[15] Others derive from patterns of organization, either of labor or of management, on the basis of such variables as the structure of production (e.g., natural monopolies or the specific kinds of assets characteristic of particular firms and markets),[16] the structure of consumption (e.g., public *versus* private goods), the structure of foreign trade (e.g., 'small country' corporatism),[17] or even a potential for protest deriving from economic vulnerability (e.g., shop-keepers).[18] Thus corporatism becomes a variable to be explained through empirical case studies of particular sectors which, whether because of historical, political, or economic factors, have been susceptible to these more collaborative and less competitive forms of organization.

The same can be said for the various levels of corporatism distinguished by Cawson.[19] Macro-corporatism, which is essentially the same as tripartism, we have already discussed. 'Meso-corporatism' seems at first to be similar to sectoral corporatism, but can also be applied to more general corporatist relations which are, however, circumscribed within a particular sub-national territory or region, as well as to *bilateral* bargaining structures at various levels (to be considered in more detail below). And 'micro-corporatism' involves the bypassing of supra-firm organizational networks or pressure groups such as trade associations, etc., and the direct collaboration of firms with the state and/or trade unions. In each of these cases, of course, the 'level of corporatism' identified by Cawson refers to the extensiveness of the production processes involved, not to the size of the inner collaborative circle or the number of individual agents included. But this does lead us on to the third further direction – the notion that corporatism does not necessarily include all of the main *corps* of advanced industrial society *per se*. It may be bilateral, and may tend, in particular, to exclude the unions.[20] At the same time, the business community has a particular fear that collaboration between labor and the state will exclude capital, despite the assertion by most writers that business interests have a particularly strong position, even in a neo-pluralist perspective.

What, then, is left of the original substance of the concept of neo-corporatism? We argue that the essence remains. Despite – and even because of – the universalization of market-based forms of exchange ('commodification'), neither pure pluralism nor instrumentalist class domination, but an analyzable combination and even fusion of the two, constitutes the structured field of action represented by the interest intermediation process. Neo-corporatism has been partially subsumed in a mixed system in which certain organized interests – capital, labor, and the state apparatus retain this status despite endogenous tensions – operate according to hierarchical and/or collaborative criteria. In other words, the interest intermediation system is itself an ongoing process of structuration – one which is particularly significant for the processing of many of the key issues facing politics and the state in the contemporary world. In attempting to identify the parameters of this process, we will first look critically at the way that neo-corporatist authors have used the concept of the state. We will then attempt to locate neo-corporatism within the wider range of 'processes of political allocation', using a more complex formulation of the problem of the 'organizational form' or structure of the state itself, derived from social and historical analyses of state formation and development. Finally, we will try to show how neo-corporatist and related 'collaborative' processes of political allocation are especially relevant for the future of political structuration.

Putting the State Back into Neo-Corporatism

The main problem with the more complex formulations of neo-corporatism discussed above, with all of their exceptions, qualifications, levels, etc. (and a problem shared by classical corporatism too), is the assumption that some ideal-type form of corporatist collaboration is actually an independent variable, driving the organizational process, usually 'from below', from the societal level, as embodied either in the holistic notion of the mode of production or in more circumscribed and specific production processes. The other side of this coin, of course, is that the state, or the political structuration process, would have to be seen, in the last analysis, as a *dependent* variable – or else corporatism would merely be a sham, a façade, for authoritarian state power. Thus in classical corporatist theory, the state forms and develops around the *corps*, which are either historically or sociologically prior to the state – even where the *corps* are not seen as fully 'natural' but to some extent conventional. This is the key element which has been resurrected in the notion of 'societal corporatism'. The original idea of neo-corporatism, then, involves a rejection of authoritarian corporatism and an assertion of the compatibility of corporatism and liberal democracy; thus when what Schmitter labels 'state corporatism' does arise, it involves a state-imposed distortion of the proper mechanisms of corporatism.

At one level, then, the state becomes a reified exogenous factor, with state actors operating functionally to establish by command or fiat a set of corporatist processes which can only work properly if it reflects the spontaneous structure of the *corps* themselves and of their pattern of interaction. In a way which is reminiscent of some forms of pluralism, the state becomes a quasi-neutral field on which the corporate actors determine by and for themselves the patterns which bargaining processes and political outcomes will take. The main function of the state is to lend its holistic *legitimacy*, as guarantor of the broad social order, to such actors in return for their acquiescence to the underlying norms of that order, i.e. to honor the 'rules of the game', and to undermine neither the symbols of social unity nor, in particular, the outward forms of liberal democracy and the territorial state. Indeed, the maintenance of the stability and effectiveness of neo-corporatism requires such legitimization and 'licensing'.

At another level, however, the state – especially in the form of the welfare state or the interventionist state (the economic and social activities of the state, as set out in Chapter 2) – constitutes a range of 'stakes' which corporatist agents are attempting to control. Of course, 'state actors' are among these corporate actors, attempting to marshal intrastate resources in order to further their own preferences. In a quasi-clientelist fashion, then, government is caught up in the competition process, sometimes pursuing 'autonomous' preferences, sometimes 'captured' by other, societal actors, and sometimes both, as state actors play 'dual roles'.[21] This rather confusing picture of the state's relationship with neo-corporatism, then, involves two roles: both an *authoritative* role which is necessary at one level in order to stabilize and legitimize the interest intermediation system, but which must be kept to a functional minimum, to prevent societal or liberal corporatism from turning into authoritarian corporatism; and an *ad hoc*, differentiated behavioral role deriving from the fact that the state is made up of a set of state actors acting to maximize their own utilities within the corporatist collaborative framework too. This very confusion has made attempts to build the state back into neo-corporatism problematic in ways which reflect assumptions about the nature of the state which are posited by neo-corporatist theorists themselves. In particular, they cannot fully take into account the process of state structuration: their structural-functionalism is too rigid at the level of the state *per se*; and their rational individualism is too dispersed at the level of agency.

For example, Birnbaum's attempt to build corporatism into his model of the state, based on the distinction between 'strong' and 'weak' states,[22] asserts that corporatism becomes possible only when *neither* a strong nor a weak state is present. He sets up two intermediate categories, once again called state corporatism and societal corporatism, but with a number of countries falling out of the corporatist model altogether – i.e., either those in the weak state category, like the United States, which is characterized as pluralist, or those in the strong state category, like France or Japan (as well as more authoritarian state forms), which are characterized by autonomous state interventionism or *dirigisme*. However, the weak state/strong state model still has problems, i.e., (a) its unidimensionality and (b) its conceptualization of the state as an authority structure *per se*. The main issue is that while this formulation constitutes a much more nuanced continuum than a simple pluralism/corporatism scale, it still treats both corporatism and the state more or less as 'orthodox structures', and explains the operation of interest intermediation systems in terms of the juxtaposition of conflicting deep-structural tendencies rather than as a process of structuration – and is not therefore able to explain the full range of variations which have led to the impasse of neo-corporatism.

But what it does do is to point us in a direction whence a solution might come. If the form of corporatism is somehow correlated with the form of the state, even if the model of the state used is inadequate, then perhaps a more complex model of state structuration will yield a way of ordering and explaining the complex forms of neo-corporatism (and its problematic offshoots) which have given rise to such a wide range of partial types. To do this, as stated earlier, we will use a more complex model of the organizational form of the state. There are several relevant dimensions to this model, but we believe that a two-dimensional representation will be sufficient to identify and differentiate between virtually all of the major forms and types of interest intermediation. There is one particular omission, for example, and in one sense the major explanatory variable favored by neo-corporatist theorists is left out – i.e., the social bases or 'raw materials' which constitute the interests themselves, whether grounded in production processes, consumption categories, belief systems, or whatever, interests which constitute a major class of 'agents' in the structuration process. A start has been made toward systematizing these interests already,[23] however, and it will ultimately be necessary to bring these and other explorations in that direction together with the analysis here.

Secondly, we will assume that, in contrast with Table 3.1, the question of types of 'goods' being sought has been controlled; in effect, we are excluding the four 'corner' boxes and dealing with the mixed cases included in the middle row and middle column only. And a third dimension which might be included, but which is partially subsumed by the model presented here, is one which measures the organizational and structural cohesiveness among endogenous state actors themselves, but we will only comment briefly on this later. For the moment, though, let us look first at two specific dimensions of state structuration and try to show how they correlate with basic types of the state/corporatism relationship. It is hoped that the plausibility of the types will lie in their capacity not only to include and to distinguish between a wide range of sub-types of corporatism, but also to link them with an explanatory framework and even to expand the notion of interest intermediation systems to include a wider variety of the most prevalent and significant 'processes of political allocation'.

Both dimensions elaborated below concern the organizational form of the state. The first dimension is based on historical state-formation, i.e., the process of structuration of the state itself and the different sorts of linkages which crystallize and develop between state actors and the socio-economic environment. Thus it deals essentially with both the general level of *exogenous* differentiation of the state from 'society' (or lack of differentiation) and the amount and kind of autonomy which state actors have.[24] In substance, it concerns the relative order in which a more complex, modern state structure, on the one hand, and an integrated national society, on the other, emerged, combined, and crystallized. The second dimension involves the *endogenous* structural centralization/decentralization of the state, as in Williamson's scale of organizational form.

The first scale is thus labeled 'Formation/Integration', and is loosely derived from the typology of states presented by Birnbaum in *La logique de l'État* and which represents a more complex version of his strong state/weak state dichotomy.[25] This is primarily a historically-based scale, chosen on the assumption that state-building is a critical historical conjuncture which establishes certain structured institutional matrices of rewards and penalties, cultural presuppositions about the nature of state/society imbrication, etc. – i.e., a complex range of clustered games – which continue to shape the strategic action of individuals and groups over time. Our assumptions include the possibility of incremental change altering such patterns, and also of paradigmatic shifts undermining them, but we agree with Birnbaum's assessment, and our discussions in Chapters 2 and 4, that the underlying patterns which he perceives continue to operate and to exert influence on actors' strategic choices.

One pole of the scale consists of the case where the institutional structure of the modern state emerged and crystallized – leaving deep legal, cultural, and organizational legacies – in an historical phase prior to the effective social and economic integration of the national territory more or less as it exists today. The other pole consists of the case where the national territory was effectively integrated socially and economically prior to the effective crystallization of a complex, modern state apparatus.* The first we label 'state precedence'; the second, 'society precedence'.† We also identify a mid-point on the scale, where the crystallization of the modern state and the socio-economic integration of the

---

*Although, in prior historical phases, early state structures, extensive 'traditional' or 'patrimonial' bureaucracies, externally-imposed colonial-type administrative structures, conflicting sub-state political networks, etc., would have existed, of course.

†These categories would seem at first glance to be close to Birnbaum's strong state/weak state cases, but the latter include a range of assumptions about structure and authority which we would not make, given earlier comments about our choice of analytical dimensions.

national territory have been broadly 'symbiotic'.* Despite our differences with Birnbaum, we share with his analysis the basic assumption that *the forms which neo-corporatism and/or collaborative behavior take* will flow more directly from choices made by state actors – what Nordlinger calls 'state preferences' – when 'state precedence' has been the case in the state formation/integration process, while it will flow more directly from choices made by societal actors in the case of 'society precedence'. The mid-point involves a relatively close linkage or even a fusion between the preferences and strategic orientations of both state and non-state elites. Thus this scale is an indirect indicator of 'state autonomy'.

The second scale is a simpler 'Concentration/Diffusion' scale, similar to the 'organizational form' scale used by Williamson and familiar to students of institutional structure through the ages. Now the organization and activity of interest groups is strongly influenced by the structure of centralization and decentralization of government, and therefore by the range of formal and informal points of access through which interests must operate.[26] This is still a critical structural feature of the state, although it subsumes a number of sub-factors the influence of which can be uneven – such as the number of key 'vertical' levels or tiers comprising the overall structure of the state (e.g., the existence of federalism or regional autonomy of some kind), the separation of powers, the relative openness of different points of access, the problem of bureaucratic 'deconcentration' *versus* 'decentralization',† etc. One pole represents centralized hierarchical structures. The opposite pole represents a structure characterized by multiple centers of power of a heterogeneous kind – either a fractionalized structure, in which many sub-units of relatively equivalent weight compete (and form coalitions) in the search for influence and power within the structure, or an uneven structure, with many different kinds of sub-units jockeying for leverage and control. For simplicity we call these 'unitary' and 'decentralized' structures, as in Chapter 3. But rather than labeling the mid-point the 'multidivisional' form, which is more apt for business firms, or 'nested',

---

*Once again, our intermediate category differs significantly from Birnbaum's, as he regards this category as involving the hegemony of a relatively unified ruling class cutting across state/society distinctions, whereas we leave that question open.

†'Deconcentration' refers to the diffusion of administrative tasks to lower levels of government, usually according to criteria established at higher levels, in order to improve organizational efficiency within a hierarchical bureaucratic structure; 'decentralization' refers to the diffusion of power to make significant policy decisions according to criteria set at those lower levels. It is usually believed that the ability to tap an independent source of revenue, especially the power for states, regions, and local governments to set their own taxation levels at their own discretion, is the most significant indicator of effective decentralization.

which is often refers to a wider range of phenomena than we do here, we will refer to it as 'homogeneous/subdivided'.

In this way, we derive a typology of structures of interest intermediation, which forms a subset of our earlier category of processes of political allocation. There are three columns. In the 'unitary' column:

(a) the most important access points for large groups of a potentially corporatist nature are near or at the summit of the structure; and
(b) the relations between different levels and component parts of the state structure (intra-organizational competition/collaboration and decision-making) are formally and/or informally controlled from the top down.

In the 'homogeneous/subdivided' column:

(a) there are available a limited range of alternative access points relatively equivalent in openness and not very different in the ways that each might be utilized; and
(b) the relations between levels and vertical components of the state operate, formally and informally, in a relatively homogeneous, cartel-like endogenous fashion to control unrelenting but limited political and bureaucratic competition over 'turf'.

In the 'decentralized' column:

(a) there exist a wide range of horizontally and vertically differentiated access points, each with its own advantages and disadvantages in terms of what resources need to be mobilized, what constraints and opportunities exist, etc. – giving 'claimants' wide but complex strategic and tactical choices; and
(b) the relations between levels and components are determined by a more open political marketplace, with outcomes determined typically by adversarial procedures.

Note that the structure of access and control is not determined wholly by the formal constitutional structure of the state, but by a combination of formal and informal structures, both 'political' (in the narrow sense) and bureaucratic.

In this matrix, then, the main types of neo-corporatism can be found, but there also appear a number of marginal types of corporatism and, perhaps even more significantly, a variety of other prevalent forms of interest intermediation which have often been misconstrued as mere subtypes of corporatism but which are in fact related but distinct kinds of collaborative behavior. It is particularly important to note that this approach helps to clarify a major issue – the relationship between corporatism, clientelism, consociationalism, *dirigisme*, etc. For corporatism and neo-corporatism are essentially subtypes of a wider phenomenon, i.e., ongoing patterns of collaboration between socio-economic categories and the state for both particular and mutual advantage. As with our typology of processes of political allocation, of which this is a subset, the categories in Table 6.1 refer to processes, any of which can be found in any country; but our increased emphasis on state structures here gives the category of organizational form a greater specificity and applicability to particular countries, which are usually seen to have predominant patterns of interest intermediation. Indeed, the sort of national stereotypes employed by a range of writers on interest intermediation in general and neo-corporatism in particular appear quite clearly and distinctly in the typology presented here.

The first thing that stands out from the table is that each of the horizontal rows in fact identifies a group of systems which are usually considered to have important common factors in their political cultures which affect the nature of collaborative behavior characteristic of that group. In the first row, state actors tend to be the senior partners in any collaborative exchanges, the legitimacy of those exchange processes themselves derives from the patronage of state actors, and corporatist and/or clientelist relationships essentially fill the gaps between more hierarchical and authoritative decision-making processes. The difference between the three subtypes in fact stems from the nature of the interstitial gaps or spaces – points of access and processes of control – in the state structure and the different constraints and opportunities which they provide for both state actors and 'societal' agents.

Table 6.1 *State structures and patterns of interest intermediation*

| Formation/ integration | Concentration/diffusion | | |
	Unitary	Homogeneous/ subdivided	Decentralized
State precedence	Strategic state corporatism and *dirigisme*/'neo-colbertisme'	Segmented state corporatism/ 'arms-length *dirigisme*'	Patronage/ patchwork state corporatism/ *caciquismo*
Symbiotic	Hegemonic societal corporatism/ tripartism	Mixed sectoral corporatism/ concertation/ consociationalism	Systemic clientelism/ pseudo-consocia- tionalism
Society precedence	Corporate 'bias' or 'temptation' (unstable over time or cyclical)	'Corporate state'/neo- pluralism/uneven meso-corporatism	Fragmented *ad hoc* corporatism and clientelism/ pseudo-pluralism

For example, the administrative systems of France, Spain, and Italy are all modeled on the centralized, *dirigiste* Napoleonic bureaucratic system. However, power has in fact historically been concentrated and/or diffused differently in each of those countries, with centralization having been more effectively realized in France – whereas in the others, local political and administrative bosses (such as the Spanish *caciques*) were able to operate in a highly independent manner, leading to the establishment of quite autonomous multiple fiefdoms, but fiefdoms in which state rules and resources have been critical in the exchange equation. And even where some of these have been 'captured' by special interests, the power of those specific interests tends to be expressed in and through the very act of capturing part of the state apparatus, and not in their independent power (derived from the 'raw material' of their socio-economic resource base) to bargain with each other in a wider field.

Political outcomes in the area of social and economic policy reflect the configuration of relationships between state actors themselves for the most part, i.e., in patterns of cooperation and conflict among politicians and bureaucratic officials. The most concentrated form is found in the notion of the 'strategic' or 'developmental' state, as those terms have been applied to Japan[27] and, in a somewhat more problematic way, to France.[28] Although a debate has been raging over whether France is 'corporatist' or 'pluralist',[29] both of these categories miss the point. In France the state apparatus is itself dominated by corporative bodies – the civil service's *grands corps* – which developed when the French monarchy was still centralizing the country and undertaking the main tasks of integrating both the territorial periphery and the variegated class system. Thus, in terms of this chapter, France is characterized by a kind of endogenous, intra-state corporatism which has dominated societal tendencies toward a traditionally extreme pluralism among the structures of capital and labor. The main question about France concerns the cohesion and concentration of the state itself – whether the French state is more of a strategic state like Japan, as Zysman argues, or what Machin and Wright have called a 'splintered state' or a state riven by intra-state cleavages and conflicts, involving the recurrence of fairly predictable and regular clashes between sections of the state apparatus itself over turf.

Japan seems to be a more straightforward case of the strategic or developmental state. The unity imposed by state elites since the Meiji period has been reflected in recent decades by the primacy of the Ministry of International Trade and Industry and the Ministry of Finance, along with a small number of other state and para-state agencies, over economic policy, and the centrality of state policy itself to the wider economic development process – as well as to relations between capital, labor, and the political system too, through the dominance of the Liberal Democratic Party over the past forty years or so.[30] Thus within the category of 'strategic state corporatism and *dirigisme*' there is variety based on the different ways that the central state and the state elite itself are structured, and their capacity to impose centrally coordinated policy outcomes on societal actors while maintaining a collaborative façade and certain collaborative practices. Of course, a more extreme form partly falling within this category, and partly falling outside the range of 'collaborative behavior' altogether, is that of central state planning as traditionally practiced in the Soviet Union and other command economies; here too, however, a certain amount of competition exists among state actors or 'Apparats'.[31]

The second category in the top row in the table, 'segmented state corporatism', implies the existence of a state structure in which major intra-state cleavages basically lead to the development of 'states within states' – both at the central level, within which relatively insulated political/bureaucratic spheres of influence develop but without policies being effectively coordinated, and at the lower levels of the state, where sectoral and regional fiefdoms can develop and persist. In virtually every state, the defense industry or 'military–industrial complex', to use President Eisenhower's phrase, is perhaps the best example of this sort of organizational tendency. Policy-making in other areas which are classified as 'strategic industries' or 'natural monopolies', but the long-term operation as well as the day-to-day running of which are left to sectoral state actors, also falls into this category. This category more closely approximates to Machin and Wright's or Hayward's view of the French state,[32] with its competition between bureaucratic *grands corps* and turf battles between sectors dominated by state actors and their selected *interlocuteurs valables*.

However widespread the tendency for sectors characterized as 'segmented state corporatism' to exist in many countries, it is rarely the case that whole states fall into this category; it requires a strong tradition of bureaucratic precedence along with sufficient cohesion not to allow bureaucratic conflicts to degenerate into endemic turf wars which further fragment state structures in centrifugal fashion. In contrast, the most diffuse form of statist corporatism, which we label 'patchwork state corporatism' or 'patronage', is found in many societies characterized by some combination of pseudo-corporatism* for popular consumption, degenerated centralized state forms, social fragmentation, and petty forms of localized repression. This can be seen in Franco's Spain, various Latin

---

*We would include in the category of 'pseudo-corporatism' various kinds of quasi-mystical, super-patriotic, and religious fundamentalist regimes which have become so popular in countries at the 'receiving end' of both internal and international conflicts (often at the same time). Such state-imposed solidarism, however, is extremely unstable, and usually either it must be propped up by ever-increasing central repression, or it will degenerate into petty corruption and localized repression – or, as is often the case, both.

American countries such as Peronist Argentina or the dominance of the Institutional Revolutionary Party in Mexico, and a range of post-colonial regimes in Africa and Asia, for example. There is also the very real danger that the Soviet Union, Eastern Europe, and China, as centralized planning is abandoned or undermined by rapid bureaucratic and social change, often of a fragmenting kind, may degenerate into such conglomerations of satrapies.

The second row contains those systems most often described as being characterized by neo-corporatism, 'consociationalism' or 'concertation'. We have already analyzed neo-corporatism in some detail. 'Consociationalism' has also been called politics by 'elite cartel' or 'the politics of accommodation'.[33] It means a system in which potential political conflict, based in deep or 'extreme' socio-economic cleavages, is avoided not by reconciling conflicting interests *per se*, but by formal or informal agreement between dominant elites *within* each social group or interest category. Such an agreement (a) would require each elite to control its *own* group endogenously in such a way as to avoid conflict with other groups, to segregate groups from each other, and to insulate politics and political culture within each group in such a way as to isolate and control disruptive influences from outside; such internal control (b) would then leave the elites of each group free in exogenous terms to negotiate and maintain what might essentially be termed political 'market-sharing agreements' with elites of *other* groups, carving up the political marketplace according to an agreed formula, like an economic cartel.

Political stability would then not be explained by social stability; rather it would be the other way around, with social stability explained by political arrangements and the structuring of the socio-economic field of action by political actors seeking assured slices of influence for their power bases. The relationship between neo-corporatism and consociationalism is a complex one, with consociationalism deriving from a general theory of elitism and elite autonomy, with a focus on group leadership and political officeholders interacting within the 'political process', while corporatism stems from a general theory of development which stresses the organizational capacities inherent in modern capitalism and in the bureaucratic state apparatuses. Nevertheless, both approaches stress the relationship between the endogenous solidarism of major social, economic, and/or political categories, on the one hand, and the exogenous cartel-like bargaining field among different categories, on the other.*

*Which is why they are sometimes confused, or used in ways which argue that one is the genus or more general category and the other is the species or more specific sub-category. This argument can be presented either way around, depending on how the wider theoretical questions are addressed with regard to the sources of either or both dimensions of endogenous 'group' solidarism and exogenous political or state bargaining.

'Concertation' is a weaker, but in some ways more generally applicable, concept, which basically leaves out the dimension of endogenous group solidarism, but focuses on attempts to generate spontaneously, or for the state to impose, a realm of *conjunctural* agreement between 'social partners' or *interlocuteurs valables*. Such conjunctural agreements are seen to arise not from underlying or 'orthodox' structural characteristics of elites, political cultures, core 'interests' of capitalist society, or the organizational imperatives of modern bureaucracy, but rather from a more incremental process of information-sharing and uncertainty-reducing around a range of specific policy issues – wage agreements, price guidelines, the maintenance of full employment, the pursuit of economic growth, avoiding political and economic instability, adjusting tax liabilities and benefits, introducing targeted welfare measures, etc.

This is often seen as an inherently informal process of cajoling and accommodation, and is what British Prime Minister Harold Wilson was talking about in the 1960s when he said that 'A week is a long time in politics.' But it can be part of a much more formal process. The process of 'indicative planning', as established and understood in France in the 1950s and 1960s, was supposed to be not a command system wherein state-determined norms were imposed by fiat on capital and labor, but rather an 'auction' system, wherein capital, labor, and the state would share information about costs, prices, expected fluctuations, and intentions to produce, invest, and/or employ; the spontaneous coordination of decision-making which would in theory flow from such an exercise would naturally improve the efficiency of the marketplace, improve business confidence and lead to a virtuous circle of growth. Indicative planning was in many ways seen to be a kind of joint forecasting exercise, the result of which was meant not to comprise organic solidarism, representational monopoly or oligopoly, the systematization of market imperfections, corporatism, or elite cartel – but rather to constitute a more efficient form of 'market-clearing' exercise.* In essence, then, 'concertation' is a vague term, which none the less implies a certain integrated, national-level set of structured inputs, mainly at the framework level of conjunctural economic decision-making, which can be included in North's 'neo-classical' conception of the state as a hierarchical promoter of economic efficiency and reducer of uncertainties (like Williamson's notion of the firm).[34]

---

*'Market-clearing' refers to a situation in which all of the commodities offered for sale in a particular market over a particular time period (ranging from a few seconds or minutes in the case of auctioning a particular commodity or trading financial securities, for example, to much longer periods, such as four-year or five-year 'indicative' plans) are actually sold, at 'efficiency prices', to willing buyers. For an excellent review of the theory of indicative planning and of its application in France, see Saul Estrin and Peter Holmes, *French Planning in Theory and Practice* (London: Allen and Unwin, 1982).

Interest intermediation processes characterized by neo-corporatism, consociationalism and/or concertation, then, involve not the imposition of norms by autonomous state actors, as in the top row of Table 6.1, but rather the capacity for different agents – state actors as well as interest agents – to perceive, and to act upon the basis of, a range of structurally and/or conjuncturally shared assumptions, norms, and goals. They require state actors and state structures at least to some extent not merely to create and maintain a framework for those processes, but also to develop a certain minimal capacity to 'steer' those processes in the direction of collective action – but not to dominate them. These processes, then, are of course found to some extent in all interest intermediation systems, but they tend to be predominant in some admixture in states characterized by 'symbiotic' socio-historical processes of formation and integration. In these countries, state and interest group actors tend to be relatively equal in the bargaining process, the legitimacy of the exchange processes derives from the success over time of bargaining *per se*, and the outcomes of neo-corporatist, consociational, and concertational exchanges tend to establish the parameters for the most important contemporary forms of resource and value allocation, an oft-noted example of which is called 'consensual wage bargaining'.[35]

The differences between these countries reflect the extent to which these bargaining processes represent either a single umbrella-like norm-setting process valid across a number of key issue-areas, or a number of more variegated processes. The closest most analysts come to identifying whole states characterized by a pure form of societal neo-corporatism usually concerns Sweden and/or Austria, which we would locate in the category labeled 'hegemonic societal corporatism'. It is a matter of argument whether the centralizing Swedish monarchy of the seventeenth century or the combination of late industrialization and the early emergence of the welfare state was the more influential factor in creating the type of neo-corporatist processes which are so central to Swedish social, economic, and political life. In any case, in addition to consensual wage bargaining and the dominance of the Social Democratic party for most of the period since 1931 (with only a short gap the 1970s), the development of Sweden's 'active labor market policy', and problematic recent moves toward setting up state-supported trade union investment funds, provide a broader activity and resource base for neo-corporatist processes.

And despite Austria's formal federal system, Austrian corporatism has a long history, on both the Catholic Right[36] and the social-democratic Left. At one level, Austria at the time of the break-up of the Austro-Hungarian Empire at the end of World War I had long been a society whose elites saw it as the cultural and social center of the Empire and in which classical Catholic corporatist traditions were being transposed to a more homogeneous socio-political unit. At another level, its interwar political cultures were built around a highly centralized, Vienna-based conflict between Right and Left, a conflict which resulted in the victory in 1934 of a pseudo-Catholic state corporatism blending indigenous traditions, the predominance of the traditional Catholic ruling class, and state forms copied from the Italian Fascist model. Austria's structures were reinforced and reshaped in the postwar period of *Proporz* – a grand coalition between the major parties, grounded in an agreement to share, in a proportional manner, ministerial posts and political appointments to the bureaucracy – which lasted until 1966, and, after that, by Socialist Party dominance for most of the succeeding period. Katzenstein attributes Austria's successful corporatism primarily to her small size and vulnerable position in world markets,[37] although other aspects of social structure, cultural and ideological quasi-homogeneity, political processes, and bureaucratic state structures could be cited.

In the category labeled 'mixed sectoral corporatism and concertation' we find a somewhat looser but recognizably neo-corporatist set of processes. For example, West Germany is often identified as a neo-corporatist society, although this has been a matter for some debate. In fact, despite the centralization of the capital and labor organizations which arose in the context of simultaneous national unification and industrialization in the late nineteenth and early twentieth centuries, the regional character of much of the political and administrative structure of West Germany is today reflected in a more mixed neo-corporatism than is the case in Sweden or Austria. In addition to some central state concertation on issues of wage bargaining, especially under the Christian Democratic Right (with its own Catholic corporatist elements) in the 1950s and the Social Democrats in the 1970s, the centralized trade union structure, in particular, has made corporatist bargaining possible, especially in traditional heavy industrial sectors. Union representation on management boards has been a key element in fostering collaboration. But much bargaining also goes on at the *Land* (provincial/regional state) level, and certain key aspects of that process such as vocational training, manpower planning, industrial policy and state investment, etc., go on at the regional level also. The Netherlands, too, subdivided less on regional or political-party than on religious and communitarian grounds, also provides a mixed case, described by Lijphart as 'pillarization'; economic crisis, however, has seriously undermined concertation and neo-corporatist bargaining processes in recent years, whereas the underlying consociational structure seems to have remained relatively stable.

Where the state itself is decentralized, and where the classes with socio-economic power and the predominant state actors have emerged more or less simultaneously, the system of interest intermediation is likely to be characterized by some combination of 'systemic clientelism and pseudo-consociationalism'. In fact, if there is a relatively closely-knit *ite*', but a decentralized state structure, then that *perse* the capacity of the elite or ruling class to control *coherent* and coordinated fashion and will lead to strong *fairly* consistent clientelist practices. Such was frequently seen *the* case in Third Republic France, where relatively homogeneous circuits of power, cutting across a state which was 'stalemated' at the center not only along the lines of party cleavage but between 'representative' and 'administrative' traditions, emerged around stable linkages between the career bureaucratic class (especially the 'prefects' who controlled administrative decision-making at departmental or county level), the 'deputies' or members of parliament (who tended to act as constituency or district representatives first and foremost and who often gained considerable seniority thereby), and local or regional influentials or *notables* (who also tended to remain a fairly stable group, given the relative stagnation of the French economy before World War II). The structure of postwar Italian politics is often said to revolve around the relative stability of its system of *parentela* and *clientela* (patron–client relationships).[38]

However, where there are more divisions between economic, regional, religious, ethnic, and other sectors or fractions of the symbiotically dominant classes (despite their overlapping predominance in socio-economic and state structures), then interest intermediation systems may be characterized by a more uneven form of clientelism, in which groups in conflict also enlist state actors and agencies in their respective causes – frequently accompanied by at least a formal ideology of pseudo-consociationalism (sometimes confused with socialism) to paper over the cracks. This is frequently the case in Third World countries, especially larger countries with more elaborate federal systems such as India or Brazil. A certain amount of asymmetric and erratic neo-corporatism may also be found here, including regional meso-corporatism, bilateral micro-corporatism, often very uneven attempts at sectoral corporatism, and even an unstable façade of economic planning and concertation at the national level.

The third row of Table 6.1 contains interest intermediation structures which Lowi would categorize as forms of 'interest-group liberalism',[39] where a weak state faces strong but competitive or conflicting groups.*

---

*Although where a more unified ruling class could be identified and where the state was seen essentially as the 'instrument' of that ruling class then the state might be thought of as an even weaker element in the equation, losing more of its relative autonomy; in essence, however, the weakness of the state *vis-à-vis* society also reduces the power of the ruling class to prevent other classes and interests from participating, even if only to the extent of their assimilation into the prevailing system. Empirically, of course, politically and economically undivided 'ruling classes' (wholly monopolistic and not divided into 'fractions of capital') are extremely rare, if not non-existent, in advanced capitalist society, so there is always scope for 'politicking' and, indeed, structuration.

While, once again, analogous structures can be found within all states, in fact the best systemic examples are found in those countries with an Anglo-Saxon tradition and political culture. In these systems, state actors are formally expected to take a back seat and must be seen to offer specific, conjuncture-linked incentives to societal groups in exchange for their participation in bargaining processes; exchange processes are legitimized by the apparent willingness of social groups to participate in them and by the acceptance of common legalistic norms and 'rules of the game'; and outcomes are only valid – both in terms of legitimacy and *enforceability* – so long as they conform to those legal and cultural norms and are not repudiated by those groups. The existence and persistence of collaborative processes are relatively unstable, and depend upon group leaders being able to demonstrate to their members the tangible benefits gained from participation. *Non-collaboration* is a real threat held over the heads of state actors by group leaders – and also held over the heads of group leaders by the rank-and-file. Nevertheless, collaborative processes do develop, in an uneven way, and, where benefits are *seen to continue to flow*, such processes may become precariously established as a 'second circuit of representation'.

In this context, the levels at which such uneven processes develop will depend critically on the formal differentiation of constitutional structures as well as the more informal lines of subdivision (decentralization and deconcentration) within the state. The most centralized example – and always a difficult case for neo-corporatist analysts – has been Britain. British state actors have for a long time operated, or at least tried to operate, a rather mild form of tripartism, without it developing into an effective form of neo-corporatist decision-making.[40] And yet British politicians (of both Left and Right), bureaucrats, and some trade unionists and businessmen have often felt that the answer to the 'British disease' of stagnation and industrial conflict would be to put more teeth into neo-corporatist processes. The problem is that the development of the British state – in Badie and Birnbaum's terms, a 'weak state' – has left capital (especially finance capital) and labor in strong, independent, and conflictual positions concerning the allocation of resources, while the British civil service, with its ethos of neutrality, has cultivated a 'logic of negotiation' which often breaks down in practice.[41] Despite the dominance of the party system and the Prime Minister in the political process, the links between the Conservative Party and business, on the one hand, and between the Labour Party and the trade unions, on the other hand, have further stymied attempts to foster neo-corporatism at the political level by reinforcing the seesaw effect rather than by stabilizing the bargaining process.

Thus British state actors are regularly tempted by corporatism or concertation – from the establishment of the National Economic Development Council by a Conservative Government as a bargaining forum in 1962, through the abortive attempt to introduce indicative planning in 1965 under a Labour Government, to various forms of both statutory and negotiated wages and prices policies introduced by governments of both parties in the 1970s. The Thatcher Government's abandonment of the neo-corporatist temptation in the 1980s may represent a turning point in undermining a process going back at least to 1911, but attempts to resurrect it in particular sectors, among certain 'neo-realist' trade unions, and in both the Labour Party and the other minor parties such as the Social Democratic Party and the Democrats (formerly the Liberal Party plus some other centrist factions), indicates that it is alive and well but just waiting in the wings for another opportunity.

Where the formation/integration process is society-centered, but the structure of the state is homogeneous/subdivided, as in a more homogeneous federal system, a wide range of neo-corporatist structures tend to develop. For example, in Canada, as many studies have shown, there is a tendency for quite strong corporatist structures to emerge at the level of regional meso- and micro-corporatism. Where the federal government is the stronger element, as in Australia, then certain forms of sectoral corporatism may emerge too. But the extent and substance of such kinds of neo-corporatism tend to be fairly isolated and vulnerable to outbreaks of competition and conflict. At a societal level, we are here in that large gray area usually called neo-pluralism, where some groups are significantly more important than others, but where a certain fluidity also prevails. There are numerous analyses which put the United States in this category, especially where political outcomes are seen to be dominated by a relatively homogeneous set of large business corporations (the 'corporate state', not to be confused with neo-corporatism), or by business–government overlap in the 'technostructure', or where central government agencies are seen to be controlled by the very socio-economic sectors which they are supposed to oversee (the Interstate Commerce Commission by the railroad or the truck industry, etc., often referred to as the 'captured state').

This analysis of interest intermediation in the United States, however, depends upon two assumptions. The first is that the American interest-group structure is relatively homogeneous at a national level, especially the structure of business interests. The second is that interest intermediation is not further excessively fragmented by the organizational form of the American state itself. If either of these assumptions does not hold – i.e., if the interest-group structure is more diversified either territorially or functionally, and/or if the structure of access fragments and weakens the attempts of large groups to influence political outcomes and, indeed, disperses their lobbying efforts into a variety of conflicting and offsetting channels – then the United States fits better into the category of 'fragmented *ad hoc* corporatism and clientelism', which is very close to certain traditional conceptions of pressure-group pluralism. We do not use the label 'pluralism' here (except with a question mark) because of the various criticisms of the concept of pluralism itself which have been cited at various points in this book. Indeed, this particular category contains many elements of (or analogous to) neo-corporatism and clientelism, but in a more fragmented form; it might be labeled 'pseudo-pluralism'.

However, those elements tend to develop around discrete parts of the state apparatus: whether it be the 'iron triangles', 'issue networks', and 'policy communities' at both federal and state levels around regulatory bodies, Congressional committees, agencies of the executive branch, the courts, etc. (these lack the external organizational apparatus of neo-corporatism, of course);[42] or whether it involve state or local governments. American state politics (i.e., at the level of the individual states making up the federal system) are often seen to be dominated by such arrangements in an even more consistent fashion, leading to – depending on the size of the individual state – extensive regional and/or local meso- and micro-corporatism.[43] Thus the United States is in reality a mixture of pluralism and of various levels of corporatism or quasi-corporatism deriving from both the society-centered character of American political development and the decentralized structure of American institutions. Once again, elements of fragmented *ad hoc* corporatism and society-centered clientelism can be found in all states; however, the particular combination of elements which makes up the overall state structure of the United States makes it by far the most salient example of this type of collaborative behavior at a systemic level.

Conclusions

The analysis and typology of interest intermediation patterns which we have constructed is based on the hypothesis that the difficulties which neo-corporatist analysis has experienced in explaining and categorizing exceptions to ideal-type, tripartite macro-corporatism has been the consequence of an inadequate theorization of the role of state structures in shaping the form of collaborative behavior which develops in different countries. The state is not merely a reified instrument of command, as neo-corporatist pathology would have it. Neither does it simply legitimize and maintain the field upon which different configurations of relations between corporative bodies impose a structured form of action; the structure of interests does not autonomously determine the form of intermediation. Indeed, the state is a far more important structuring variable – especially insofar as collaborative bargaining processes represent the interaction of state actors with interest 'agents' who must transform the 'raw material' of socio-economic resources into relevant political resources which can be effectively deployed within the 'structured field of action' constituted by the state if desired political outcomes are to be generated.

Once again, the state is best theorized as a process of structuration, a varied set of interactive games the stakes, rules, and dynamics of which shape and skew outcomes. The autonomy of this state lies in its structural form rather than in the autonomy of state actors to impose their wills. When theorized and applied in such a way, a structural analysis of the state provides a surprisingly accurate guide to forms of collaborative behavior, including different types of corporatism and neo-corporatism, *dirigisme* and patronage, consociationalism and concertation, pluralism and neo-pluralism, 'iron triangles' and clientelism, and the like, which have emerged not only in advanced capitalist states but in a wide range of other structural settings too. It clarifies the relationship between corporatism and other forms of social bargaining and social control, indicating that neo-corporatism, far from having reached an impasse, is just one manifestation of a wide range of deeply-rooted social, economic, and political processes of a collaborative kind. Finally, the kind of collaborative processes analyzed in this chapter are widely called upon to deal with many of the most significant issues faced by the state both in the past and today. Whether they can cope with the challenges of the twenty-first century lies at the heart of the problem of the changing architecture of politics.

Notes

1. Schmitter, 'Still the Century of Corporatism?', *op. cit.*, pp. 85–131.

2. *Ibid.*, p. 96.

3. *Idem.*

4. *Ibid.*, pp. 93–4.

5. John H. Goldthorpe, 'The End of Convergence: Corporatist and Dualist Tendencies in Modern Western Societies', in Goldthorpe, ed., *Order and Conflict in Contemporary Capitalism* (Oxford: Oxford University Press, 1984), pp. 315–43.

6. P.G. Cerny, 'Foreign Policy Leadership and National Integration', *British Journal of International Studies*, vol. 5, no. 2 (April 1979), pp. 55–89.

7. See Henry Tudor, *Political Myth* (London: Macmillan, 1972).

8. See the classic treatment by Louis Hartz, *The Liberal Tradition in America: An Interpretation of American Political Thought since the Revolution* (New York: Harcourt Brace, 1955).

9. See Chapter 8.

10. Cf. A. Grant Jordan, 'Corporatism: The Unity and Utility of the Concept?', Strathclyde Papers in Government and Politics, no. 11 (1983); and R. Martin, 'Pluralism and the New Corporatism', *Political Studies*, vol. 31, no. 1 (March 1983), pp. 86–102.

11. See Ronald H. Chilcote, *Theories of Comparative Politics: The Search for a Paradigm* (Boulder, Colo.: Westview Press, 1981), ch. 6.

12. Alan Cawson and Peter Saunders, 'Corporatism, Competitive Politics and Class Struggle', paper presented to the annual conference of the Political Sociology Group,

Political Studies Association of the UK and the British Sociological Association, Sheffield, January 1981; see also Cawson, *Corporatism and Welfare, op. cit.*

13. Gerhard Lembruch, 'Neocorporatism in Western Europe: A Reassessment of the Concept in Cross-National Perspective', paper presented to the XIII World Congress of the International Political Science Association, Paris (July 1985), and Alan Cawson, ed., *Organized Interests and the State: Studies in Meso-Corporatism, op. cit.*

14. See John T.S. Keeler, 'The Corporatist Dynamic of Agricultural Modernization in the Fifth Republic', in William G. Andrews and Stanley Hoffmann, eds., *The Fifth Republic at Twenty* (Albany, N.Y.: S.U.N.Y Press, 1981), pp. 271–91, and Keeler, 'Corporatism and Official Union Hegemony: The Case of French Agricultural Syndicalism', in Suzanne Berger, ed., *Organizing Interests in Western Europe: Pluralism, Corporatism and the Transformation of Politics* (Cambridge: Cambridge University Press, 1981), pp. 185–208.

15. See Jacques Gansler, *The Defense Industry* (Cambridge, Mass.: M.I.T. Press, 1980). For an historical analysis which effectively focuses on both of these elements, see R.J. Holton, *The Transition from Feudalism to Capitalism, op. cit.*

16. Many economists focus on the technological imperatives which lead to economies of scale, while Williamson, in particular, focuses on the 'specificity of assets' characteristic of particular firms. Cf. Williamson, *Markets and Hierarchies, op. cit.*; and Scherer, *Industrial Market Structure, op. cit.*

17. See Peter Katzenstein, *Corporatism and Change* (Ithaca, N.Y.: Cornell University Press, 1984), and Katzenstein, *Small States in World Markets* (Ithaca, N.Y.: Cornell University Press, 1985).

18. J.T.S. Keeler, 'Corporatist Decentralization and Commercial Modernization in France: The Royer Law's Impact on Shopkeepers, Supermarkets and the State', in Cerny and Schain, eds., *Socialism, the State and Public Policy in France, op. cit.*

19. Cawson, *Organized Interests and the State, op. cit.*, and 'Is There a Corporatist Theory of the State?', in Graeme Duncan and Robert R. Alford, eds., *Democracy and the Capitalist State* (Cambridge: Cambridge University Press, 1987).

20. See Martin A. Schain, 'Corporatism and Industrial Relations', in Cerny and Schain, eds., *French Politics and Public Policy, op. cit.*

21. See I. Scholten, ed., *Political Stability and Neo-Corporatism: Corporatist Integration and Societal Cleavages in Western Europe* (London and Beverly Hills: Sage, 1987).

22. Pierre Birnbaum, 'The State versus Corporatism', *Politics and Society*, vol. 11, no. 4 (1982), pp. 477–501; cf. Bertrand Badie and Pierre Birnbaum, *The Sociology of the State, op. cit.*

23. See Lembruch, 'Neocorporatism in Western Europe', *op. cit.*, and Lembruch, 'Concertation and the Structure of Corporatist Networks', in Goldthorpe, ed., *Order and Conflict, op. cit.*

24. Using Nordlinger's formulation of the problem of autonomy; *Autonomy of the Democratic State, op. cit.*

25. Pierre Birnbaum, *La logique de l'État, op. cit.*

26. See Chapter 1; also see Pennock, 'Responsible Government', *op. cit.*

27. The term 'developmental state' was applied to Japan by Chalmers Johnson, *M.I.T.I. and the Japanese Miracle, op. cit.*

28. Cf. John Zysman, *Governments, Markets, and Growth, op. cit.*, and Howard Machin and Vincent Wright, eds., *Economic Policy and Policy-Making under the Mitterrand Presidency, 1981–1984* (London: Pinter, 1984).

29. Cf. F. Lee Wilson, 'French Interest Group Politics: Pluralist or Neocorporatist?', *American Political Science Review*, vol. 77, no. 4 (December 1983), and J.T.S. Keeler,

'Situating France on the Pluralism–Corporatism Continuum', *Comparative Politics*, vol. 17, no. 2 (April 1985), pp. 229–49.

30. Cf. Jon Halliday, *A Political History of Japanese Capitalism* (New York: Monthly Review Press, 1975); Chalmers Johnson, *M.I.T.I. and the Japanese Miracle, op. cit.*; and Zysman, *Governments, Markets, and Growth, op. cit.*

31. See Ionescu, *Politics of the European Communist States, op. cit.*

32. Cf. Machin and Wright, *op. cit.*, and Jack Hayward, *The State and the Market Economy: Economic Patriotism and Industrial Development in France* (Brighton: Wheatsheaf, 1986).

33. Lijphart, 'Typologies of Democratic Systems', in Lijphart, ed., *Politics in Europe: Comparisons and Interpretations* (Englewood Cliffs, N.J.: Prentice-Hall, 1969), pp. 46–80, and *The Politics of Accommodation: Pluralism and Democracy in the Netherlands* (Berkeley: University of California Press, 1968).

34. North, *Structure and Change, op. cit.*; Williamson, *Markets and Hierarchies, op. cit.*

35. See Peter Lange, 'Unions, Workers and Wage Regulation: The Rational Bases of Consent', in Goldthorpe, ed., *op. cit.*

36. Diamant, *Austrian Catholics, op. cit.*

37. Katzenstein, *Corporatism and Change, op. cit.*, and *Small States in World Markets, op. cit.*

38. Joseph LaPalombara, *Interest Groups in Italian Politics* (Princeton, N.J.: Princeton University Press, 1964).

39. Lowi, *The End of Liberalism, op. cit.*

40. Cf. Middlemas, *The Politics in Industrial Society, op. cit.*; Hall, *Governing the Economy, op. cit.*; and Graham K. Wilson, *Business and Politics: A Comparative Introduction* (London: Macmillan, 1985).

41. Cf. Hall, *op. cit.*, and A. Grant Jordan and Jeremy Richardson, 'The British Policy Style or the Logic of Negotiation?', in Richardson, ed., *op. cit.*

42. See Hugh Heclo, 'Issue Networks and the Executive Establishment', in Anthony King, ed., *The New American Political System* (Washington, D.C.: American Enterprise Institute, 1978), pp. 87–124.

43. See Susan E. Clarke, 'State-Centered and Society-Centered Models of Local Economic Development Policy-Making in American Cities', paper presented to the XIII World Congress of the International Political Science Association, Paris (July 1985).

7

The Paradox of Civil Society:
De-differentiation and Re-differentiation in
the Contemporary State

The development of the complex structure of games which constitutes the contemporary state, on the one hand, and the development of the aggregation of structures and activities which constitute the 'raw material' of socio-economic interests and the distribution of resources between them, on the other, are inextricably intertwined or imbricated on myriad levels both historically and structurally (diachronically and synchronically). The structuration of society itself, however autonomous its component games may be in principle, and however weak state 'power' or dependent state actors are in practice, cannot ever be effectively isolated or detached in practice from the political structuration process and the architecture of the state. State development constitutes critical boundaries and conditions for social structuration, especially as it establishes and underpins (a) the cultural concept of the 'nation' itself and (b) the 'playing field' onto which socio-economic 'raw materials' are transposed and where they are transformed into stakes, bargaining chips, payoffs, game-winning trump cards – and handicaps. Thus the shape of civil society is in a wide range of critical ways molded to the shape of the state. In this chapter we will look first at the way that the 'structural power' of the state shapes socio-economic interaction; then we will examine some issue-areas which illustrate how state and social development are imbricated in everyday life; and finally we will interpret these interactions as an ongoing dialectical process of 'de-differentiation' and 're-differentiation' of the state. This will lead directly into a consideration, in Chapter 8, of structural trends in state economic intervention at the end of the twentieth century.

The Structural Power of the State and the Structuration of Civil Society

The impact on civil society of this centrality and 'structural power' of the state, which together represent a cumulation of the three levels of structure outlined in Chapter 4, can be seen as analogous to the 'three faces of power' as set out by Steven Lukes.[1] The first face of state 'structural power' concerns the ways that non-state actors find the scope and range of their rational choices bounded and channeled by the rules and resources embedded in the structured field of action which constitutes the state and by the state actors which populate that field. Thus the freedom of socio-economic actors to exert relational or structural power over other agents is limited, and can be actively constrained, not just by other agents – including state actors – but by the state structure itself. In the second place, those state structures are not in themselves neutral, but privilege certain forms of action and certain sorts of *outcomes* over others, 'selecting in' some forms of political action and the goals represented by those forms of action, and 'selecting out' other forms of action (and goals), both in discriminating between different exogenous inputs and in the way that intra-state processes deal with them as *withinputs*. State structures, like all structures, are inherently and implicitly biased (in addition to any explicit, conscious normative bias). And finally, state structures, as we have argued, operate in effect in *anticipatory* fashion, linguistically and corporally constructing (and deconstructing) expectations, perceptions, values, norms, goals, etc., prior to the specific conjunctures in which power is actually and actively exercised. They represent 'investments' in 'power resources'[2] or 'governance structures'.[3]

But even this elaboration of the notion of structural power suggests that power is itself an 'essence', a thing in and of itself, and not – as we have argued – a structured set of clusters of games. Power, and structural power in particular, can only be seen in its genuinely problematic form by looking at the phenomenon of powerlessness, as Gaventa has done.[4] In the relatively more pluralistic context of the first face of power, we are confronted with those non-state agents (and the non-state structures which they occupy) who are not able to perceive or manipulate the rules and who are underprivileged in the unequal distribution of resources; whose strategic position means that they are unable to make a wide range of choices within the structured field of the state (and find bias strategically mobilized *against* them); and who therefore appear more as objects than as subjects in power relationships, while other agents within the field, i.e., state actors in particular (and states to the extent that they can operate as virtual subjects, as argued in Chapter 4), are also acting as subjects and not merely standing by in the form of a neutral field. That is why there is only strength in organization for such relatively powerless agents.

In the context of the second face of state structural power, non-state agents and structures find that biases appear and are 'mobilized'[5] – that their 'deviant' perceptions, goals, and actions are 'selected out' – at all three of the levels of structure which were outlined in Chapter 4. Their capacity to use the rules and the resources which they do possess is constrained by their position, as other 'simple structures', threatened by the challenge, mobilize in a quasi-automatic way against them. Their movement within the structured action field is limited by their lack of strategic choices while others within the field, believing themselves threatened by this deviant behavior, bring their superior positions into play to constrain *even otherwise legitimate* challenges. And at the overall structural level, state actors interpret state rules and mobilize state resources – symbolic and material – in ways which will not only least threaten their own structural position but also frequently strengthen the state itself in structural terms. What is most important at this level is that challenges to the state which are perceived as 'deviant' can (and usually do) actually *let the state in* – i.e., draw upon state rules and resources, capture the attention of state actors, and lead to the emergence and structuration of *new* games and clusters of games. These new game structures are not only intertwined with the state but virtually constitute extensions of the state structuration process itself – in ways which can ensure that challengers end up even worse off in a structural sense than when they started, or at the very least, that they are drawn closer into the system and absorbed more and more into the playing of games the parameters, and often the substance, of which are defined on the state's own terms.

And finally, in the context of the third face of state structural power, the very expectations and perceptions through which less powerful non-state agents and structures discern their position and calculate their choices between rational alternatives in the context of the state and its central position in society mean that they will likely *underestimate* their potential power – whether in regard to rules and resources, to their strategic position in a structured field, or to their ability to challenge the state as subjects in their own right. Their bounded rationality, when combined with their pre-existing understandings of the structured nature of power – drawn from past experiences, socialization, the cultural memory of their class, ethnic group, gender, local networks, etc. – channels their interpretation of particular situations and conjuctures, even sometimes paralyzing them through a dread of defeat and the worsening of an already bad situation. The power and autonomy of state structures and state actors, which are also inextricably intertwined with expectations of a very different kind, are inverted, in a wholly contingent fashion, reinforcing the powerlessness and lack of autonomy of underprivileged agents.

Thus the structural power of the state can become a self-fulfilling prophecy – unless the coherence and consistency of the structuration process itself are undermined. But changes in social structure, for example the development of a modern capitalist class system, do not in and of themselves determine changes in state structure. Rather, they constitute 'raw material' which must be transformed into politically relevant resources, resources which must in turn be mobilized in such a way as to impact critical zones of indeterminacy within the state structure itself – the interstitial gaps and tensions embedded within it. If they are so mobilized and transformed, they must then normally dovetail with structural developments within the state which allow them to exploit contingent and conjunctural 'rents in the fabric'. New challenges are only likely to be successful where they confront relevant structural *vulnerabilities* in specific conjunctural game situations. These can include the decay of the state structure, critical challenges from other, more powerful non-state structures or exogenous structures (e.g., other countries), or a new consciousness of alternatives leading to more efficacious challenges such as those based on the organization of the powerless (e.g., early trade union struggles).

If these lead to successful challenges in specific, strategically significant conjunctures, this may create situations where the challenging structures can themselves become structurally self-reproducing, sufficiently 'central', and autonomous. *But these conditions are strict, and rarely fulfilled.* Both non-revolutionary and revolutionary challenges to the state, then, if they fail, 'let the state in'. Even if they succeed, however, they must continue to succeed in a sufficiently effective way either to change the balance of the state structure itself or to replace that structure with a new one. Thus far in history, such challenges have generally reinforced or expanded, rather than undermined, the state. We must see power, then, as a contingent relation between agents *and structures*, and not as a property which can be measured other than historically. Only by contrasting power and powerlessness can this be done; only then can the structural power of the state, and its developing *de facto* imbrication with society, be properly analyzed and assessed.

The structural power of the state *vis-à-vis* society is therefore always in the process of structuration, as is the structure of the state itself. This process involves (a) the relationship between the state and other large social structures (which also possess a measure of structural power),* (b) the relationship between each structure and its associated and constituent elements (agents and substructures), (c) the relationship between those structures and agents which are relatively powerful and those which are relatively powerless, and, of course, (d) any cross-cutting relationships which may link particular sets of agents and substructures across the first three. Thus the structural power of the state involves an ongoing situation of tension at all of these levels. Note that this is a situation of tension, and, indeed, of multiple tensions, and not one of 'necessary contradiction' – defining 'contradiction' in the strict dialectical sense of a relationship which will lead inevitably to the eventual undermining of

---

*As neo-corporatist analysts would claim for capital and labor (as well as for the state).

the overall structure itself.* Therefore rather than asserting, for example, that the tensions present in capitalist society represent merely the 'surface level' of deep structural contradictions, we would argue that the presence of a set of significant and ongoing tensions between the various levels of the structural complex outlined above can be seen as constituting a set of games of great strategic consequence for processes of political and social structuration, providing the most significant foci for political action. Actors with power will give priority to controlling games which revolve around those tensions; actors without power should, in theory, focus on such 'rents in the fabric', but are likely to be at a severe structural disadvantage, as argued above.

The focus of actors on such major tensions, however, can lead to what might be called the 'hyperdevelopment' within any large structure – especially a central structure such as the state has become – of the features of that structure which are regularly affected by such tensions. Those tensions are significantly interpenetrated with and affected – whether pacified or exacerbated – by issues involving systems of economic stratification, sets of religious beliefs and institutions, ethnic cleavages and kinship networks, territorial disputes, or some combination of a wide range of tensions deriving from the ongoing process of structuration itself. For example, the role of class in capitalist society can be seen from one angle as merely one manifestation of the general problem of the unequal impact of rules and the unequal distribution of resources in *all* societies. But in capitalist societies it is exacerbated by the universal character of markets and the commodity form (that human relations are relationships more and more rooted in processes of buying and selling, with values determined by money prices rather than by intrinsic notions of worth), by the (relatively) exclusive right of private property ownership, and

*Nevertheless, in varying situations of tension, depending on the concrete historical character of the structures and agents involved and the complex of relationships between them, certain features of that complex and of the tensions characterizing it can appear to behave as 'contradictions' (in the strict sense). Such a perspective is destined to remain hypothetical, as real contradictions can only be identified historically, i.e. with hindsight, as part of an *ex post facto* explanation of real historical situations. Of course, the analytical assertion that tensions within a society actually constitute contradictions is a perfectly rational and proper analytical exercise, provided that it is recognized that such an assertion can be falsified by later history. At the same time, however, the assertion that real contradictions do exist can act as a self-fulfilling prophecy if taken on board in the perceptions and expectations of potentially powerful agents and structures in a way which leads to the perception that an alternative structural complex or configuration of games is achievable and if it also leads to the appropriate strategic behavior on the part of those agents/structures in a situation where the large structure (or the central structure of the state) is sufficiently *vulnerable*. This is, of course, the central problematic of the Marxist analysis of the contradictions of capitalist society and the capitalist state, and it is 'scientific' so long as it involves not categorical assertions but falsifiable hypotheses.

by the predominance of wage labor in the production process.[6] Thus the core structure of capitalist society, which for historical reasons is constituted in the *state* – and not, we argue, the capitalist ruling class – exhibits 'hyperdeveloped' features which reflect the dynamically expanding capitalist economic system.

Nevertheless, this does not make the state in capitalist society into a purely 'capitalist state'. Indeed, as we have argued above, the opposite process is the predominant one. Capitalist economic structures, while dynamically expanding, are of course not auomatically or holistically self-regulating, given fundamental 'tensions', for example between market and hierarchy, the need for *a priori* institutional preconditions for the establishment of the market in the first place, or the ongoing problematic of market failure, and this allows (and often requires, for both political and economic reasons) the state to be 'let in' to the structures of the capitalist economy more and more. Thus not only is the state 'in capitalist society' not *necessarily* capitalist in and of itself, but furthermore the process of state structuration revolves in critical ways around a key tension between the so-called 'functional requirements' of capitalism, on the one hand, and a range of other social and political utilities, on the other, at the same time.

Nevertheless, within these parameters, the range of ways in which the state is imbricated with the capitalist economy – whether managing and strengthening it, on the one hand, or distorting it and weakening it, on the other – gives the state part of its specific character as a structure, indeed the central structure, of a society also characterized by a capitalist mode of production. This is true both endogenously – as the state responds to the stresses and dysfunctions of capitalism ('market failures') and/or shapes the economy through processes of political allocation within the state-defined 'national' society – and exogenously, or internationally – as relations between states have more and more to do with adjusting rivalries derived from internally-generated imperatives (whether economic or not) to the growing integration and interpenetration of the capitalist world economy. The 'capitalist world-system' is a system of powerful but tension-ridden (non-self-regulating) capitalist markets intertwined with nation-states with their own autonomous sources of structural power.[7] The relationship between the changing and expanding structure of the transnational capitalist economy, on the one hand, and other intertwined social and political processes embedded in the nation-state, on the other, leads not to the functional, evolutionary, or long-term supremacy of one or the other set of variables, but to an ongoing *problematic* – a critical cluster of games – constituted by their dynamic interaction through the agency of state and non-state actors.

Thus the state in capitalist society is not so much different in kind from earlier forms of the state (or non-state central structures), as different in degree – in the range, scope, and complexity of its characteristic tensions and hyperdeveloped features. It is not, then, as contemporary sociological theorists in the tradition of Marx and Weber tend to assert,[8] a tension between 'private appropriation', on the one hand, and 'socialized production', on the other, which is the central tension (or contradiction) of contemporary capitalist society. It is rather a tension (although not a full-blown contradiction) between private appropriation, as represented in capitalism and legally sanctioned in the modern state (with its forerunners in Roman Law, etc.), on the one hand, and *socialized national identity*, as represented in the very fact that the state as central structure has come, as we have already argued in Part I, to 'stand for' the society itself, on the other. This is at the core of the state's structural power today – the fact that it not only mediates between, but actually shapes, through the process of structuration, the linkages between private appropriation and socialized national identity.

This can also reflect the state's structural *weakness* – in a world where capitalist economic relations interpenetrate with the state structuration process at countless levels. This can be seen both endogenously, as individuals, interests, classes, etc., pursue their economic utilities, and exogenously, as trade links, international production patterns (the complex international division of labor), institutions such as multinational corporations (some of which possess more resources even than many middle-sized states), spreading Western cultural patterns, the rapidly integrating 'global 24-hour financial marketplace', etc., continually test and often break through the capacity of states and state actors to initiate policy or to respond to change. Nevertheless, class internationalism, liberal pluralism, institutional internationalism (with the exception of certain international 'regimes', the significance of which is debatable),[9] and the like have all failed to supersede the nation-state. And the responses of the state, whether as strategic policy or tactical *bricolage*, have actually expanded the reach of its activities and its structural power and autonomy in many ways. In the next section we will look more closely at how the structured field linking the state and capitalist economic development reaches right down into the everyday life of ordinary people, constructing and deconstructing a range of both socio-economic games and personal choices – illustrating how the state is inseparable from the development and structuration of civil society itself.

The Macrocosm within the Microcosm: The State in Everyday Life

The paradox of civil society is that, in contrast to the image portrayed in social contract theory, the rational choices faced by individuals and groups in many everyday situations – games which affect personal circumstances in an immediate way – are directly or indirectly structured by and through the state. Now this is not a new point, of course. But analysts who emphasize the influence of the state on everyday life tend to focus on the impact of macro-level policy changes: on the one hand, the development of attempts at more coherent state intervention in the economy through fiscal and monetary policy, industrial policy, trade policy, and the like, which are intended to control the pace and structure of economic activity; and on the other hand, the development of the welfare state, which directly affects workers, women, poor people, and even large sections of the middle and lower middle classes (whether as claimants, as lower-level civil servants or public sector employees, as businesspeople dependent upon the patronage of welfare recipients, etc.) in terms of subsistence, lifestyle, and expectations. Of course, these are central and obvious components of state/society imbrication. But here we will instead look at aspects of life which come to be taken for granted, which are not so much seen as 'governmental outputs' as accepted as part of the socio-economic fabric itself. The key to understanding the imbrication of the state and everyday life requires, at bottom, a critical reappraisal of the cultural conceptual distinction between the spheres of the 'public' and the 'private'.

For the development of modern society and the structuration of the state as we know it have involved a complex expansion and intertwining of both the public sphere and the private sphere, with the growth of each enabling the other to grow too. In ways analogous to the interlocking development of states and markets, the development of the public sphere has enabled the private sphere also to develop. Indeed, without the growth of an independent public sphere – whether through the spread of legal systems, currencies, the protection of rights not only against infringement by the state but against infringement by other individuals and groups, or any number of other factors – there would have been no way for a predominant private sphere to emerge out of the collectivist, organic world of families, extended kinship networks, and other *gemeinschaftlich* social bonds. And the converse is true also. The development of a private sphere, and of the activities which have been nurtured within it, has created a potential for conflict, or at least for disorganization, which has required the formulation of new rules and the allocation and reallocation of new and old resources – i.e., the formation of new clusters of games the intersection of which constitutes the state. Therefore to assert that modern politics involves a struggle between the public and the private, whichever one might be seen as 'good' (or the other as 'bad'), is to miss the point. And the point is that they are different sides of the same coin, and maybe not all that different, at that.

An example of the imbrication of public and private, of state and society, of political and personal, can be seen in probably the central symbol of contemporary American cultural life (after the cowboy, which represents a mythical 'world we have lost', and could similarly be subjected to critical analysis) – the car, and the roads on which it travels. Now the ways in which people and things physically move from place to place are key aspects of social structure. Changing forms of movement are at the heart of the development of societies and economies. Geographers see patterns and forms of movement in terms of a 'field' – a more physically and materially concrete field in some ways than politics or the state (although these too have their materially concrete features), but none the less a structured field of action, and one continually in the process of structuration. As with other forms of structuration, the structuration of movement involves choices by agents made within bounded and historically contingent parameters, parameters which themselves can be reinforced and/or restructured through the aggregate effect of complex mosaics of choices (clusters of games). In this context, the structuring of patterns of movement of people and things can be presented as a metaphor for the intertwining of state and society, the existential reality of the state at the personal level, the macrocosm within the microcosm.

The imbrication of private and public, as a key manifestation of the paradox of civil society, can be seen at four levels: the level of cultural symbolism; the level of personal choice; the level of state structure and rule-making; and the level of socio-economic development in the setting of the economic and social activities of the state. Perhaps the cultural symbolism of the car is most developed in the United States, where it has replaced other forms of transportation more fully than in other countries. In a society where a deeply rooted value structure focuses on the individual and the private as the source of society itself (*via* the social contract), of authority, and of legitimacy, the shift from mass public transportation (railroads, urban mass transit, etc.) to individual car ownership and use has formed into a powerful archetype or condensation symbol of a wide range of processes which constitute social development. For the car, to its owner/driver, is a dramatic extension of personal space. The car encloses the driver, cocooning and protecting her or him from the outside world, while at the same time constituting a physical extension of the driver's conscious action in the wider world in a direct and psychologically immediate way – whether in love (dating), *gemeinschaftlich* cooperation (the 'family car'), or conflict (the car as a weapon in the concrete jungle). Perhaps the two most important expressions of this in contemporary culture – and two of the most central developments in American mass culture generally –

are images of cars and roads* in rock and pop music, and the centrality of the 'car chase' to television plots (more of which later).

The look and power of a car, however mass-produced or styled, are seen by the owner to reflect his or her personality in much the same way that an individually-owned house would. One only needs to see the reactions of drivers to perceived errors or slights by other drivers to understand the depth of this personal bond. Unlike a house, however, which is immobile, the personal space and statement which the car represents moves along with the driver, not only making that space and statement mobile, but also virtually compelling aspects of the wider society to conform to the utilities and self-expression of the individual personality in a very direct way. The car seems to empower the individual, and not only in American society. Other societies have continued to become more and more dependent on automobile transportation, whether because of its superior allocative efficiency, as economic theory might suggest, on the one hand, or, on the other, because of the decline of public transportation (as in much of the developed West), or of the lack of adequate existing infrastructure (as in much of the Third World), or of centrally-planned economic priorities which, by restricting use to, e.g., Soviet party elites, inadvertently make the car a symbol of status, paradoxically desirable however difficult and expensive to obtain and maintain.

And yet the car can also be seen as a symbol of the way that the notion of 'the personal' is limited and structured by the state. For along with the coming of such an individualized, 'private' mode of transportation, have also come rules and regulations, collective allocation decisions, and patterns of socio-economic development which constrain choices in everyday life and 'let the state in' to a supposedly private sphere. Perhaps the most salient dimension of this side of the coin is the fact that for most people, with the probable exception of poor urban dwellers, the most continuing direct personal confrontation – or awareness of potential direct personal confrontation – between 'private' individuals and agents of the state usually involves parking offenses, traffic violations, etc. The most manifest signs of state control are traffic signs – stop signs, speed limits, parking restrictions, traffic lights, and many more – and the real or imagined omnipresence of the highway patrol car, its siren and flashing lights, and its threatening yet order-maintaining occupant. The use of a

*A somewhat contrasting image, of course, is that of air travel, which has greater power as a technological/cultural image, but in which individuals are usually portrayed as victims or virtual prisoners (in films such as the 'Airport' series or its parody counterpart, 'Airplane'). Television also seems more at home with cars and car chases, with their rapid movements, individualized action sequences, and variety of road patterns (which bring a 'small screen' to life), than with the more static frame provided by the airplane or airport. The analysis here focuses primarily on mass culture, of course, although it should be possible to undertake an analogous critique of, e.g., books, magazines, newspapers, etc.

car is doubly licensed by the state (both the car and the driver normally require licensing). Compulsory insurance laws provide a cushion against personal liability as well as constituting an effective additional tax. And a host of key personal choices and decisions, which make up the warp and woof of everyday life, concern the relationship between the driver (and his or her car) and the state: whether or not to break speed limits, for myriad reasons from self-indulgence to a sense of moral *force majeure* (lateness for a crucial appointment, need to take a woman in labor to the hospital, etc., etc.); whether to drink alcohol in a private social setting prior to driving; whether to break or bend rules in a context where the probability of detection may be low; and the like. These examples and metaphors could be greatly extended, of course, for example to notions of class identity and consciousness, which we will mention again later.

One of the reasons why this imbrication of the private and the public is so densely structured, of course, is that the development of the role of the individual automobile ('private car') as a form of transportation is not the result merely of personal choices. It is also the result of patterns of state development. In their concern to amalgamate 'private appropriation' and 'socialized national identity', state actors (and their non-state interlocutors) throughout history have of course pursued the development of infrastructure, whether we are speaking of the links between empire-building and road-building in Roman times, of the role of the *corps* of road and bridge engineers (*Corps des Ponts et Chaussées*) in the course of bureaucratic development and state-building in France, of railroad-building in many First World countries in the First Industrial Revolution (and into the Second), or the work of colonizers in the Third World, whose most concrete legacy (so to speak) was often a network of roads, bridges, and railroads (whether adequate or inadequate, whether suitable for colonial administration or economic development).

The integration of national societies has involved infrastructure-building at many levels: building a sense of common identity through a geographically centripetal transportation system ('all roads lead to Rome', or Paris, or London); increasing the capacity for trade and the integration of the national market in order to increase national wealth; maximizing military mobility in a strategically and technologically changing world (often the crucial catalyst and motor-force in the development of road systems, such as the expansion of the Interstate Highway System in the United States after World War II); or the efficient administration of the state, such as tax collection, police surveillance, information gathering, monitoring local government and administration, etc. The almost umbilical tie between state-building and infrastructure-building, despite many national variations, can be exemplified in the way that, while wage labor had spread to most corners of Western capitalist economies, road-building was still organized as a quasi-feudal obligation to the state, from the *corvées* of *ancien régime* France to the 'statute labor' system in the American states in the late nineteenth century.[10] And where roads were built privately, the expansion of motor traffic and economic integration, along with the scale of operations which state road-builders could undertake, led to their absorption into a state-built and state-planned system – a system which would have been unprofitable for the private sector, but which was to provide business with increasing profits not only from contracting for road-building itself, but also by altering the structure of economies of scale and market opportunities in the wider economy.

Thus the very development of the state can in part be traced through a history of its road-building activities. In France, the attempt by administrators both before and after the Revolution to construct a systematic grid of national roads on the Roman model, followed by a certain stagnation and localization of such concerns in the late nineteenth and early twentieth centuries, ultimately superseded by public sector/private sector partnerships in the building of expressways from the 1960s onwards, reflect styles of decision-making and economic intervention characteristic of the succession of French constitutional regimes. The massive program of railroad-building in Imperial Germany, followed by the centralized construction of the *Autobahn* system in the Nazi period of the 1930s, are characteristic of the development of the German state. The British model of parish responsibility with a state regulatory framework after 1555, followed by the development of the private turnpike system (with turnpike privileges individually authorized by Parliament), ultimately superseded by the state taking over the road network in 1936 and the postwar construction of national motorways, reflect the incremental development of state economic intervention and the emergence of the welfare state there.

And in the American model, in which early federally-sponsored 'internal improvements' in the road system were later virtually abandoned in favor of first canals and then railroads by the late nineteenth and early twentieth centuries, road-building policy was made and carried out (a) by active state governments increasingly dominated by well-organized state highway engineers, and (b) through the expansion of the Federal highway program reflecting an alliance of Federal agencies (from the Post Office to the Pentagon), highway interests, and 'rational' planners from the Federal to the urban level. As railroads and mass transportation declined, often the result of the division of powers between agencies and levels of government – preventing, for example, the nationalization of the passenger rail network until the late 1960s – the incremental growth of highways came to dominate the physical pattern of transportation, reflecting the structure of the American national state. And the decline of the interstate highway system, from the late 1960s onwards, has also been testimony to the patchwork structural pattern characteristic of the American governmental system. In different countries, then, the various structural frameworks and constraints which have shaped the parameters of 'private car' usage have mirrored state development. Analogous analyses could be offered of the development of the state/road/automobile/driver nexus in other parts of the world.

Finally, it is important to analyze the way in which this set of developments is also intertwined with wider patterns of social and economic change and structuration. On the one hand, the development of infrastructure is obviously a key element of the development of economies in general, and capitalism is of course no exception (except insofar as the intensive development of the forces of production and the need for ever-increasing capital accumulation intensify and speed up those processes in multiplier fashion). The automobile and road construction industries are significant components of these processes. On the other hand, however, the configuration, in different countries, of the processes of political allocation which we introduced in Chapter 3 and elaborated upon in Chapter 6, provide us with some clues to the linkages here. Cars are seemingly quintessential private goods; but the roads which they need to drive on can, in different circumstances, be seen as private goods, semiprivate goods, or public goods, depending on their size and length, their interconnections with other roads and highway networks, the economies of scale which accrue to either or both road-builders and/or road users from existing and planned roads (or from road maintenance and repair), the means chosen to pay for them (public funds, private funds, tolls, or some combination of these), the transaction costs involved in their construction and maintenance, and the like. Thus the organizational form of the state and the structure of state actor/non-state actor relations are crucial determinants of political outcomes.

The position of road engineers in the state – both their structural position, on the one hand, and their 'relative autonomy' as state actors in relation to highway interests (automobile manufacturers, contractors, highway user pressure groups, environmental groups, etc.), on the other (i.e., dimensions analogous to the two scales in Table 6.1) – would seem to constitute the site of the most important cluster of games in the highway issue-area. And usually this cluster of games shares structural similarities, deriving from the wider configuration of the elements of state structure, with other clusters of games within the system. Road engineers in France, as part of the central *grands corps* structure, or state highway engineers in the United States, in their sometimes conflictual, sometimes symbiotic relationship with Federal agencies and planners, are archetypical. The 'policy communities' or 'issue networks' which form around these sets of games, with a *dirigiste* dynamic in the former case and a 'psuedo-pluralistic' dynamic (swinging, in particular, between regulation and 'deregulation') in the latter, reflect ongoing patterns not only of endogenous state structuration but also of the central role of the state in shaping wider patterns of social and economic structuration.

This, in turn, reflects back into and shapes the level of the 'private'. This can happen in several ways. For example, the development of a far-reaching highways program can crowd out other transportation alternatives, whether one considers the decline of urban mass transit and the altering of neighborhood and settlement patterns in many older core cities – a key example being the impact of the urban planning of Robert Moses on New York City, even leading to the sort of urban blight characteristic of the South Bronx since the 1960s – or the atrophy of other forms of long-distance travel. The legendary difficulty of developing strategic, integrated transportation planning is a salient example of the stalemate which can form. Such a development obviously has the paradoxical effect of limiting the scope of personal choice and requiring transport users to purchase automobiles even where other alternatives might be more rational in economic or personal terms (not to mention ecological terms). At another level, of course, the development of the automobile industry has been a lynchpin of the Second Industrial Revolution, as the main user of steel (and thus supporter of that 'strategic industry'), a major user of rubber and glass, the core of the development and expansion of the oil industry for automotive products, etc., and even as an adjunct to the development and viability of many defense industries.

Thus the state's imbrication with such large-scale economic developments shapes the possibilities and potential parameters of social and personal relationships. The cultural act of desiring a car as an extension of personal space is also the other side of the coin, the individuation, of large-scale structural developments. The spread of the car, and the increased individuation of the person which the car represents culturally, mirrors the ongoing, intertwined structuration of both the state and capitalism. Thus while the representation of the car as idealized individual action in American television series, the car chase formula, at one level embodies the ideation of mass capitalist 'man' (his or her freeing from the physical limits of place), at another level it represents his or her socio-political boundaries – for the fleeing driver is always apprehended, either losing control of the vehicle, getting lost in the maze of alleys and dead-end streets, or being cut off, surrounded, and disarmed by the police or their private allies (e.g., the 'private eye'). The car, the ultimate in privatization, is strictly bounded by the most basic level of the 'public' – the 'police power'. Furthermore, of course, individual identity is still never individual identity, it is also class identity. The kind of car you drive, and in the United States the kind of college alumni sticker you put in the rear window (remember that educational level is regarded by sociologists as the closest concrete correlate of class for categorization purposes), indicate the pecking order of society in a culture which denies the relevance of class. The car, as nexus of public and private, is not exceptional, but characteristic of the paradox of civil society in today's world.

The kind of analysis which we have attempted with regard to cars and roads can be replicated in a range of structured fields within civil society. Recent social historians of science have specifically targeted these linkages, and their work highlights the way that the personal, the political, and the economic interact. Another change which has, of course, transformed everyday life (as well as industry, communications, etc.) is the spread of electrification, which is usually seen in the context of technological innovation and the natural progress of science. However, in his study of the development of electrification in the United States, Britain, and Germany in the late nineteenth and early twentieth centuries, Thomas P. Hughes focuses on the nexus of technological innovation, economic organization, and political structures – and the key role of particular agents such as inventors, engineers, entrepreneurs, and state actors (both political and bureaucratic). From these he generates an analysis of patterns of growth, setbacks, and change – of the structuration of what he calls, appropriately enough in view of our focus on the state, 'networks of power'.

The patterns which he elaborates are closely analogous to the sort of processes of structuration discussed in this book, with particular reference to structural comparisons between different national state forms – especially their local urban manifestations in Berlin, London, and Chicago, as well as the development of wider attempts to rationalize electrification systems at national level following World War I. He concludes that economic factors constitute only what he calls 'a soft determinism', and furthermore that the alteration of technical factors can only work effectively if 'sociotechnical systems' also change:

> If only the technical components of a system are changed, they may snap back into their earlier shape like changed particles in a strong electromagnetic field. The field also must be attended to; values may need to be changed, institutions reformed, or legislation recast.[11]

The 'field' which he refers to, like geographers' treatment of transportation systems in terms of a 'field–center nexus',[12] is analogous to a 'structured field of action'; although the physically fixed components seem at first glance to structure the field, these components are in fact continually changing, evolving or being compelled to change, incrementally or abruptly, according to criteria and parameters the logic of which is frequently non-technical or even non-'economic' in the narrow sense.[13] It involves the coming together of a range of different dynamics in structured clusters of games with different if overlapping endogenous rationales, interstitial gaps, and tensions. Change requires political action, action relevant to and converging with other sources of dynamic tension and change. Again, civil society is structured in and through the centrality of the state.

Other areas of study – again, usually interdisciplinary study – which focus on the intertwining of public and private, of state and civil society, include the amazingly rich investigations which have developed out of both the intellectual and the political forces at work in the feminist movement. The development of language structures, education systems, legal norms, economic practices, welfare state structures, and the like, has been highlighted in ongoing research and debate which frequently revolves around the concept of patriarchy; such studies often succeed in detailing and analyzing the relationship between such hidden structures of power and wider developments in the intertwined field of society, economy, and state in original and highly significant ways. Nuanced philosophical analysis and detailed empirical studies demonstrate the subtleties of the intricate webs of relations which have formed historically and which are reconstituted through a structuration process. Although there has sometimes been a tendency to reify the concept of patriarchy, especially when presenting it in ideological terms – seeing it as what we have called an 'orthodox structure' rather than an ongoing process of structuration – most sophisticated feminist analysis sees patriarchy rather as a more complex social construct. Also, recent trends have focused more on the state in the extended structural terms which we adopt here.[14]

Thus recent intellectual trends in the social sciences and certain interdisciplinary fields, ranging from the 'new social history' through feminism, the history of science and technology and political economy to the 'new institutional economics', all have come to privilege not just the macro-structures of state, economy, and society, but the intricate interweaving of macro-structures and micro-structures in complex agent/-structure relationships (or clusters of games). They have highlighted the 'macrocosm within the microcosm', but in ways which recognize and integrate into their analyses not only structural continuities but also the complex patterns of indeterminacy which are the other side of the structural coin. In this context, the 'paradox of civil society' is that the rediscovery of civil society which many analysts have perceived has been at one and the same time a rediscovery of the state. It is an infinitely more complex state than before, one not simply intervening more or getting weightier, but one also drawn into the structures of everyday life by the changes and gaps and tensions in everyday life itself – while the private and personal have expanded (and contracted) too, in complex ways. To 'get the government off our backs', as President Reagan wished to do, often paradoxically requires more intervention, not less.[15]

De-differentiation and Re-differentiation

The result of the continuing process of state structuration has thus been both multi-dimensional and characterized by unanticipated consequences. On the one hand, there has been a process of 'de-differentiation' of the state.[16] In this process, the very success of the state and state actors – whose relative autonomy emerged out of the original differentiation of nation-state structures from other social structures from the post-feudal to the advanced capitalist epochs – in expanding the range, scope, and complexity of the state have meant that non-state agents and other structures seeking to influence the state are less likely to approach it as a whole – as political philosophy would prescribe, and as traditional political parties and relatively homogeneous elites or political movements might do. Rather, the actions of non-state agents and other structures in relation to the state have increasingly tended to involve approaching it in a partial way, creating pressure groups, policy demands, issue networks, and political allocation processes on single issues or limited clusters of issues.

In this context, the state itself and state actors find it harder to pursue coherent packages of policies, thus fragmenting ideologies and being tempted by the notion of deregulation, of lowering its sights and seeming to reduce its autonomy in order to prevent the undermining of its structural power. Furthermore, ideological revisionists have frequently attempted to alter the focus of their strategic action away from the state – concentrating on the notion of action through civil society, an approach which finds echoes in the developmental and educational strategies of Ivan Illitch, the religious strategies of 'liberation theology', or the 'post-socialism' of French sociologist Alain Touraine.[17] Indeed, such an approach was the core of the 'counterculture' of the 1960s, with its ideology of 'doing one's own thing',[18] although the alternative structural focus varies from the individual to the primary group, the commune, the grass-roots social movement (as with Touraine's concern with environmentalism, feminism, and the new trade unionism of the late 1970s), the religious group (including the roots of the Moral Majority and the Islamic neo-fundamentalism of the 1980s), etc.

On the other hand, however, there has been an equal and opposite process of *re-differentiation* of the state at various levels. In the first place, in order to counteract the diffusion of the structural power of the state, new internal struggles have been adopted by very different kinds of states and state actors. While the French state in the early 1980s sought to extend the public sector in industry and finance, the British state, through the extension of its monetary policy and strict financial controls on public spending, centralized a whole range of services previously carried out by local government and severely restricted the autonomy of local government to make financial decisions on those services it retains (including public transportation).[19] Although the Reagan Administration sought to 'deregulate' the American economy, that deregulation has often had the effect of creating new regulations, and the need to manage a greatly enlarged federal budget deficit has brought the American state into closer liaison with and control of not only the internal American financial system but also the world financial system. The Swedish government has been extending its 'active labor market policy' in order systematically to counteract the growth of unemployment (in contrast to the British government's laissez-faire approach to the subject).

In a whole range of newly-industrializing countries, of course, the state is playing a far more salient role in the creation of successful capitalism than has normally been attributed to their industrial predecessors.[20] In countries which have been characterized by instability and upheaval, such as Argentina, the re-legitimization of the state has been the first order of business – a difficult task to accomplish in the context of the Third World debt crisis. And in the Soviet Union and other communist countries, the process of openness and restructuring – *glasnost* and *perestroika* – has required the recentralization of the authority of the state in liberalizing elites and leaders such as Mikhail Gorbachev and Deng Xiao-ping in order to undermine the stalemate and stagnation embedded in the party bureaucracy. But this pattern has been a partial one, as de-differentiation and re-differentiation often take place in different ways at the same time, creating denser networks and webs of relations which enmesh state and social structures more intensively and extensively.

More important, however, is the fact that the process of re-differentiation is perhaps less homogeneous within individual states than it is *between* states. Re-differentiation has come about primarily through the development of the role of the state in promoting economic competitiveness – as the main method of reconciling private appropriation with socialized national identity in a more open international marketplace. This happens on two levels. On the one hand, the convergence of economic models of industrial society (and the homogenization of politics within them) which was seen to be a central characteristic of the post-World War II industrialized world and which was sustained by the 'long boom' of economic growth until the mid-1970s[21] is now widely interpreted as giving way to a 'divergence'. In this context, more traditional distinctions between state formations (and their pattern of economic intervention) have re-emerged and been reinforced by the variety of measures which governments have taken to promote economic recovery and the restructuring or redeployment of industry.

This new divergence has been analyzed by Katzenstein and others with regard to foreign economic policies, by Zysman with regard to financial systems and the promotion of industry, and by Goldthorpe and others, with regard to varieties of neo-corporatism.[22] Two major paradoxes arise out of this. In the first place, there would seem to be some evidence that in an open world economy with its 'openness' guaranteed by a 'leading economy' (a relative economic superpower), those *other* economies which have the best capacity to manipulate 'competitive advantage' in their favor are those with a large repertoire of tools and mechanisms of industrial and foreign economic policy inherited from an earlier 'autarchic' phase. And in the second place, it may well be the case that the 'leading economies', in taking on the responsibilities – and privileges – of being such, may be sowing the seeds not only of their own long-term relative decline (as is often said to have been the case with Britain in the nineteenth century and the United States in the twentieth) but also of growing tensions and conflicts within the world economic system. Such tensions can be engendered by the uneven impact of openness on different countries and regions, and this may in turn lead to pressures to return to protectionism and autarchy which threaten to undermine the very openness of the system itself. However, such pressures may actually have the effect of extending and deepening the network of reciprocal relations or the 'web of contracts', paradoxically reinforcing both the state and international economic and political interdependence.[23]

This process is perhaps best represented by the contrast between the United States in the 1980s, where the Reagan Administration sought to reduce government intervention in the economy and has encouraged an internationalist viewpoint on foreign economic policy (e.g., the reform of the General Agreement on Tariffs and Trade, the opening up of foreign capital markets, etc.), and Japan, arguably the most successful capitalist economy even though it has the most thoroughly bureaucratic and *dirigiste* structure of all. Japanese businessmen, even when competing aggressively abroad, do it not in the name of global prosperity or individual utility, but in order to strengthen the Japanese economy and the position of the Japanese nation-state in the world; furthermore, Japanese firms approach international competition through a search not so much for short-term profits as for market share. But they do these things in the context of consensual understandings with each other and with the developmental priorities of the state. At the world level, then, the state has been making something of a comeback. The legacy of the autarchic bureaucratic state has proved itself to be alive and well in the current world marketplace. We will have more to say on these issues in Chapter 8.

On the other hand, and closely linked with the above, has been the relative lack of success of transnational political experiments, whether on a complex level like the European Community – although the project of a single market by 1992 may change the equation somewhat – or the New International Economic Order proposed by Third World states in the 1970s, or on a simpler level, such as the annual summit meetings of the heads of state and government of the leading industrial countries. Despite the thaw in the Cold War since the coming to power of Mikhail Gorbachev, the relative decline of the superpowers has reduced their ability to control world events.[24] And there is also the return of protectionism through a range of non-tariff barriers competitively erected and frequently threatened. Thus states, in pursuing what at one level are more complex and 'de-differentiated' strategic goals at home, have at another level sought to reaffirm and reinforce their autonomy and structural power in various (and often conflicting) ways at the same time and in an inextricably intertwined process – while at the same time diverging increasingly from each other and reasserting their rivalry. The economic consequences of this process are complex to evaluate, as we will see in the next chapter, but one clear socio-political result has been the renaissance in some countries, particularly the United States and Britain, of the awareness of national identity, whether it be the 'new patriotism' of Reagan's America at the time of the Statue of Liberty centennial in 1986 or the British example of the Falklands/Malvinas War. Re-differentiation at global level interacts with de-differentiation at the grass roots.

By juxtaposing the unevenly interacting processes of de-differentiation and re-differentiation, we can catch a glimpse of the sorts of interstitial gaps and tensions which characterize the structural power of the state in a capitalist world and see how the various hyperdeveloped features of that state operate within the larger ongoing process of structuration. The core features of that state are not determined by a reified social formation such as a class structure or by an essential first principle such as *potestas*, but by the contingent centrality of the state, the *de facto* development of its autonomy through pattern-creating historical accidents. The nation-state as a predominant unit of political structure has lasted as long as it has because its centrality in the complex period since the seventeenth century has ensured that its rules and resources have expanded, that other structures have increasingly been compelled or drawn into working within its structured field of action, and that the ability of state actors to act in a coherent and autonomous fashion has been reinforced by the widespread perception that the nation-state has come to stand for society itself. Even in the highly integrated world capitalist economy, the state has retained its centrality, penetrating further into everyday life and maintaining and even renewing social identity in contradistinction to other states.

The centrality of the state is unlikely to be undermined unless an alternative structure can not only challenge it, but also replace it. And in a world where other structures have their own weaknesses, to replace the state would require not only the emergence of a potential 'challenger', but also the decay of state structures and their inability to cope with critical conjunctures. The list of alternative structures, from markets to civil society, seems unlikely to include one with a sufficient potential scope of structural power across the range of elements of structure elaborated in Chapter 2 to be successful (although the re-emergence of theocracy in Iran poses certain questions *vis-à-vis* religious structures). And some states, through the twin processes of de-differentiation and re-differentiation, have in recent years proved remarkably capable of the kind of 'virtually subjective' strategic action which has been able to maintain, restore, and even to re-invent, their structural power. The roots of the state grow deeper in civil society even as its reach grows more complex. The state does not look like fading away. At the same time, however, each different state's capacity to 're-differentiate' itself is structurally influenced by the changing international context. On the one hand, there is a more integrated and interpenetrated world marketplace. But on the other hand, the role of states in promoting competitiveness within that marketplace requires yet further and more structurally complex patterns of state economic intervention if nationally-based industries, services, and economic growth are to be systematically fostered.

Thus the state structuration process reflects, although it is not determined by, the increasing 'hyperdevelopment' of the transnational dimensions and structures of capitalism. As state structures seek to adapt to these rapidly developing challenges, and state actors seek to find ways to control such developments – whether in the pursuit of political power or of other socio-political goals and ideals (such as 'justice') – the architecture of politics, from the grass roots to the apex of the state, is not so much transformed, but is in the process of transforming itself, efficiently or inefficiently, successfully or unsuccessfully. But whereas political actors, as discussed in Chapter 5, have limited and structurally bounded opportunities to influence these key political outcomes, and in a context where the structured 'interfaces' of collaborative behavior have become more central to political allocation, the structure of constraints and opportunities which states and state actors in general confront will be critically affected by specific types of issues – international economic competition and national economic survival. And, as we have tried to demonstrate in this chapter, the position of the state 'at the crossroads' will increasingly affect not only state actors and 'high politics', but also the very intertwining of public and private. The process of structural reconversion or transmutation represented by the development of the 'competition state' is not only a phenomenon of a reified state 'superstructure', but one of the 'state-in-civil-society' too.

Notes

1. Lukes, *Power*, *op. cit.*

2. Korpi, 'Power Resources Approach', *op. cit.*

3. Oliver E. Williamson, *The Economic Institutions of Capitalism* (New York: Free Press, 1985), pp. 17–18.

4. John Gaventa, *Power and Powerlessness*, *op. cit.*

5. See Peter Bachrach and Morton S. Baratz, *Power and Poverty: Theory and Practice* (Oxford: Oxford University Press, 1970).

6. See Karl Polanyi, *The Great Transformation* (New York: Rinehart and Co., 1944).

7. See Immanuel Wallerstein, *The Capitalist World-Economy* (Cambridge: Cambridge University Press, 1979).

8. E.g., Giddens, *Central Problems of Social Theory*, *op. cit.*

9. Cf. Krasner, *Structural Conflict*, *op. cit.*, and Susan Strange, *States and Markets: An Introduction to International Political Economy* (London: Pinter, 1988).

10. Albert C. Rose, 'The Highway from the Railroad to the Automobile', in Jean Labatut and Wheaton J. Lane, eds., *Highways in Our National Life: A Symposium* (Princeton, N.J.: Princeton University Press, 1950), ch. 8. This section draws upon several chapters of this book, as well as on John B. Rae, *The Road and the Car in American Life* (Cambridge, Mass.: M.I.T. Press, 1971), a book closely connected with the roads lobby; Mark H. Rose, *Interstate: Express Highway Politics, 1941–1956* (Lawrence, Kan.: Regents Press of Kansas, 1979), a study of pressure group and allocative politics; and Ben Kelley, *The Pavers and the Paved* (New York: Donald W. Brown, 1971), an anti-highway development argument by an ex-highway administrator allied with the environmentalist movement.

11. Thomas P. Hughes, *Networks of Power: Electrification in Western Society, 1880–1930* (Baltimore and London: Johns Hopkins University Press, 1983); quotation is from p. 465.

12. See Walter Firey, Charles P. Loomis, and J. Allan Beegle, 'The Fusion of Urban and Rural', in Labatut and Lane, eds., *op. cit.*, ch. 13.

13. Notice the similarity to Williamson's comments about economists who consider the scale of the firm to derive predominantly from technological factors; *Economic Institutions of Capitalism*, *op. cit.*, and *Markets and Hierarchies*, *op. cit.*

14. Cf. R. Amy Elman, 'Sexual Politics of Swedish Neocorporatism', paper presented to the meeting of the New England Political Science Association, Cambridge, Mass., 8 April 1989; Kathleen B. Jones and Anna G. Jonasdottir, eds., *The Political Interests of Gender* (London and Beverly Hills: Sage Publications, 1988); R. Emerson Dobasch and Russell Dobasch, *Violence Against Wives: A Case Against the Patriarchy* (New York: Free Press, 1980); Sylvia Walby, *Patriarchy at Work: Patriarchy and Capitalist Relations in Employment* (Minneapolis: University of Minnesota Press, 1986); Annette Kuhn and AnnMarie Wolpe, eds., *Feminism and Materialism* (London: Routledge and Kegan Paul, 1978); Catharine A. MacKinnon, *Feminism Unmodified: Discourses on Life and Law* (Cambridge, Mass.: Harvard University Press, 1987); Linda Gordon, *Heroes of their Own Lives: The Politics and History of Family Violence* (New York: Viking, 1988); and Eileen Boris and Peter Bardaglio, 'Gender, Race, and Class: The Impact of the State on the Family and the Economy, 1790–1945', in Naomi Gerstel and Harriet Engel Gross, eds., *Families and Work* (Philadelphia, Pa.: Temple University Press, 1987), pp. 132–51.

15. See P.G. Cerny, *The Financial Revolution and the State* (Oxford: Oxford University Press, forthcoming), and for an exploration of the theme of the interdependence of 'deregulation' and 'reregulation' in contemporary state economic intervention.

16. Pierre Birnbaum, 'Sur la dé-différentiation de l'État', *International Political Science Review*, vol. 6, no. 3 (1985), pp. 57–64.

17. Touraine, *L'aprés-socialisme, op. cit.*

18. See Lyman L. Sargent, *New Left Thought: An Introduction* (Homewood, Ill.: Dorsey, 1972).

19. Cerny, 'State Capitalism in France and Britain and the International Economic Order', in Cerny and Schain, eds., *Socialism, op cit.*

20. Nigel Harris, *The End of the Third World* (Harmondsworth, Mddx: Penguin, 1986).

21. For a well-known interpretation of this process, see Andrew Shonfield, *Modern Capitalism: The Changing Balance of Public and Private Power* (London: Oxford University Press, 1965).

22. Cf. Peter Katzenstein, ed., *Between Power and Plenty: The Foreign Economic Policies of the Industrial States* (Madison: University of Wisconsin Press, 1978); Zysman, *Governments, Markets, and Growth, op. cit.*; and Goldthorpe, ed., *op. cit.* See also Cerny, 'State Capitalism in France and Britain and the International Economic Order', *op. cit.*

23. Cf. Strange, *States and Markets, op. cit.*, and Edmund Dell, *The Politics of Economic Interdependence* (London: Routledge and Kegan Paul, 1988).

24. See Cerny, 'Political Entropy and American Decline', *op. cit.*

8

Transnational Structures and State Responses: from the Welfare State to the Competition State

The architecture of the state, through the processes of de-differentiation and re-differentiation, is changing. At one level, this can be seen as an episode in the ongoing process of structuration which is the theme of this book. But at another level, it can be seen as a particularly significant phase of state development, for it involves a much closer interpenetration of the internal field of state structure, essentially the domestic nation-state, with its external field, which comprises not only an international system of states but also an increasingly open and integrated transnational economic marketplace. Now this external field has always been an intertwined political/economic system. But the density and variegation of transnational linkages has been highly circumscribed by the nation-state order – the territorial sovereignty of the state and the much greater internal integration of domestic markets than transnational ones. At the end of the twentieth century, that order is not so much threatened or undermined as it is changing. The greater density and complexity of international economic and political linkages and interactions constitutes a problematic for state structures and state actors, and they are experimenting, sometimes fitfully, sometimes systematically, with a range of both traditional and innovative measures – in terms of policy, in terms of culture and ideas, and in terms of structural changes – to respond to and deal with that problematic.

As we have already seen, responses to this problematic affect the state structuration process at all levels, in different ways in different arenas. With regard to the political process, the repertoire of responses of political actors is becoming increasingly constrained and their collective impact increasingly marginal – further deepening the existing structural constraints examined in Chapter 5. Furthermore, however, the complexity and centrality of the kind of political allocation processes examined in Chapters 3 and 6 are expanding, as transnational interpenetration alters a growing range of factors in the dynamic equation linking the structural principles of market and hierarchy. And finally, transnational interpenetration – at one time mainly confined to the 'cosmopolitan' elite level or, for the rest of the population, to times of war – has been extending and expanding deeper into civil society, in ways discussed in Chapter 7. The overall configuration of the state structuration process –

the patterning and clustering of ongoing games which are played by state and non-state agents separately and together – has been undergoing, and will continue to undergo, considerable change, as the dynamic interaction of agency and structure reflects new interstitial gaps and tensions, and as state actors seek to control new sources of indeterminacy.

The focus of these pattern shifts, then, is not on patterns of party politics or even of domestic interest group intermediation. The focus is on the way that forms of state economic intervention – or, in its broader form, the economic and social activities of the state (as elaborated in Chapter 2) – change in the attempt to respond to, and to shape and control, growing international economic interpenetration and the transnational structures to which it gives rise.[1] A major theme of the argument of this chapter will be that international factors have forced three sorts of changes to the fore: (a) a shift from macroeconomic to microeconomic interventionism, reflected in the conceptualization and operationalization of 'industrial policy'; (b) a shift in the focus of that interventionism from the development and maintenance of a range of 'strategic' or 'basic' industries – which traditionally are supposed to underpin and sustain the overall 'comparative advantage' of a national economy and which presumes that each nation-state must possess some minimum level of industrial self-sufficiency – to one of flexible response to competitive conditions in a range of diversified and rapidly evolving international marketplaces (what has been called 'competitive advantage');[2] and finally (c), a shift in the focal point of party and governmental politics from the general maximization of welfare within a national society (full employment, redistributive transfers, and social service provision) to the promotion of enterprise, innovation, and profitability in both private and public sectors – a shift with significant ramifications for liberal democracy.

Economic Theory and Policy: Some Cases

Before going on to look at the nature of these contemporary challenges, it is worth pointing out that the economic 'policy cultures' or 'policy styles'[3] of particular nation-states, like the wider state structures in which they are embedded, reflect not only different historical and political structures, but also different understandings about the very nature of economics and therefore the potential range and scope of policies themselves. For example, in the case of Britain, both the classical economics of Adam Smith and its twentieth-century Keynesian variant were home-grown products, which emerged in the context of British economic development, and which intellectualized particular problems facing British capital and the British state in quite specific historical circumstances. British policy culture reflects their assumptions about the possibilities for, and limitations on, state action and intervention. The same tradition flourished also in the United States, but with some significant differences. Some aspects of these assumptions are particularly relevant to outline briefly here, although they will be familiar to many readers.

The action of the state is crucial to the logic of classical economics, but the notion of state 'intervention' is essentially a pathological one. In the first place, the state by certain of its actions establishes the basic conditions for markets to work freely, as we have already argued. Unlike the abstract 'state of nature' of Lockean political philosophy, post-feudal society was not characterized by the predominance of free and spontaneous market relationships. The emerging 'modern' state, then, for a variety of reasons which are the stuff of theoretical and historical debate, attacks and undermines certain key restraints on market activity. Among other things, it establishes exclusive property rights, it constructs a legal system based on the sanctity of contract, and it consolidates a larger, national base for market activities through administrative structures and common standards (especially a national monetary system) as well as helping those activities to penetrate abroad through imperialism, the Open Door, etc.

But, once these foundations have been established, the normative role of the state in classical economic theory is to take a back seat, for intervention in increasingly complex market activities is seen to be inherently counterproductive. There are several reasons usually given for this, of which two are particularly important. The first is that the efficiency of the market as an allocative mechanism depends by definition upon the spontaneous fixing of price levels, for in classical economic theory there is no effective measure of relative values other than price. But the structure of the state is said to be based on authority relations, not market relations, and thus there is thought to be an inbuilt tendency for state intervention to involve the fixing of prices by fiat rather than by spontaneous market signals.[4] The second reason is that the ultimate 'market discipline' is the threat of bankruptcy, which the state in theory does not face. The result is the assumption that, to use a well-known phrase, 'civil servants make bad businessmen'.

Nevertheless, there will always be obstacles to the efficient working of markets. On the one hand, market rigidities can appear at macroeconomic level, if demand and supply do not automatically adjust to each other (as Say's Law would prescribe). Indeed, market uncertainties, such as a lack of reliable information, differing cultural predispositions, or the presence of unclear or conflicting market signals, have been seen as a major source of rigidities, although these are generally dismissed by 'rational expectations' theorists. On the other hand, specific markets at the mesoeconomic level can develop institutional/organizational charac-teristics which make them operate less as theoretical markets should and more like 'political' institutions, i.e., through authority or rule-based structural logic. Capital markets, labor markets, and product markets are seen by many to exhibit such organizational characteristics, making them more like political institutions than like ideal-type markets.[5] Or, finally, microeconomic structures may behave in market-dominating rather than market-clearing fashion. There are two aspects to this.

At one level, it is well known that individual firms are actually endogenously structured, in theory as well as in practice, on the basis of authority or hierarchy (popularly referred to as 'the right of management to manage', based on property ownership) rather than ideal-type market relations. Thus there will be a natural temptation for individual firms to attempt to use their market power to prevent markets from clearing if market-clearing outcomes will be disadvantageous to the particular firm in a competitive environment (leading to unprofitability, declining market share, or bankruptcy). This tendency is usually interpreted in classical and neo-classical economic theory as a market-inefficient tendency to monopoly.[6] The development of 'monopoly power' is of course only the most extreme end of the scale of such behavior. At another level, groups of firms not infrequently cooperate systematically with each other, for example in formal or informal cartels or 'price-fixing rings'. Oligopoly, too, is simply one extreme example of such 'political' market behavior.

Now the main justification for state intervention, in mainstream economic theory, is of course applicable where that intervention is seen to attack or restrict the effect of such obstacles to efficient market behavior. Keynesian economics, for example, is aimed at controlling macroeconomic rigidities through the use of fiscal and monetary policy, but its legitimacy is most crucially undermined when it is seen as leading to new rigidities, for example in leading to a spiral of intervention which becomes less and less effective with each new increment of policy manipulation; in this way, Keynesian policies were judged to be responsible for the combination of stagnation (unemployment) and inflation characteristic of much of the 1970s in most developed capitalist economies – a phenomenon known as 'stagflation', and previously thought to be avoidable by using the right policy 'mix' of reflation, on the one hand, and austerity, on the other. This perceived failure was the core not only of neo-liberal critiques from the Right, as in 'monetarist' Thatcherism or 'supply-side' Reaganomics, but also from a range of 'post-Keynesian' and neo-Marxist critiques from the Center and the Left. As for Keynesianism at macro-level, so government regulation has been intended to control and lessen the effect of rigidities at the mesoeconomic and microeconomic levels; here, again, critiques of new rigidities created in turn by the rules, practices, and agencies of regulation have led to widespread attempts at 'deregulation', mainly from the Right, but from the Center and the Left too (although deregulation has often meant changing the substance of regulations rather than merely eliminating them).

A further exception to the rule against state intervention is the argument that some activities are simply not amenable to being organized and run according to market principles. Either the internal organization of particular production or consumption processes is unsuited to the market; or else the provision of certain goods and services is seen as being so essential to the maintenance of the 'basic conditions' of the system that they cannot be allowed to fail without endangering other market activities. An example of the first would be a 'natural monopoly', where the production process itself is seen to be in some crucial way indivisible, particularly where economies of scale demand a single production process. Another variant is the concept which we have already come across in Chapter 3, the 'public good', where the consumption of that good cannot be limited to particular buyers but would automatically be available to much larger numbers who would thus get it 'free'. This would potentially leave no incentive for any individual buyer to appear, and provision would consequently become dependent upon collective provision financed authoritatively through taxation; street lighting and national defense are oft-quoted examples, although perhaps the most basic example is the provision of a currency system.

An important extension of these principles is the notion that it is essential for a national economy to possess, and therefore for the state to promote and/or maintain, certain 'strategic industries' in sectors where the outbreak of war or the erection of trade barriers would make essential commodities unavailable. This category usually includes some critical raw materials, especially energy, some capital goods – steel, chemicals, machinery, infrastructure, etc. – and some technology and productive capacity basic to the defense sector. The activities which are justified according to classical economics, then, are essentially pathological. The market mechanism is seen to be 'natural', while the state is an artificial imposition to remedy specific defects – 'market failures' – but the interventions of which are prone to serious opportunity costs for wider market efficiency.

The 'welfare state' is usually seen to consist of a combination of such interventions, linked with and mobilized by more specifically political (i.e., non-'economic') factors such as the organizational and electoral clout of the working class, welfare-type goals of social solidarity, the special interests of minorities or the poor, and the like. Social services, for example the provision of health services, are often justified by a combination of the narrower rationales set out above. Thus macroeconomic demand management is operationalized through welfare spending, especially if implemented by political parties with a working-class base (on the Left) – or alternatively through defence spending (if by the Right).

Market-enforcing regulation, such as anti-monopoly legislation or stock market regulation, is justified by norms of 'public interest' and the desire to prevent 'unfair competition' resulting from the unequal market power and the *anti-market* behavior of firms, cartels, or even other organizations such as trade unions. Even indicative planning is rationalized as a market-clearing exercise.[7] And more direct, non-market control or regulation is legitimized by reference to the need to organize production by natural monopolies, the provision of public goods or services, or the need to maintain basic or strategic industries through public ownership, subsidy, government procurement, and the like. This is a powerful package of potential interventions indeed, especially when galvanized by a political objective such as full employment. However, it is necessary to remember that, in mainstream economic theory, whatever the weight of the welfare state (for example, the proportion of Gross Domestic Product represented by public expenditure), its rationale is incremental, and specific interventions must be justified in specific terms.

Such an economic ideology dovetails closely with the structural characteristics of the British state and the cultural norms of British policymaking as we have dealt with them in various places in this book. The primacy of the private is in fact reconciled with the expansion of the range of activities involved in the development of the welfare state. Indeed, the 'logic of negotiation' characteristic of the British policymaking process provides an almost ideal structural field for this reconciliation, for intervention could expand without significantly altering the structures of capital, labor, or production. The price has, of course, been the prevalence of what has been called 'stop-go' economic policy, i.e., periodic deflation to maintain the value of the currency or to counteract surges in the rate of inflation, followed by periodic reflation to counteract industrial stagnation and endemic low wages, and to ensure the success of negotiation and consensus. Indeed, the political party debate on economic intervention takes places within similar parameters, although some changes, which we will come back to later, have taken place in the 1980s not only in the Conservative Party, in government since 1979 under Prime Minister Margaret Thatcher, but also in the Labour Party and the center parties. British economic theory, as well as the ideology of the ruling party, has rediscovered and highlighted the residual character of state intervention; and the myth of the nineteenth century, when free trade and Victorian values ruled, has been clearly identified as the normative core of the British policy culture.

In contrast, the cultural force of these theoretical limitations on state intervention is for the most part simply lacking in the French and Japanese economic policy traditions. Whether the French state exhibits an underlying strategic cohesion on economic policy, or whether it is a 'splintered state', the pure logic of the market takes a back seat to a pragmatic predisposition to assume that civil servants can take a longer-range, more synthesizing view of the public interest, and that they ought at least to try to ensure that what are seen as selfish and myopic private interests take that public interest into account. Not only is the history of the French state – the myth of the seventeenth century and *colbertisme* – read in such a way that the state is seen as a positive force in economic development, but market rigidities are more often seen as inherent and natural, not pathological. The private sector, traditionally seen either as timid, fragmented, static, and inefficient in allocating capital, or as predatory and market-distorting, protectionist, and cartel-prone, has been widely thought to have insufficient potential for long-term growth and development; while the public sector has been widely seen not as residual but as a strategic resource in the pursuit of economic growth and international competitiveness. The same is true for Japan, where *dirigisme* was consciously copied from the European experience (especially the German experience) in the late nineteenth century and has been applied even more rigorously to guiding economic development.

In this context, the very concept of the welfare state in France is less inclusive as a label than has been the case in Britain.[8] In the postwar period, Keynesian macroeconomic policy generally took a back seat to planning and more direct state promotion of specific sectors; government regulation has tended to depend on direct, authoritative measures such as price control and credit control; and the central objective of intervention was not more effective domestic competition, but the promotion of mergers and the creation of sufficient economies of scale for effective international competitiveness (although the former did not always produce the latter). No 'arm's-length' relationship here, but rather a bilateral quasi-corporatism (with unions generally excluded) between civil servants and businessmen – many of whom were trained as, and began their careers as, civil servants themselves. There was a general expansion of social and public services, of course, but the welfare state appeared simply as a new set of functions grafted onto the traditional interventionism of the state, a new dimension to *colbertisme*. In Japan, where the welfare state is still usually seen to be underdeveloped in comparison with Western Europe and the United States, the expansion of state activities and state expenditure have been directed even more systematically to promote industrial expansion and adaptation.

The contrast between the British and French policy cultures is therefore quite clear. It is not as clear, however, as the contrast between the American and Japanese policy cultures. On the one hand, the United States obviously lacks even the degree of political and bureaucratic centralization which characterizes the British state, and has not been penetrated so systematically by the welfare state – the organization of health services providing a particularly well-known paradigmatic contrast. The private is, if anything, even more salient in the U.S., the civil service less autonomous and insulated (the persistence of clientelism), and economic policy more piecemeal. Public expenditure represents a much smaller proportion of G.D.P. (about two-thirds of the British percentage). On the other hand, Japan has, if anything, a much more centralized state than France, dominated by a single (right-wing) political party since the late 1940s, characterized by an even more tightly woven, state-centric elite network with a super-*colbertiste* ethos, interpenetrated with a quasi-oligopolistic business community oriented to export growth, and underpinned by a densely structured, nationalistic social order and class system. But in Japan, too, public spending represents a smaller proportion of G.D.P.; the welfare state is less developed than in France, although it has been expanding considerably since the 1970s, and state intervention in the economy rather takes the form of strategically targeted and integrated industrial and trade policy. Our two European cases, then, lie somewhere in between the current rivals for the title of 'leading economy' in the world system.

Nevertheless, the contrast between Britain and France becomes much starker when placed in the perspective of their relative economic performance since World War II. Whereas the British economy has been in a long-term decline since the late nineteenth century, reversed only during short periods of international upturn, especially in the 1950s (the jury is still out on the 1980s),[9] France has experienced both structural development and economic growth through most of the postwar period.[10] British-style state interventionism has frequently been blamed for the former, whether from the sweepingly anti-statist perspective of Keith Joseph and Margaret Thatcher, or from neo-Marxist perspectives which see the British state as the prop of a peculiarly stagnant capitalist class.[11] However, French-style intervention – especially the planning system, but also industrial policy, science policy, and credit allocation – despite its limitations, has frequently been credited with leading the growth process.[12] There is, of course, a certain paradox to this contrast from an historical point of view. Britain, the workshop of the world, was the dynamic powerhouse which spread free trade and capitalist production across the globe in the nineteenth century, while France, divided by political and social conflict, was at that time a center of culture and intellectualism, but a country falling behind its main economic competitors.[13] Why have their roles apparently been reversed?

These changes are unlikely to derive from purely domestic developments inside Britain or France; indeed, a study of British or French policy cultures would emphasize underlying structural continuity rather than change – even in the 1980s. Rather they have come from changes at the international level: from the changing requirements of political relations with other countries, which mean that neither country is burdened to the same extent as before 1945 with the problems of being a 'big power'; but even more from the changing structure of international economic relations. The United States – the first 'superpower' – was determined from the outbreak of World War II to use its new-found role of world leadership not only to prevent war in the traditional military sense but also to eliminate what many of its elites saw as the underlying *economic cause* of twentieth-century wars: the economic competition between autarchic states, which was believed to lead inexorably to the use of military means to conquer resources and markets.[14] For the newly dominant 'internationalists' in a succession of American administrations, Lenin's 'highest stage of capitalism' – the competitive imperialism of (mainly European) nation-states – was to be followed by an even higher stage. This stage would be characterized by an 'open' world economy.

The Challenge of Openness in Advanced Industrial Societies

In an open world, conditions for success would prove to be rather different from those previously faced either by nineteenth-century Britain, as an early leader in a world where competitors were still relatively weak, or by France, which for social and political reasons chose not to compete head on. Their respective state structures, like those of other states with many different characteristics, have therefore been faced with much greater challenges in the contemporary world, where these external pulls and constraints themselves create and exacerbate not only exogenous but also endogenous tension and conflict. Indeed, the very capacity of a state to act autonomously derives to a great extent from its interaction with its external environment. Now the range and variety of responses which contemporary states and state actors can adopt are wide, and involve a number of different dimensions and levels. It is none the less possible to set up two polar ideal-type modes of response – 'openness' and 'closure'. Now these contrasting modes are not characteristic only of today's world. They have been just as characteristic of the responses of societies in earlier history to the external challenges of the 'modern' world of their own times – but in today's world the external pressures are stronger, more variegated, and more all-pervasive.

Of course, if one were looking at the world through the perspective of the 1930s, without the benefit of hindsight, it would be difficult to imagine that the wave of the future would be found in a more open world economy. Indeed, the trends of the interwar period pointed in exactly the opposite direction. Britain, the champion of free trade through the power of its navy, the dominance of its merchant fleet, and the extent of its free-trading empire – not only the industrial 'workshop of the world' but also the financier of world trade through the commercial activities of its financial center, the City of London, which provided backing and guarantees for trade between third parties as well as for that involving British merchants and which acted as the world monetary center through the close link between the pound sterling and the gold standard – was in structural decline. In response to the Great Depression, Britain closed off its Empire through the imposition of imperial trade preferences (the 'Ottawa system') and devalued its currency. The United States, still basically locked into its vast internal market and unwilling to play the role of guarantor of a new free trading system, blamed the Depression on external economic forces and tried to cut itself off through the Smoot–Hawley Tariff and later through certain aspects of the New Deal; however, the Reciprocal Trade Agreements Act of 1934 marked the beginnings of an American shift towards a more universal Open Door policy. France, in the midst of long-term economic stagnation and torn between Left and Right at home, vacillated, but generally erred on the side of protectionism.

At the same time, the main ideological thrust of the period was toward a very intense form of autarchy or closure – represented by the rapid rise of Fascism, Nazism, and other forms of autarchic imperialism on the Right, and by the shift of Soviet communism from a global revolutionary perspective to the Stalinist forced march toward 'socialism in one country'. What was to be called 'totalitarianism' was in effect a drastic and ideologically powerful rejection not only of democratic and liberal politics, but also of the brand of open, cosmopolitan capitalism represented by Britain and the United States. It involved a drive for economic self-sufficiency, even if that meant conquering territories and creating dependent spheres of influence – mainly in contiguous regions (Hitler's notion of *Lebensraum*, or Japan's Greater East Asia Co-Prosperity Sphere) – in the attempt to create vast political and economic heartlands with enough raw materials, production facilities, labor resources (often forced labor), and markets to create a full-blown advanced industrial society without depending on outside sources. External trade would be carried on increasingly by barter, with political alliances and rivalries the central motive, rather than merely profitable exchange. Only the United States in the nineteenth century has been able to exist in some form of splendid economic isolation, and even it depended on outside investment and trade during crucial phases of development.

But in the 1930s the new autarchic imperialism, underpinned by racist ideology and organicist, ultra-corporatist forms of nationalism, seemed to be the force of the future. And in addition to pure racial hatred, the main ostensible reason for the Nazis' persecution of the Jews was because they were seen to be too 'cosmopolitan' – a term of derision associated not only with traditional images of Jews being linked to trade and finance (which by definition, in Nazi demonology, made them parasites) but also because they were accused of being at the core of a centuries-old worldwide conspiracy to control 'superior' nations and races like the 'pure' Germans by making them dependent on capitalism. Furthermore, Stalin's purges, whether from paranoid madness or simply evil, were also accompanied by increasing xenophobia, which sat uneasily alongside the Leninist discourse of proletarian internationalism. Japan's expansionist policies were also accompanied by a certain amount of racism and xenophobia, although the Japanese at times sought to play the role of Asian liberator from the white capitalist imperialists from Europe and America too; and it was America's refusal to supply the one raw material that Japan needed most, oil, unless the expansionism stopped, which led to Pearl Harbor. Finally, the drive to carve up the world into autarchic empires was further echoed in the United States by isolationists, many of whom saw Latin America (and the Western Hemisphere in general) as the natural U.S. sphere of influence (since the Monroe Doctrine).

Thus by the time that the Roosevelt Administration had come full circle since its early unilateralist, domesticist days, and had embraced the need (in America's national interest as well as the interest of peace and prosperity in the world) for free trade – and for the U.S. to take up the guarantor role which Britain could no longer play, often called America's 'reluctant leadership' – the rest of the world seemed heading in the opposite direction. Indeed, just before and during World War II, it often seemed that the United States was also at war with its allies, Britain – whose imperial preference system was under attack from the time of Lend-Lease until the General Agreement on Tariffs and Trade was signed in 1947[15] – and even the small but growing Free France organization, whose leader, General de Gaulle, was suspected of quasi-fascist tendencies. In the early postwar period, the British Labour Government was suspected of having a socialistic orientation toward 'state trading' rather than free trade. The postwar economic settlement, consisting of the Bretton Woods Agreement of 1944 which set up the International Monetary Fund and the World Bank, the General Agreement on Tariffs and Trade, and, indirectly, the Marshall Plan, in effect divided the world into a sphere in which free trade and currency exchange would increase under the stabilizing *pax Americana*, on the one hand, and an expanded autarchic alliance, the 'Communist Bloc', on the other. The Cold War was thus rooted in economic policy as much as, and perhaps more than, in political philosophy.

'Openness' means just what it says – that the necessity or desirability is accepted of the penetration of the home society by external pressures. Obviously, in any ideal type, all such pressures will be welcomed, whether they impinge on the state, the society, or the economy; however, not only are such pressures differential in their impact but states may wish to welcome certain pressures but not others. In the contemporary world, for example, it is often pointed out that the relatively open capitalist system established after World War II was dependent not only on, for example, trade and a stable system of currency exchange, but also on the military integration of the Western Alliance, on the spread of 'stable liberal democracy', or on the adoption of Keynesian economic policies. These were seen as required in order to maximize economic growth, secure the territorial base of the system, and minimize social disruption in ways which were compatible with the system's key guarantee, American 'leadership' – the lack of which was widely blamed for the failure of the interwar system. Britain, France, Japan, Germany, and other countries reacted with a range of mixed responses. Nevertheless, these all proved to be broadly compatible with American aims, and became more so as trade expanded, the Cold War turned into a stalemate, and economic growth and full employment provided an 'offer they couldn't refuse'.

It is now widely taken for granted – despite a decade from the mid-1970s to the mid-1980s of growing unemployment, widespread recognition of the limits of Keynesianism, and wider political conflict – that the disadvantages, both political and economic, of protectionism and autarchy proved so great in the 1930s as to make even relatively minor breaches highly suspect (although still widely utilized, often in 'hidden' ways, in particular political and economic circumstances). For France, and even more so, Japan, this openness was more or less an innovation, while for Britain, and for the United States itself, it reflected traditions of free trade and the Open Door.[16] But in all of these societies since the war, the relative level of openness and interpenetration has become higher than ever before despite certain limited 'neo-mercantilist' trends. And this openness, which is indeed drawing in the Third World ever more closely and even extends to more and more of the Communist world, has had a multiplier effect on the international economy, reinforcing the expansion of trade and capital flows (and the political interactions which are linked with them) and increasing the 'penetrating power' of the world capitalist system itself.

Closure or 'delinkage' involves the attempt by a state to resist the penetrating power of external pressures. Again, as an ideal type, this would involve total closure – political isolationism and economic autarchy or self-sufficiency. Even in the early stages of the development of capitalism, states found it difficult to resist external pressures of the sort we have been talking about. Long before the development of absolutist monarchism Europe was closely linked in trade, religion, politics, and culture. Absolutism itself was partly an attempt to resist or control external penetration – and often, as in the case of *colbertiste* France, Imperial Russia, or Meiji Japan, to construct an alternative order based on mercantilism, which, as we have seen, involved a much closer control of trade and economic development by the state (or by corporative bodies) rather than by market forces. Indeed, the United States itself in the nineteenth century underwent long periods of economic protectionism (combined with the internal empire-building of Manifest Destiny), but once having started to play a larger world role in the 1890s also embraced the Open Door policy.

In the 1930s, as we have seen, closure became the most widespread option for a while, with even free-trading Britain attempting to retreat behind the wall of imperial preferences. But the Cold War brought with it the division of the world economy into the 'open' capitalist sector and the 'closed' Communist bloc; political and economic structures within each bloc were more tightly interwoven than ever before. Neutralism became an anomaly, for it required economic (and not just political or military) choices which meant involvement with one bloc to the general exclusion of the other; to stand genuinely alone meant that a country had either to possess vast internal resources (such as the huge labor reserves of Maoist China) or to accept backwardness (like Albania). Third World revolutions based on dreams of delinkage foundered on the need for trade and aid. And even China, with Mao dead and Deng's 'four modernizations' beckoning, has turned to the West. Of course, most states have vacillated between openness and closure, trying to find a mix that meets domestic claims for both development and protection given the external pressures of the time.

In the case of Britain after the repeal of the Navigation Acts and the Corn Laws, openness became the real dynamic core of the myth of the nineteenth century, despite the encroachments of imperial preference. But since Britain's loss of world economic leadership, its openness, while remaining for the most part an article of faith, has often been a major source of vulnerability to foreign competition. Britain's economic structure even in the middle of the twentieth century has been seen by economic historians to be the legacy of her early industrialization in several ways: a lag in the adoption of more efficient and technologically advanced production processes; management concerned more with social status than with efficiency; the lack of articulation between the provision of finance and the investment needs of industry; maintenance of safe trading patterns and the avoidance of competition; and rigidly entrenched labor market structures. To such market rigidities has frequently been attributed Britain's failure to adapt and to respond to growing competition from later industrializers, especially the United States and Germany.[17] The state played a relatively consensual role in this process rather than seeking to promote change through autonomous action. And despite the changing international environment after 1945, both economic structures and the state continued to behave in much the same way.

In contrast, French responses to external pressures coming from the development of the capitalist world economy tended at crucial times toward the closure option, especially in terms of trade protection. At one level, the stabilization of the state has often been linked to resistance to external pressures, as with the obstacles to change embedded in the 'stalemate society' of the Third Republic with its mix of instability and immobilism. But at another level, the legacy of closure, paradoxically, has been to further entrench the structural position of the French state – not only as one of the most significant obstacles to modernization, but also, paradoxically, as the main modernizing force.[18] If the state itself is unstable and confused in its direction, or if it becomes an explicit or implicit bulwark of stagnation, then the weakness of forces working for economic modernization in French civil society tended to act as a buffer to insulate the state from internal political pressures. In this context, it was the impact of external forces upon the French state, rather than any internal modernizing dynamic (whether inside or outside the state) which provided the essential cause and catalyst for both political and economic modernization.

For Western Europe in general, as for many other parts of the world in the longer run, the postwar economic settlement quite simply meant that the sorts of closure which France and other states had relied upon to maintain the internal balance would not be possible much longer. Greater economic integration in Western Europe was foreshadowed by the establishment of the Organization for European Economic Cooperation, promoted by the United States for coordinating the allocation of Marshall aid, and the boom of the 1950s was the crucial dynamic factor which permitted the consolidation of the new system. Of course, the most striking first impression was one of relative convergence in an Atlantic system under American patronage. The combined stimuli of the infusion of capital under the Marshall Plan, the Korean War spending boom and the reduction of trade barriers led to economic growth, the expansion of trade, and the consolidation of the welfare state. Thus the combination of the new, American-sponsored openness (despite frequent *de facto* flouting in detail) with the spread of liberal democracy and the 'mixed economy' was thought to be the core of a new and lasting world order which would not be subject to the trade wars and depressions – and associated attempts at closure – of its predecessors.

But the impact of the boom was different in different countries. In Britain, paradoxically, it tended for the most part to give traditional structures and ways of doing things, in both the economy and the state, a new lease of life. The focus of the state was on establishing and expanding, or, later, maintaining, the welfare state, on playing its ever more important consensual role in tripartite relations, and on mediating between the often conflicting objectives of Keynesian economic management and of maintaining international confidence in the currency with the latter winning the major battles.[19] But though traditional businesses boomed, they often did so despite their relatively poor competitive position; prosperity, combined with the entrenched structures of state and society, inhibited the need to restructure and retool, as investment would restrict short-term profits to shareholders as well as wage rises. And though workers found their wages growing, they often did so less than their counterparts elsewhere in the industrial world; the maintenance of traditional craft methods, strict demarcation and overmanning saved certain jobs but limited productivity gains. A classic example of this syndrome was shipbuilding, where old methods on both management and labor sides contributed to the crumbling of the industry in the face of Japanese mass-production methods introduced by the end of the decade.

The British state was happy provided that growth, labor peace, and currency stability remained. Thus it was the very prosperity which came from the long boom and the open world economy (modeled on lines already etched in British culture), which seemed to reinforce Britain's independent position in Europe, her 'special relationship' with America, her new Commonwealth ties (as preferences provided *de facto* advantages for otherwise uncompetitive British goods), and her model welfare state with its pioneering advances. By the early 1960s, however, consciousness of Britain's relative stagnation was growing, but it had yet to find a practical echo in the financial center (the City of London, Britain's Wall Street), the civil service, the unions, the political parties, or even the ranks of industrialists, who were not doing badly at all.

France in the 1950s was also a country with a façade and image rapidly being undermined by its collision with the open world economy. It was an image of stagnation, both political and economic.[20] Continuing governmental instability and protectionism along with inflation threatened to undermine the most ambitious French project of the time, European integration.* Business was still fragmented and defensive, fearful of the competition which the E.E.C. would bring, and labor was both industrially weak and politically aggressive, with its largest union confederation allied to the electorally strong Communist Party. But state actors played a major role in providing a structural focus for increased investment, industrial restructuring, and international competitiveness – first through the planning system, then through European integration, and finally through the policy of encouraging industrial concentration, referred to as the creation

---

*European integration, manifested in the European Coal and Steel Community and the European Economic Community, was an attempt to manage increasing external pressure by permitting a certain amount of closure at European level – a customs union and later the Common Agricultural Policy – in a trade-off for internal industrial free trade.

of 'national champions'.[21] The Fifth Republic has widely been seen as giving the new *colbertistes* pride of place in both prestige and strategic political resources in the new regime.[22] Thus by the end of the 1950s, with economic growth and investment strong, backed by a state committed to pro-business interventionism, the traditional image of France as Britain's poor relation was being overturned.

This situation lasted through the 1970s, but the position of each of these countries was worsened, and the consequent structural problems exacerbated, by the end of the long boom and the recession which lasted from the oil crisis of 1973–74 until the mid-1980s. In Britain, calls from the Right to dismantle the welfare state – in the name of greater openness – echoed calls from sections of the Left for more protectionism and a 'siege economy' (i.e., closure) although the latter have subsided since the heavy defeats for the Labour Party in the 1983 and 1987 general elections. Restructuring in the 1980s has come through labor-shedding, bankruptcy, takeovers, and an increased share for profits in national income. But Britain's balance of manufacturing trade fell into deficit in 1983 for the first time since the Industrial Revolution, and heavy current account deficits have become chronic in the late 1980s as oil exports have begun to shrink.

In France, the period can more easily be divided by the oil crisis. The trends in state intervention in the 1960s were reinforced and extended in the early 1970s, but there were problems and setbacks: mergers often did not result in real restructuring;[23] wage rises helped fuel inflation; the planning process was thrown more and more off course;[24] and the 'national champions' policy was plagued with problems in key sectors like electronics, while never really solving the problem of what to do with unprofitable 'lame ducks'. The biggest setback was the oil crisis, given France's huge dependency on imported oil, further exacerbating all of these problems. Private investment fell, and industrial policy became more selective and targeted, despite a phase of reflation and ambitious state-led projects initiated under the Socialist Government from 1981 to 1983.

Nevertheless, the French growth rate remained higher than her neighbors' until 1983, when it began to lag behind as other countries recovered from the recession. France's reaction to changes in the international environment were thus mediated through traditional structures, with all of their strengths and weaknesses. Both the Socialists from 1983 to 1986 (and again since 1988), and the right-wing government from 1986 to 1988, however, have pursued a strategy based on a new belief in the need to encourage the market. Indeed, probably the most decided group of actors supporting liberalization of both public and private sectors has been the higher civil service, previously the core of the state's economic primacy. For example, the deregulation of French financial markets came about not through pressure from market actors (who were closely tied to the state in quasi-corporatist fashion) but because of the new liberal mood of state actors; some of the key instruments of *dirigisme* in France have, paradoxically, been dismantled because state actors, both civil servants and politicians of Left and Right, have come to believe that further modernization can only come from opening France to the forces of the world marketplace.[25]

From the Welfare State to the Competition State

Openness, then, has of course had negative consequences as well as positive ones, both for individual states and in periods where international trends are themselves negative, such as the global recession from the oil crisis to some time in the mid-1980s (with the phase of 'recovery' varying from country to country and region to region). But at another level, openness has brought with it a greater structural interpenetration of the national economies with each other and with worldwide market forces, an interpenetration which runs through the structures of production (especially in the form of multinational corporations), of finance, of trade, of information and communication, and at many more levels. Through these emerging 'transnational structures', it becomes increasingly impossible to isolate national political allocation processes. At the same time, the capacity of any one state to supervise or guarantee the stability of this network of interactions grows less and less; the *pax Americana* not only becomes less and less effective, but also less and less relevant. Neither state actors nor non-state actors can separate their objectives and their strategies from their international context; the games which they play, and the way that those games are clustered, are to a greater and greater extent transnational games by definition, although the socialized national identity of both state and non-state actors is often strengthened at the same time by the rigors of competition.

It is essential at this point to emphasize the consequences which the international recession has had for the economic policies of advanced industrial states generally, and for 'intermediate economies' such as Britain and France in particular. For it has tended to undermine a range of policy measures which we earlier identified with the notion – broadly defined – of the 'welfare state'. This involves not only the provision of welfare services, but the use of Keynesian macroeconomic policy with the objective of maintaining full employment, and also the maintenance of basic or strategic industries (including natural monopolies and public goods) through regulation, subsidy, and/or public control. These elements are linked primarily through the manipulation or 'fine tuning' of public expenditure on social programs and economic policy, along with some monetary controls, especially through the use of deficit financing – pump-priming or reflation – in order to maintain a sufficient level of demand to promote recovery. Nevertheless, the key element in such an analysis remains the market. It was not intended to substitute state management and/or ownership for private capital, which, as in the classical model which Keynes criticized and adapted, still provided the fundamental dynamic mechanism for self-sustaining economic growth and development.

The underlying thrust of government measures is thus to influence the evolution of demand and its impact on industry as a whole, as well as to provide basic energy resources, intermediate goods, some transportation, communication, and other services (with the role of social services and transfer payments a variable element), and regulatory frameworks necessary to counteract dysfunctional tendencies in markets – not to replace those markets. But despite the increasing openness and interpenetration of the world economy, those measures are still essentially national, and their political legitimacy rests on their appeal to and impact upon the body politic of a particular nation-state. And at the same time, transnational integration has made those policies more and more difficult to effectuate at national level. The experiences of recent decades have therefore undermined the confidence of many analysts on both Left and Right in the Keynesian package. The continuing decline of the British economy, for example, and the stubborn post-1974 recession in the industrial world generally, have led to the view that slumps had in a sense become immune to Keynesian remedies, and that this development was in part the result of new rigidities built into governmental measures themselves – rigidities which prevented private capital from playing its proper role in its own sphere. The stagflation of the 1970s came to be seen as relatively impervious to reflationary measures, and the need for restructuring involved in the Third Industrial Revolution based on electronics and related new technology to be beyond the capacity of private investment to fuel in such conditions.

Thus state intervention of the 'welfare state' variety finds its limitations in the structural rigidities constraining its conjunctural measures – as in the concepts of 'structural unemployment' and 'structural inflation' – although the result is not seen to lie in the emergence of a repressive 'command economy' so much as in a lumbering, muddling, 'overloaded' national state – a state the activities of which are increasingly seen to hinder, rather than to reinforce, international competitiveness. The 'overloaded state' is seen to bump up against four main types of constraint. In the first place, chronic deficit financing by governments in a slump period is seen to soak up private investment and raise interest rates in ways which 'crowd out' private investment and channel internationally mobile resources into non-productive financial outlets. Secondly, nationalized industry and tripartite wage bargaining are blamed for maintaining 'wage-push' inflation and preventing rises in productivity and/or the shedding of newly-redundant labor (given the obsolescence of much fixed capital and the pressing need for reconversion), lowering profitability through labor market rigidities. Thirdly, attempts to maintain overall levels of economic activity – to maintain demand, infrastructure, and employment – are seen to lock state interventionism into a 'lame duck' syndrome in which the state takes responsibility for more and more unprofitable sectors of the economy.

And fourthly, all of these rigidities, in an open international economy, have negative consequences for the balance of payments and for the exchange rate: protectionism as a response may invite retaliation and/or simply act as a drag on international trade generally; while devaluation (supposedly automatic in an international regime of floating exchange rates such as the one which has existed since the breakdown of the Bretton Woods system in 1971–72, but which is in fact manipulated in various ways) can have a knock-on effect, exacerbating the other three. All four of these constraints interact in recessionary conditions to restrict the capacity of private capital to perform its supply-side or productive function. The state itself is capable only of more *ad hoc* regulation, which demonstrates not so much the authoritative nature of the state as the inefficiencies of bureaucratic overplanning. Thus the challenge for the Keynesian state (and especially its social-democratic variant) is to realize its limitations and to combine a measure of austerity with the retention of a minimal welfare net to sustain some degree of consensus, while occasionally making forays into industrial policy to help restructure old industry and to encourage the new, particularly in targeted 'growth sectors'. Ability to carry out the latter, however, will depend upon success in putting across the former without destroying the socio-political consensus which had formed around the welfare state – or at least the class alliance upon which winning elections is based. Many false starts and internal conflicts are built into such a strategy (or set of new tactics). Nevertheless, in the industrial world generally, this sort of strategy has led to major changes in government policy, changes which have serious consequences for the welfare state model.

At the most general level, there has been a change in the focus of economic policy in general, away from macroeconomic demand management towards mesoeconomic and microeconomic policies. In an open world economy, the equilibrium point of macroeconomic policy can no longer set by a domestic political target such as full employment, but results from competitive conditions and terms of trade in the international economy. Macroeconomic policy can therefore be counterproductive – especially if, at the simplest level, it merely increases import penetration. Governments can, however, through targeted industrial policies, alter some of those conditions – encouraging mergers and restructuring, promoting research and development, providing or guaranteeing credit-based investment where capital markets fail, sponsoring the development of export marketing organizations, developing active labor market policies, and the like. Of course, the question of 'picking winners' is highly problematic in a shifting international marketplace, although Japan is seen to have done it effectively in the past. Another problem is that favored sectors must be chosen against other sectors – the other side of the coin is 'picking losers'. The price is higher unemployment, as uncompetitive industries fail or shed labor, for even if more competitive industries could eventually take up the slack – a problematic hypothesis given that most analyses of the Third Industrial Revolution suggest that labor-saving and more flexible production systems are fundamental to its very structure – there would inevitably be a much higher level of residual unemployment in the intervening period, unless that short-term slack could be absorbed by measures such as retraining, being tried in many Western countries, or by oligopolistic redeployment, as in Japan.

In Britain, however, such an approach has only been applied in a very limited and piecemeal fashion, under both Conservative and Labour governments. There have been three major constraints. Firstly there has been the structural rigidity of public expenditure, especially on the entrenched structures of the welfare state, e.g., as unemployment compensation rises to erode other cuts and prevent the redeployment of resources elsewhere. Next, effective mesoeconomic and microeconomic policies, unlike macroeconomic policy, depend upon the industrial know-how and policy activism of civil servants, which we have earlier argued is lacking in the British case. And finally, for such an approach to succeed on a strategic level, it requires the political intention and will to apply it, and this is undermined on the one hand by the Labour Party's commitment to maintaining most of the existing structure of the welfare state and the temptation of many sections of the party and its allied trade unions to favor protectionism, and, on the other hand, by the Thatcher Government's assumption that *all* intervention (except monetary controls, which have been a problematic tool) is counterproductive and market-distorting. Nevertheless, as we shall argue later, the British state has taken on a crucial but paradoxical *indirect* role, mainly in connection with the process of preparing state-owned industries for privatization.

In France, of course, both Right and Left have attempted in neo-*colbertiste* fashion to develop such a strategy. The limited hold of Keynesianism on economic management and the sectoral activism of civil servants linked into the *grand corps* networks have privileged such an approach in theory, and to some extent in practice. However, this has run up not only against the problem of the rigidity and counterproductiveness of increasing public expenditure *per se* (as the first year of the Socialist experiment underlined), but also against the internal compartmentalization and other limitations of the bureaucratic apparatus which we have described earlier. None the less, it has, somewhat paradoxically, encouraged a kind of new state capitalism which has played a significant role in the recovery of the French economy since 1983.

However, it must also be remembered that both France and Britain have particular disadvantages in economic and industrial policy in comparison to their strongest competitors, the United States, West Germany, and Japan. The former are 'intermediate economies', and this becomes increasingly significant as openness and transnational structural interpenetration increase. France has in effect been an intermediate economy since the nineteenth century, while Britain's movement into such a category is, on the whole, more recent, as we have seen earlier. In the context of the world economy, an intermediate economy is one which is structurally less advanced than the most advanced economies and more advanced than the great majority of less developed ones. This does not simply refer to growth rates – which are only relative to existing levels of output and income – nor to macroeconomic indices – which can conceal a wide range of contrasting trends and performances in different sectors and subsectors. Rather it refers to the types of goods which are produced and exchanged with (and received in exchange from) structurally different categories of national economies.

It means that in those sectors which are economically most advanced in terms of both technological sophistication and productive efficiency (particularly the productivity of capital), there is a structural gap between an intermediate economy and those of the most advanced countries, a gap reflected in the composition and terms of trade not only between those countries themselves but also between each of them and third countries. An intermediate economy is thus structurally underdeveloped in such sectors. At the same time, an intermediate economy is considerably more advanced – not only in those sectors, but in a number of others, generally technologically more traditional and more labor-intensive – than less developed economies.

In reacting to the policy problems embedded in the 'intermediate economy' structural position, national policy-makers have a range of potential responses with which to work. Each of these responses has potential benefits for the national economy, but each can also have severe disadvantages in the context of the world economy. These include: trade policy, including tariff protectionism, 'hidden' protectionism, reciprocity, export promotion, and the like (often bending or even breaking multilateral rules);[26] fiscal and monetary policies of a Keynesian type; exchange rate policies; etc. We have already looked at some of these problems. Now the important point is that countries in a strong structural position can often resist these binds, at least for a time; but those in a weak structural position – such as intermediate economies (not to mention the structurally much weaker underdeveloped economies and stagnating autarchic economies like those of the Soviet Union and China, now attempting to adapt to greater openness) – have less room to maneuver. Striking a balance between growth and competitiveness is difficult when shifting external conditions predominate. Policy-makers are continually having to navigate between policy combinations which, in particular conjunctural conditions, may prove to be not only ineffective and internally incompatible, but also counterproductive and involving significant opportunity costs (a 'Hobson's choice').

Of course, in a worldwide boom period, such questions may not seem to be of the same degree of centrality. Not only is there more money in the kitty with the international economic 'engine' pulling the weaker economies along behind, but in fact the very 'intermediate' position can be an asset. Their production can not only add fuel to the engine, complementing its productive repertoire and increasing trade in general, but also provide the essential linkage mechanism to articulate the expansion of the 'core' industrial economies with those of the underdeveloped world, avoiding the more brutal intervention of the two superpowers. Indeed, the latter analysis could be found on both sides of the debate in the 1950s and 1960s between proponents of European integration and supporters of the Gaullist conception of a *Europe des États*. In any case, the engine is seen to pull an ever longer train behind it. Needless to say, such structural complementarity, in a way which is perhaps analogous at the world level to the role of Keynesian policies at the national level, can become a factor of rigidity in the more competitive, zero-sum world of an international recession. In this situation, what had appeared to be an efficient division of labor turns into competition over stagnant or declining markets.

The intermediate economies thus find their positions eroded on both the 'upmarket' and 'downmarket' sides; growth sectors elude them, and 'captive markets' (e.g., neo-colonial outlets) are no longer secure. Trading partners and currency markets pull in opposite directions, as capital flows – less and less inhibited as currency markets become more and more open (exacerbated by the floating exchange rate system) – follow competition over interest rates in less regulated financial markets like the Euromarkets. Tight monetary policies, on the one hand, which are supposed to reduce inflation and costs (in the long run), also hit both investment and exports, thus reducing output and creating unemployment. Looser monetary policies and reflation, on the other hand, increase inflation and costs in a way which also reduces profitability, thus also hitting investments and exports, but also propping up uncompetitive enterprises. The question becomes one of which is the necessary evil: high unemployment and a reduction in output and capacity, in the hope that improving market conditions abroad will pull investment into new, more competitive firms and sectors once

npetitive ones have fallen by the wayside (the Thatcher gamble);
aintenance of a large, uncompetitive sector, in the hope, again,
proving market conditions abroad will increase overall demand
sur.... ntly that markets can be found anyway, starting from a broader
industrial base too (the gamble taken by the French Socialist Government
in 1981–83, and the one which would have been taken by the British
Labour Party had they come to power in 1983).

Experience of the 1970s shows that the second approach, based as it is
on the Keynesian principles which sustained the long antecedent boom,
tends to be adopted first. This was true in Britain in 1974, with the Labour
Government's 'Social Contract', and in France, too, under the first Chirac
Government (1974–76). Its failure leads to the adoption of some version
of the first approach, painfully at first under the Wilson and Callaghan
Governments after 1975 in Britain, but more abruptly under the Thatcher
Government, and the other way around in France, with the early austerity
of the conservative Barre Government (1976–81) incrementally giving
way to a more pragmatic policy of assisted 'redeployment'. But the
similarities go deeper than this, and reveal a central paradox of contemporary industrial policy in intermediate economies. This paradox rests in
the fact that the most extensive *restructuring* of industry which has taken
place in the 1980s in both Britain and France has stemmed not from the
spontaneous operation of market forces, although these indeed tended to
squeeze both countries from above and below, weakening their position,
and especially the position of private capital in both. Rather it has come in
those sectors most directly controlled by the state. At first, however, one is
most struck by the contrast between the Thatcher Government's approach
to industrial policy and that of the French Socialists.

Of course, by extending the nationalized sector to include the country's
main industrial groups and the remainder of the non-nationalized banking sector, the Socialist Government in France in the 1981–83 period
sought precisely to make the state sector the spearhead of any new
boom. This was intended to make possible greater access to long-term,
high-risk capital investment, energetic government-backed efforts in
research and development in the high technology field, state support
through planning agreements for the targeting of specific growth sectors,
and the restructuring of firms in the public sector (as well as certain
traditional industries in the private sector), and thus to reconcile the
sometimes conflicting requirements of competitiveness at both national
and international levels with those of product specialization and more
effective organizational integration. The complexity of the task was
exemplified by the problem of arranging for nationalized firms to swap
subsidiaries in such a way as to avoid the inefficiencies of dependency
upon a monopoly supplier in the domestic market, while still integrating
and streamlining the firms sufficiently to increase their international

competitiveness. This dilemma was illustrated by the policies ado͵ in the telecommunications sector after nearly two years of discussio͵ policies still having controversial ramifications today. None the less, the government even after 1983 continued to pursue a modified version of this state-led strategy (with different emphases under different Industry Ministers), despite unanticipated costs and a reduction of the overall level of real public expenditure from 1984 onwards, until the Right came into power in 1986.

The Thatcher Government has been just as fully committed, in contrast, to a broad and deep reduction in the size of the public sector, returning as much of it as possible to private ownership. This goal has gone hand-in-hand with a strong austerity program virtually since taking power in May 1979,* involving, in particular, the setting of firm cash limits to the expenditure of public sector industries and services and of local governments, although some monetary and fiscal stimulation was added, especially by increasingly ignoring certain monetary targets (although there has been a clampdown since mid-1988) and by cutting income taxes to partially compensate for the rise in Value Added Tax in 1979. The core has, of course, been the privatization program, which has involved the full or partial sale of a wide range of firms, including British Telecom, British Aerospace, the British Oil Corporation, British Airways, British Petroleum, British Steel, British Gas, the airports authorities, the local water boards, and, next on the list, the electricity industry. In some cases, especially British Gas and the water authorities, public monopolies are simply turned into private monopolies. Parts of the social and public services have been opened up to private subcontracting (provision of laundry and cleaning services to National Health Service Hospitals, local refuse collection, etc.), bus and coach services have been widely deregulated, and, in 1986, the 'Big Bang' took place in the financial services sector.

What is most interesting, however, is that these industries, before they were privatized, were actually turned by their state shareholder from lame ducks into efficient, profitable concerns. This was done by the standard methods – labor-shedding, some capital investment, extensive changes at managerial level, the closure of unprofitable activities, and the like. Those public sector industries which are too deeply dependent on the state to be sold – e.g., coal or the railroads – have also been drastically rationalized and reduced in size through management changes, labor-shedding, and expenditure ceilings. Even where a public service has already been restructured and rationalized, as with the local government-controlled water authorities, the central government has set a firm face against even

---

*Except for the periods preceding the elections of 1983 and 1987, when classic 'political business cycles', including monetary laxity, prevailed.

productivity-based wage rises, which, along with limiting the amount that local authorities can raise through property taxes ('rate capping'), has further eroded the scope of local autonomy. Thus despite the reduction of the public sector and extensive deregulation, however, the Thatcher Government's approach in practice has confirmed the state's central role in industrial restructuring.

For the British private sector has been no more attracted to the lure of domestic investment and expansion than the French. The rush to purchase shares in British Shipbuilders or British Telecom on the Stock Exchange was not an indicator of a new vitality of British industrial capital, but, like the vertiginous rise in trading of nationalization compensation bonds on the Bourse in the months preceding the French nationalizations in early 1982, represented private capital taking a free ride on the state. British manufacturing decline is continuing, and the recent rise in interest rates and deterioration in the balance of payments have increased fears of a recession despite a consumer boom fueled by tax cuts. Unlike the United States, which has financed its budget and trade deficits through capital flows from outside, especially from Japan, the British economy is more constrained by its structural position. Yet many of the success stories – British Telecom, British Airways, British Steel – are past or present nationalized industries whose recovery has been achieved while still in public ownership. This mirrors the success stories of French nationalized industries in the 'competitive sector', which for a time too made the Chirac Government's privatization program an easy one in the sense that profitable, going concerns were being sold off. And the boom in small business in both countries – especially in the service and high-technology sectors – has also benefited from extensive government start-up schemes.

The track record of state intervention, then, has been remarkably good in both countries in the 1980s, in comparison with the mixed record of private capital. This reflects the problems faced by private capital in an intermediate economy. But it also reflects the fact that the state, rather than 'crowding out' the public sector, has in many ways been 'sucked in' – not only into civil society but also into the competitive rat race of the open world economy. For the state is making market decisions too, and sometimes making them in more efficient ways than private capital can, in intermediate economies as well as in Japan.* And despite the resilience

---

*In the United States, of course, some individual agencies may have a wider impact. It has been suggested, for example, that the 30-year-old Defense Advanced Research Projects Agency 'has had an impact on the nation's technology development well out of proportion to its size'; Andrew Pollack, 'America's Answer to Japan's M.I.T.I.', *The New York Times* (5 March 1989). Similar comments have long been made about the development of integrated circuits, the predecessor of the microchip, in the 1950s, also treated as a military project.

of welfare *per se* – social services and the welfare safety net – which has not been cut significantly in terms of the proportion of G.D.P. spent on it (despite well-known cuts in salient sectors), significant elements of the broader welfare state model outlined earlier in this chapter have been squeezed out by the structural constraints of economic policymaking in the intermediate economy. Directly or indirectly, hard decisions of industrial policy have come to predominate.

This change from the welfare state to the competition state has a number of other dimensions which go beyond state-led restructuring of industry, however, and which demonstrate some of the possibilities and constraints of such developments. Deregulation of financial markets has often involved an attempt by governments to force cozy clubs of stockbrokers to adapt to world market conditions – despite resistance from major sectors of the financial system. Measures to combat unemployment no longer come in macroeconomic packages; they tend to appear either as merely the side-effect of the promotion of industry or in terms of promoting labor market adaptation, as with the remarkably similar youth temporary employment and training schemes in both Britain and France (and their variations in other countries). Control of the wages and conditions of labor, whether directly or indirectly (as in the British case of trade union legislation and the defeat of public sector unions in confrontations over the course of the 1980s), is an even more important element than before, in order to avoid the negative effects of cost-push inflation and/or currency devaluation. And direct support for research and development in high-technology sectors is crucial; here the record of the French state would seem to be better than the British in many fields. These dimensions merely underline the complex impact on advanced industrial economies of contemporary international challenges.

Conclusions

Contrasts between Britain and France, then, must not obscure a certain paradoxical convergence too. Furthermore, the Japanese model, despite a certain amount of liberalization and the revaluation of its currency against the dollar, is alive and well. Not only has dollar devaluation not reversed the Japanese trade surplus with the United States, but the health of Japanese industry has been demonstrated by further state-led restructuring away from industries and services losing their competitive advantage and toward those becoming increasingly competitive (including financial services). Furthermore, of the four so-called 'Asian tigers' – South Korea, Taiwan, Singapore, and Hong Kong – the first three have followed a path of state-led growth not dissimilar to the Japanese model.[27] Other countries in Southern Europe and the Third World are attempting to shift from earlier plan-led models of development to this kind of private sector/public sector interpenetration (although for the latter the debt crisis is often a crippling obstacle). In the Communist world, of course, after years of stagnation, as the forced gains of the Stalin period were replaced by bureaucratic entropy, painful and halting steps are now being made to liberalize – both politically and economically.[28] The state is no longer in a position anywhere to pursue the general welfare as if it were mainly a domestic problem. As the world economy is characterized by increasing interpenetration and the crystallization of transnational markets and structures, the state itself is having to act more and more like a market player, that shapes its policies to promote, control, and maximize returns from market forces in an international setting.

In effect, the economic and social activities characteristic of the welfare state, as its name implies, still conformed to the image of the state as an authoritative actor (or set of actors), the main effect of the intervention of which was to *take certain activities out of the marketplace* – especially to attempt to prevent and counteract market failure – and to 'socialize' them. The state, in this sense, structurally speaking, was still primarily a *decommodifying agent* in the wider economy. But what we are seeing in the world today, the main impact of increasing openness on the state and on state actors, is the reverse – the re-emergence of the state as a *commodifying agent*, a role which it was often seen to play in the emergence of capitalism itself in the post-feudal period and the years of mercantilism. A new state capitalism will come to the fore. The dividing line between public and private, in this context, is being eroded, making possible not just the further development of the world marketplace as an arena of private capital, but also, and perhaps more importantly, the emergence of a changing world order. This order would be based not on the clash between autarchic powers and open capitalist nations, nor on the dominance of a benevolent 'hegemonic superpower', but on a more complex web of relations in which states will remain primary actors, in dense and cross-cutting relations with each other, with their economies, and, of course, with their civil societies, with which they will become more and more inextricably intertwined.

In this context, paradoxically, the total amount of state intervention will tend to increase, for the state will be enmeshed in the promotion, support, and maintenance of an ever-widening range of social and economic activities. De-differentiation and re-differentiation will continue to be at the heart of the structuration process. But state actors will find it more difficult to operate in the planned, coherent way that traditional state theories posited, whether based on the notion of *potestas* or authority, or on the state as the coercive agent of a relatively unified capitalist class (or even as the 'ideal collective capitalist'). The domestic redistribution of wealth and power in favor of disadvantaged domestic constituencies, which is at the heart of the social-democratic welfare state, will become more difficult and complex to achieve. Macroeconomic policies will be more difficult to implement, and mesoeconomic and microeconomic policies will become more and more central. And the world order itself will have to adapt – not only to the imperatives of world markets, but also to a new and more complex configuration of state interaction. The changing architecture of politics, then, will mean that the state structuration process will be more and more enmeshed in transnational structuration processes, that shifting cross-border connections between market and hierarchy will complicate processes of political allocation, and that agents will have to learn to play new sets of games.

Notes

1. The concept of 'transnational structures' is best treated in Strange, *States and Markets, op. cit.*

2. See John Zysman and Laura Tyson, eds., *American Industry in International Competition: Government Policies and Corporate Strategies* (Ithaca, N.Y.: Cornell University Press, 1983), especially chs. 1 and 9.

3. See Richardson, ed., *Policy Styles in Western Europe, op. cit.*; and Hall, *Governing the Economy, op. cit.*

4. These issues are treated in Lindblom, *Politics and Markets, op. cit.*

5. Cf. Hall, *op. cit.*, and Zysman, *Governments, Markets and Growth, op. cit.*

6. In the 'new institutional economics', however, such behavior is seen as a search for greater efficiency by 'internalizing transaction costs'; Williamson, *Economic Institutions of Capitalism, op. cit.*, and *Markets and Hierarchies, op. cit.*

7. See Estrin and Holmes, *French Planning, op. cit.*, ch. 1.

8. See Catherine Jones, *Patterns of Social Policy: An Introduction to Comparative Analysis* (London: Tavistock, 1985).

9. Cf. Eric J. Hobsbawm, *Industry and Empire, op. cit.*, and Andrew Gamble, *Britain in Decline: Economic Policy, Political Strategy and the British State* (Boston: Beacon Press, 1981).

10. See Jean Fourastié, *Les trente glorieuses, ou la Révolution invisible de 1946 à 1975* (Paris: Fayard, revised edn, 1979).

11. See Sam Aaronovitch, Ron Smith, Jean Gardiner, and Roger Moore, *The Political Economy of British Capitalism: A Marxist Analysis* (London: McGraw-Hill, 1981).

12. Cf. Stephen Cohen, *Modern Capitalist Planning: The French Model* (Berkeley and Los Angeles: University of California Press, 1969); Robert Gilpin, *France in the Age of the Scientific State* (Princeton, N.J.: Princeton University Press, 1968); and John Zysman, *Political Strategies for Industrial Order: Market, State and Industry in France* (Berkeley and Los Angeles: University of California Press, 1977).

13. The classic comparison is Charles P. Kindleberger, *Economic Growth in France and Britain, 1851–1950* (Cambridge, Mass.: Harvard University Press, 1964).

14. Cf. Richard N. Gardner, *Sterling–Dollar Diplomacy in Current Perspective* (New York: Columbia University Press, revised edn, 1980); Lloyd C. Gardner, *Economic Aspects of New Deal Diplomacy* (Boston: Beacon Press, 1971); and Fred L. Block, *The Origins of International Economic Disorder: A Study of United States International Monetary Policy from World War II to the Present* (Berkeley and Los Angeles: University of California Press, 1977).

15. See Gardner, *Sterling–Dollar Diplomacy, op. cit.*

16. See William Appleman Williams, *The Tragedy of American Diplomacy* (New York: Dell, 2nd edn, 1972).

17. For a useful survey of the literature, see Hall, *op. cit.*; cf. Tom Kemp, *Industrialization in Nineteenth Century Europe* (London: Longman, 1969).

18. Cerny in Gaffney, ed., *France and Modernization, op. cit.*

19. Cf. Middlemas, *Politics of Industrial Society, op. cit.*, and Ingham, *Capitalism Divided?, op. cit.*

20. Cf. Hoffmann, 'Paradoxes of the French Political Community', *op. cit.*, Herbert Lüthy, *The State of France* (London: Secker and Warburg, 1955), and Jacques Fauvet, *La France déchirée* (Paris: Fayard, 1956).

21. Cf. Zysman, *Political Strategies for Industrial Order, op. cit.*, and Suzanne Berger, 'Lame Ducks and National Champions', in Stanley Hoffmann and William G. Andrews, eds., *The Fifth Republic at Twenty* (Brockport, NY: Suny Press, 1981), pp. 292–310.

22. Cf. Ezra Suleiman, *Politics, Power and Bureaucracy in France: The Administrative Elite* (Princeton, N.J.: Princeton University Press, 1974); and Cerny, 'Gaullism, Advanced Capitalism and the Fifth Republic', in David S. Bell, ed., *Contemporary French Political Parties* (London and New York: Croom Helm and St Martin's Press, 1982), ch. 2.

23. Peter Holmes and Anne Stevens, 'The Framework of Government-Industry Relations and Industrial Policy Making in France', Working Paper Series on Government–Industry Relations, no. 2, University of Sussex (June 1986).

24. Diana M. Green, 'The Seventh Plan – The Demise of French Planning?', *West European Politics*, vol. 1, no. 1 (February 1978), pp. 60–76.

25. See P.G. Cerny, 'The "Little Big Bang" in Paris: Financial Market Deregulation in a *dirigiste* System', *European Journal of Political Research*, vol. 17, no. 2 (March 1989), pp. 169–92.

26. For a recent justification of 'neo-mercantilism', paradoxically in the name of *deepening* economic interdependence, by a former British Trade Secretary, see Edmund Dell, *The Politics of Economic Interdependence* (London: Routledge and Kegan Paul, 1988).

27. See Nigel Harris, *The End of the Third World, op. cit.*

28. See Peter Rutland, 'Gorbachev, Economic Reform, and the West', paper presented to a colloquium at the Department of Politics, New York University, 2 March 1989.

Epilogue: Political Structuration and Political Ideas in the Twenty-first Century

The architecture of politics, then, represents neither an 'orthodox structure' (nor a function of such structures); nor is it simply an 'aggregation of interests' or of individual choices in a market-type context. Rather it is constituted by and through the outcome of myriad historical 'accidents', which create structures of constraints and opportunities. These sets of constraints and opportunities in effect form structured fields of action upon and within which agents make choices. In the words of General de Gaulle, 'Nothing is ever built upon a *tabula rasa*.' To the extent that the outcomes of the 'games' which agents play are structurally indeterminate, then those agents' choices are real. For structures – in the sense of sets of constraints and opportunities – are riddled with interstitial gaps and structural tensions between the rules, resources, and other factors which are embedded in different interactive games. In addition to choices being potentially more or less 'real', however, it is also true that some choices will sometimes impact on the structure of the field itself, whether in ways that are intended, or with unanticipated consequences.

The first half of this book has been an attempt to elaborate this interaction of agency and choice, on the one hand, and structural constraints and opportunities, on the other, through the concept of 'structuration'. At the same time, we have tried to explain why (and how) the core political structure as it emerged from this contingent historical process – the 'state' – has over the long run of modern history become the predominant and central structure in socio-economic development. Thus the state, itself made up of the interaction of different clusters of interactive and 'nested' games, has been central to the formation and structuration of the wider social field too. The second half of the book has been an attempt to identify several arenas or 'regions' of the ongoing political structuration process in the twentieth century, arenas which cut across the main categories of state structure and which represent particularly critical clusters of games for shaping the structured action field itself. The most critical games involve a shift of structural power from national political actors to those state actors and non-state actors who might be described as the 'gatekeepers' of the interface between transnational markets and structures, on the one hand, and 'nationalized social identity' (and nation-state resources), on the other. The outcomes of the games which they play – whether those outcomes are intended or unanticipated – will be decisive in shaping the future of the state and of the architecture of politics in general.

The sorts of changes which this book anticipates include neither the transcending of the state from above – whether through the organization of the world economy, or the development of significantly more inclusive transnational regimes or institutions of governance – nor its transcendance from below through civil society – whether by significantly more decentralized, grass-roots forms of collective action, democratic participation, or community life. However, they do include important elements and dimensions of structural change within the state itself, between states, between states and international market structures, and between state structures and a wider range of those social and economic structures which comprise civil society. For example, the goods which approximate to public goods in a relatively closed national state are often transmuted into semiprivate goods or even private goods in a wider world economy. At the same time, a new class of world public goods – support and nurturing of stable and expanding international markets, the maintenance of peace, the protection of the environment, etc. – will be guaranteed not by a monopolistic political authority such as an international state, nor by a heterogeneous collective body such as the League of Nations or the United Nations. Rather, politics in the twenty-first century will be characterized by rapidly de-differentiating and re-differentiating state structures. The role of state actors will change, but their critical location in the increasingly interpenetrated transnational structured field of action will actually increase the impact of state structures in complex ways. Let us look at how these changes may impact upon different kinds of national state regimes, the structure of the world order, and the ideological alternatives which will characterize politics in the twenty-first century.

Comparing Regimes: the Diversification of Structures

Whatever the type of 'regime' which is seen to be characteristic of a nation-state – whether 'democratic' or 'authoritarian' in terms of voting, representation, relative levels of repression, etc., or 'developed' or 'underdeveloped' in economic terms (not to mention various other potential classificatory schemes) – the structural trends discussed in this book have had, and will increasingly have, a significant impact on political outcomes. In order roughly to gauge their effects, let us look first at the categories set out in Table 4.1, and then at trends in

Table 4.1 (reprise)   *Types of state autonomy/regime structuration*

	Externally autonomous	Externally dependent
Internally strong	Autonomous	Satellite
Internally vulnerable	Private/instrumental	Penetrated/diffuse

the different arenas of comparative and international politics usually referred to as the 'Three Worlds' – advanced capitalist states, 'socialist' or 'communist' states, and the Third World (or the Third and Fourth Worlds). Now the categories set out in Table 4.1 referred to 'types of state autonomy'. They represent the intersection of the internal and external structuration processes, and the dynamic balance (or imbalance) between those processes. In effect, they represent types of 'regimes' in a typology which classifies regimes according to the principles of structuration.

The impact of the sorts of changes, both internal and external, which we have been discussing in Part II of this book, bear directly upon the issue of state autonomy and on the ways that structuration processes affect different kinds of nation-state regimes – for they directly affect the sets of constraints and opportunities confronting both state and non-state actors. The combination of increasing limitations on political power discussed in Chapter 5, the growing significance and complexity of the kinds of market/hierarchy fusion represented in the political allocation processes examined in Chapters 3 and 6, and the increasing interpenetration of state, civil society, and transnational structures treated in Chapters 7 and 8, all are in various ways interacting with *existing* state structures (clusters of games, structures of constraints and opportunities, etc.): colliding with existing rules, resources, practices, expectations, and the like; worming their way into interstitial gaps and spaces; exacerbating structural tensions, fault lines, and 'rents in the fabric'; and altering the balance of structural and institutional patterns – even, in certain circumstances, destabilizing and undermining those patterns altogether. This process will therefore have a differential impact upon each regime type, despite the fact that the overall pattern on a broad structural level – in the context of growing transnational interpenetration – comprises the same sorts of trends across countries and regimes.

Where the regime is penetrated and diffuse, then these trends will tend to be destabilizing. It will be more difficult for political leaders to create stable and/or effective regimes by trying to increase state power – although, as Krasner, among others, has pointed out, the first and most natural reaction of state and non-state actors alike in vulnerable states is to try to reduce both political and economic dependence on the outside world. In contrast to Krasner,[1] we see the failure in the 1980s of attempts in the 1970s to create a 'New International Economic Order' as an indication of the failure of state-builders in the most vulnerable areas to avoid the consequences of transnational interpenetration – as seen most vividly in the Third World debt crisis and in the emergence of a 'Fourth World' of the poorest states, often caught more than ever before in the vicious cycle of poverty. Nevertheless, 'satellite' states have been shown in recent years to possess a certain margin for maneuver – although that margin depends significantly upon the nature of their dependence. East European states, until recently strictly circumscribed by structural constraints deriving from Soviet political, military, and economic dominance, have had difficulty orchestrating political liberalization and economic opening at the same time, and are now floundering somewhat in the face of the rapidity of change in the U.S.S.R. But those American dependencies which have adopted Japanese-style industrial policies, such as South Korea and Taiwan, have been able to increase their autonomy significantly by riding the waves of transnational economic interpenetration.

States which are externally autonomous but internally fragmented, especially the United States, find that cross-cutting transnational pressures elude the capacity of the state to formulate policies which deal with either their causes, for example through a coordinated and targeted industrial policy, or their consequences, in terms of the increasing unmanageability of aggregate balances (e.g., the twin deficits). And states which are both internally strong and externally autonomous, such as Japan, find that they have an initial advantage in their pursuit of international competitiveness. In this last set of cases, however, things are more complex, because the very fact that they are pulled further and further into international markets also increases the constraints upon the state's capacity to 'go it alone' in an open world indefinitely. The 'competition state' is a two-edged sword. Just as Britain and the United States ultimately found that their early home-generated industrial lead and momentum was undermined by their very success in world markets – and by the competition which that success generated elsewhere – so Japan seems to be beginning to find that its industries and services may in the future have to respond more to international demands and constraints than to domestic 'administrative guidance' and concern with consensus. At the same time, the re-emergence of trade unions there, and the very recent appearance of a new Japanese consumerism, both perhaps reflecting a certain fatigue at earlier deferment of gratification, may also push – as well as pull – Japan into becoming a more complex kind of 'competition state'.

The most obvious effect of all these changes can be seen in the advanced capitalist states of the United States, Western Europe, and Japan. Whether it is financial market deregulation, trade negotiations, technology transfer, or whatever, the challenges are more complex and cross-cutting. International negotiations on such issues tend to be more and more *ad hoc*, sectoral, and based on complex webs of competitive power and reciprocity, rather than the sorts of overarching and multilateral frameworks once thought to be the wave of the future. This is because, at the same time that networks of interpenetration are increasing, state intervention – also *ad hoc*, sectoral, and based on complex webs of 'political allocation' – is also increasing in order to try to cope with the situation in an adaptive, sequential manner (as in Williamson's hierarchical mode). States are market actors, both in the sense of themselves representing a kind of national 'firm' or cartel operating directly in the transnational environment, and also in the sense of promoting the competitiveness and market-orientation of other, non-state, domestic firms and economic activities. Even new layers of state regulation, intervention, etc., are being constructed in the name of openness and competition, as in the European Community's single market.

But in the advanced capitalist states, such changes are merely the uneven consequences of longer-term processes of change promoted by the 'leading economies' and 'hegemonic powers', Britain in the nineteenth century and the United States in the twentieth. In the 'second world', the 'socialist' or 'communist' states, these changes are very dramatic indeed. Of course, it can be argued that the bases of continuing autarchy have been becoming more and more fragile for some time, as manifested by increasing Soviet dependence on imports of Western grain or by the economic stagnation of the Brezhnev period. But the rapidity of change since the coming to power of Gorbachev in 1985 has caught everyone by surprise, not least the satellite states of Eastern Europe, and more so in a dependent state such as Cuba. China, too, has seen a rapid swing from the spiral of chaos of the Cultural Revolution to rapid but uneven modernization and international integration since the death of Mao.

And finally, in the Third World, these changes are having the widely-noted effect of undermining the very concept of 'Third World' itself. With the worsening poverty of countries like Chad, the worsening internal conflict in countries as different as Mozambique or India, the almost complete destitution of the state in countries like the Lebanon, or the rise of state forms and movements based on the cult of anti-modernism itself such as certain kinds of Islamic fundamentalism, we can contrast the rapid development of Pacific Rim countries and other industrializing areas or the hesitant extension of democracy in places like Argentina or Chile. Differentiation between nation-states is growing in the Third World, and this trend reflects the differential capacities of particular Third World states and state structures to utilize and exploit any existing competitive advantages they might possess in a wider world marketplace, or to nurture, promote, and develop new competitive advantages, whether in old but restructuring sectors like textiles, or in new and rapidly changing areas like consumer electronics. Each Third World country is now more and more of a special case, with its particular state structure the key to its ability to adapt to more complex forms of openness. Neocolonial dependency was also, in a way, a form of security; state and non-state actors knew that so long as they continued to sell their colonially-established products in their former 'parent country's' markets, they would at least know what to expect. Now they can expect less, and have to scramble for more.

Transnational Interpenetration and State Structuration: American Decline?[2]

At the broader international level, as the United States and the Soviet Union attempt to get to grips with the strategic and economic tensions which have absorbed so much of their energy and resources over the past 45 years, it has become clear that it is not their strength that has led to their recent rapprochement, but their relative decline. Both superpowers have been realizing that their nuclear arsenals are not only unusable, but also an intolerable burden – most critically, in a global context in which other countries have been catching up with them economically, and in which they find that their writ does not run to most of the world in terms of a capacity to control critical events and structural changes of a political and social nature. This situation has frequently been described as the decline of superpower 'hegemony'.[3] Hegemony has often been seen as either a necessary condition, or at least the major *de facto* structural outcome, of the development of an international system of states since the seventeenth century. However, hegemony is a complex and contested concept,[4] and there is not space to deal with it at any length here. Most conceptions of hegemony have in common, however, the criterion that the leading state (or states) in the international system are not simply the strongest, but also have the capacity to set – *and enforce* – the international rules of the game.

This requires economic power; the 'hegemon' must be the leading economy[5] and be able to shape international structures of trade, finance, production, consumption, etc. It requires cultural power, in which there is a widely accepted identification of national interests with universal or supranational goals. It requires military power – the capacity to use force to sustain the system when economic or cultural discipline fails or when external challenges arise. Perhaps most of all, however, it requires the decisional capacity of the state to coordinate the above three types of power in order to establish and maintain a coherent set of rules and sanctions. Thus the hegemon must enforce those rules, paradoxically, in a transnational or even supranational fashion. It is this *decisional power*, which we discussed in Chapter 1, which holds the key to hegemonic power – and decline. Therefore neither the arms race nor any underlying economic weakness is the central cause of superpower decline, although each is a major symptom. The real cause has been stagnation and stalemate in the superpowers' respective state structures. The impact of Brezhnevian entropy and stagnation in the Soviet Union is a more spectacular example, given the recent rapid rise of *perestroika*. But we must continually remind ourselves of the endemic weaknesses of the American state too.

In this context, the configuration of states – and of their interpenetrated structures – which characterizes the world in the twenty-first century, post-*pax Americana*, will depend upon the structuration of decisional capacity in a more complex field than ever before. This is an environment in which the relative decline of American power will have crucial ramifications for the future of the American system of government itself – as well as for the future structuration of world power. Still, few Americans, whether on the Right, Left, or Center, perceive external challenges in terms of a complex, potentially unstable yet densely interpenetrated and cross-cutting multipolar world rather than through the tunnel vision of superpower bipolarity. Yet this very decay of the bipolar illusion (bolstered as it has been by the 'logic of nuclear terror') is the central question. It has been at the heart of the most important structural changes in international relations over the past 30 years.[6] Despite the rearguard actions of President Reagan, it has returned to center-stage since the mid-1980s.[7] The decline of American hegemony has led to debates over the possible stability of such a multipolar world.[8] But any future stability will depend upon the way that the United States adapts to both multipolarity and interpenetration. And it is this capacity to adapt – to *manage* inevitable hegemonic decline – which is called into question here.

The three legs of the American hegemonic stool since World War II – the spread of American-backed regimes in the world, the pursuit of nuclear deterrence and American-dominated alliance systems, and the economic Open Door – all depended upon American superiority, not so much with regard to the Soviet bloc, but in *relations with the West* (and to a growing extent, the South). These in turn depended on the coherence of American foreign policy and of the American role in the international economy. That coherence, furthermore, depended upon the capacity of the foreign political and economic policy-making process of the United States, which, as we have seen at various points in this book, is an extremely problematic issue. That process has, moreover, depended on (1) the development of the 'imperial presidency', (2) the maintenance of congressional bipartisanship, and (3) the capacity of the executive to coordinate certain aspects of economic policy with the requirements of transnational regimes in areas such as trade and monetary policy. Finally, therefore, the erosion or breakdown in these three aspects of the U.S. policy process has undermined American capacity to manage hegemonic decline. The intractability of the American 'twin deficits' (budget and trade) is a salient example of this lack of decisional capacity deep within the structure of the American state.

The result is that policy outcomes are blocked, that crisis management and 'end runs' around the political process become the normal way to solve problems, that normal conflicts and choices quickly turn into crises, and that crises themselves quickly become unresolvable as the political capital needed for crisis management is quickly used up. This raises particular questions in the light of the evolution of the international system. Of course, different scenarios can be envisaged. The United States in the twilight of the twentieth century, like Britain in the twilight of the nineteenth, has a capacity for muddling through which derives from the strength of its existing economic resources, backed up by the stability and deep-rootedness (if not the decisional capacity) of its state structure. This is reinforced by the relative strength of American elites and interests in the transnational structures of the contemporary world.[9] Germany and Japan are economic giants but military midgets (so far). But they have systems of government which may be better structured to respond to the questions of internal adaptation and competitive advantage than the United States, although they do not have recent experience of international responsibility. And finally, the United States no longer has either the power or the decisional capacity to impose solutions, but still has tremendous strength to oppose and virtually veto solutions proposed by others.*

Given the seeming intractability of this situation, a relatively positive scenario would involve the emergence, in a cumulative and *ad hoc* way, of a tissue of partial accords and *de facto* practices which would suck Japan and Germany (along with the rest of Western Europe, in a analogously problematic way) into specific kinds of decisional roles, aiming to find compromises which could overcome U.S. veto power. There would emerge, essentially, a 'three-tier' world. The top tier would operate through a series of quasi-Gaullist, *ad hoc* big (economic) power accords with greater but still strictly limited institutionalization, on the model of the Plaza and Louvre Accords on exchange rate stabilization since 1985, the Yen–Dollar Agreement, the Economic Summits, and so on. The second tier, much predicted but still embryonic, would be a limited regional realignment of the world economy of a 'trilateral' nature: (1) the United States, perhaps with the problematic 'sphere of influence' of Latin America, as envisioned by imperialists and isolationists alike in the

---

*As in the recent conflict between the Japanese Ministry of Finance and U.S. Secretary of the Treasury Nicholas Brady on how to deal with the Third World debt crisis.

nineteenth century; (2) Western Europe, partially led by West Germany (although this would be contested by the other European countries) and also having special ties with the Lomé countries (especially Africa); and (3) the Japan-led Pacific Rim – again, often contested by others, and with China being in a problematic position. Such a realignment could not go too far, however, because of intra-regional conflicts of interest plus the lack of enforceable military discipline. The rapidly globally-integrating Soviet Union, with its problematic satellite states seeking more independence, might be a somewhat unstable fourth region.

The third tier would involve the consolidation of what we have called the 'competition state' – with the state increasingly using new forms of economic intervention intended to 'marketize' the state itself as well as to promote the competitive advantage of national industrial and financial activities within a relatively open world economy. In contrast to images of 'neo-mercantilism', the economic-promotional activities of the state would strengthen rather than block the transnationalization of the capitalist world economy through making networks and webs of interdependence deeper and denser. The complex layering of such an interdependent, multipolar scenario would, however, require considerably more 'decisional capacity' on the part of leading states than before, in terms of both transnational coordination and internal adjustment. Thus the United States may not play a positive role in its emergence, given the structural position of the U.S. in the world and its internal tendency toward entropy. American political debate has not even begun to address the problem, and even most political scientists seem to think that America will muddle through. Most probably, the United States will continue to use its veto power whenever transnational solutions impose costs on American vested interests and threaten to undermine the brittle entropic equilibrium of the American state.

This image of a new world order is perhaps most interesting for what it leaves out. It leaves out, first of all, a return to the traditional idea of the nation-state, with its capacity for comprehensive, coherent political control, and its ability to operate as a unitary actor in an 'anarchic' international states system. Thus both of the dimensions of the traditional notion of 'sovereignty' are undermined. At the same time, it leaves out comprehensive internationalism – whether the grand multilateralism of the postwar period, the United Nations, or the purist's notion of Free Trade, on the one hand, or the highly specific kind of economic policy coordination which economists are calling for today, on the other. State policy-making will become more differentiated, and international cooperation will be based more on vague understandings, conjunctural experimentation, and 'fuzzy logic'. The networks of interpenetration which cross-cut both of these levels will probably reduce major conflicts. At the same time, however, conflicts at the margins will be likely to

increase. Border wars, ethnic conflicts, jockeying for regional predominance (as between, for example, India, Pakistan, and China, as reflected
in India's recent development of a medium-range ballistic missile),
and more, will reflect increasing differentiation. Growing transnational
interpenetration and competition will intensify the pain of the losers. But
although the writ of the superpowers will have less and less effect in such
an environment, the threat of full-scale world war may decrease.

At the same time, however, there is one particularly paradoxical way
that the U.S. might be seen to be a 'model' for the new world order.
And that is that the competition state, wherever it develops in the world,
will look somewhat less like the protectionist, autarchic model of prewar
'organized capitalism' or of Japan's 'developmental state', and more like
individual American states in their wider federal union. For, in effect,
American state governments have been 'competition states' within the
federal context – i.e., within an open external marketplace environment
consisting of the United States as a whole – since the eighteenth century.
When they have intervened in the economy, they have not been able to
manipulate the currency, establish trade barriers, or keep out out-of-state
industry or finance. They have had to use indirect measures, such as tax
policy, urban planning, regional policies, education or manpower training,
support for research and development, infrastructure development, and
many more, to attract, keep, and promote economic activities. Of course,
the American states do not possess the rule-making capacity or resource
base that independent national states possess. However, as international
market barriers become more porous, these ostensibly limited and *ad hoc*
forms of state intervention will become more and more the rule in the
world economy. Thus as the unified, reified model of the nation-state
gives way to transnational interpenetration and the rise of the new
'competition state', so the 'weight of government' and the role of state
structures and state actors will paradoxically increase too.

Political Ideas and Structural Change

The main political ideas of the nineteenth and twentieth centuries,
especially the division of visions into those of capitalism and socialism
and of democracy and authoritarianism, will be more difficult to mesh with
the structured field of action which is likely to characterize the twenty-first
century at both national and transnational levels. Categories like Right,
Left, and Center will be more difficult to define, representing more a
vague sort of sympathy for particular groups or classes, and a perception
of 'popular' *versus* 'elite' style, rather than a clear doctrine or program.
Neither civil society, nor the state, nor transnational structures, will
provide broadly favorable opportunities for political action. Single-issue
pressure groups, especially 'insider' groups and special interests, will

continue to be more effective vehicles than broad democratic participation or the pursuit of societal-level transformative goals. 'High politics' will be dominated by 'low politics'. Political frustration will be endemic in such a situation. Nevertheless, micro- and meso-level political action will become ever more needed in the development of transnationally-linked circuits of power which are coming to constitute the state. Horizons will in some ways be lower, and the fields of action more complex, but this will, paradoxically, require increasing knowledge and vigilance on the part of state and non-state actors alike.

These changes will alter the face of the Right–Left scale of political ideas which has dominated the period since the French Revolution. On the Right, the expansion of markets and capitalist institutions which will characterize the 'competition state' will be accompanied by an increasing weight of state intervention, whether to support industrial, agricultural, financial and service sectors in international competition, or to reflect the much broader and deeper consequences of 'market failure', or to undertake a range of new collective tasks which only make sense in a transnational setting, including some specific forms of international cooperation. A salient example of the latter, of course, is environmental protection, which, as a public good, can only be protected from the free-riding of *other states* when it is pursued transnationally. In this sense, environmentalism, traditionally a preserve of sections of the Left, is likely to become a 'valence issue', i.e., an issue which cuts across the Left–Right scale.[10] However, it is only to the extent that right-wing governments come to see transnational environmental protection as a precondition for national competitiveness – or, more probably, to see environmental deterioration as a growing drag on competitiveness and profits in an interdependent world – that environmentalism is actually likely to benefit from the changes which we have discussed. The same is true of feminism, as more women enter the labor market. It has always been the case, of course, as historians have frequently shown, that governments of the Right have not shied away from pro-business intervention designed to counteract market failure or protect their constituents' special interests. This may lead in new directions in the future.

The Left is faced with a much deeper crisis, as the ideas constituting socialism and social democracy have had a curious relationship with, and even an interest in maintaining and exploiting, the state structures which, historically, have emerged in conjunction with capitalist development. In the first place, socialist politics, whether in the form of 'decommodifying' certain economic activities through the welfare state in order to provide real gains and an increased voice for the poor and/or the working class, or in the form of capturing the state, transforming it into something other than a capitalist state, and ultimately causing it to 'wither away', have seen the state as the main target of and framework for political action and organization. In the second place, however, utilizing and/or capturing the state is but a means to an end, an end which involves changing society and creating the conditions for a more just 'social base' around fundamentally different social bonds and principles of economic interaction; transcending the state and transforming society itself, whether through the state, through civil society, or through proletarian internationalism – the 'Workers of All Countries, Unite!' of *The Communist Manifesto* – is the ultimate goal. But the development of the 'competition state', quite simply, not only makes the state into an even more inappropriate field for pursuing such a strategy, but also, through its interpenetration with civil society, cuts off alternative routes, routes which have traditionally involved action 'at the base'.

In terms of the democratic socialist Left which has been the dominant form in Western capitalist societies – and which may also be the form towards which 'second world' leaders now hope to evolve – there are three problems which stem directly from the structural form of the competition state. In the first place, the state is becoming a more and more complex and difficult field in and through which to attempt strategically to organize systematic policies of *redistribution* from a group as large and diverse as the 'bourgeoisie' or the 'middle classes' to an ever more diverse 'working class'. Divisions between elements of the working class – between skilled and unskilled workers, between the employed and the unemployed, between organized trade unionists and the unorganized, between the proletariat and the poorest-of-the-poor (the 'lumpen proletariat'), between workers 'by hand' and workers 'by brain', between different ethnic groups of workers, etc. – have always bedevilled the Left in its attempt to gain political power. And such divisions, within the upper and middle as well as the working classes, can only grow in the increasingly differentiated and cross-cutting world marketplace. In the second place, the limits we have outlined on political power will make it more difficult for even well-organized parties and successful party leaders in office to pursue coherent redistributionist policies, as is all too evident in the recent evolution of the French Socialist Party, the British Labour Party, and many other examples.

And in the third place, state actors and their main non-state *interlocuteurs* are more likely to see whatever redistribution takes place as requiring that priority be given to *capital* through microeconomic and sectoral policy, rather than to workers. Although it is unlikely that the welfare state – in the narrow sense of providing social and public services – will be significantly rolled back overall, say in terms of the proportion of G.D.P. which is allocated to transfer payments and welfare institutions, it is already happening that such services will be cut at the margins, required to operate according to much stricter criteria of 'managerial efficiency', faced with the expansion of privately-provided services for the better-off, and have their take-up and usage monitored more closely. The emergence of the new homelessness in the United States and of the 'new poor' in France and elsewhere, and the growth of waiting lists for health services in Britain, are but the tip of the iceberg. In the United States, welfare services are often seen by right-wing analysts today as more appropriately being targeted on a permanent 'underclass', rather than being available to all. Social services in the communist world are also seizing up, and in many parts of the Third World are not only deteriorating but non-existent. Targeted tax breaks for business and subsidies for worker retraining, for research and development, or for industrial restructuring, are the new wave on both Right and Left.

Developments in the transnational sphere are no more promising for the Left, with the possible partial exception of environmentalism. The attempt by the President of the European Commission, Jacques Delors, to envisage the advent of the 'single market' at the end of 1992 as a potential opportunity to create a 'European social space' is likely to bump up against not only the opposition of right-wing governments in Britain and Germany, for example, but also against the problem of the highly constrained rules and resources which characterize the structures of the European Community itself. The E.C. has in the past been an agent of commodification, not an agent of decommodification, and it is highly unlikely that this situation will change appreciably except in certain areas where valence issues such as environmentalism and feminism cut across the Left–Right scale. The same can be said to an even greater extent of other international regimes and institutions. The World Bank, the General Agreement on Tariffs and Trade, any new agreements such as the Basle Agreement on banking rules, or the sectoral 'regimes' for shipping, air transportation, etc., have nothing at all to do with any project that could be vaguely described as left-wing – unless support of domestic industries, limited protectionism, etc., are seen as left-wing because they involve state intervention (a false analysis, as we have shown). Similar comments could be made about the way that so-called 'left-wing' or Marxist guerrilla movements or 'revolutionary regimes' in the Third World operate with regard to trade questions, multinational corporations, and the like – for example Angola's relations with Gulf Oil. And the increasing transnational integration of the 'second world' will have analogous effects.

Thus the Left is faced with Hobson's choice: either it remains true to traditional socialist projects and tries to recreate a coherent, interventionist, and redistributionist state somehow insulated from the ever more open world marketplace, a strategy which has already proved difficult and even, of course, counterproductive in terms of creating inefficient and authoritarian regimes like those in the Soviet Union or Maoist China; or else it focuses on 'valence issues' such as environmentalism and feminism, in which case it becomes increasingly difficult to differentiate Left from Right – except insofar as the Left might be seen as better at managing a 'capitalism with a human face'. Now it may be thought that the Center could benefit from this evolution. However, centrist parties, whether social democratic, Christian Democrat, left-Gaullist/nationalist, or moderate 'liberal' (as in the British Social and Liberal Democrats or the American Democratic Party) really have no project at all any more, except to argue that voters really want a balance between Left and Right and a defense of the gains of the welfare state era. Political ideas, and the possibilities for putting them into action, will be confronted with an increasingly difficult and complex world. The most significant games will rule out a wide range of classical solutions and visions of a better world.

Conclusion

Thus it is not merely the state which is at the crossroads. It is also human political ingenuity. It is wrong to accuse traditional visions of intellectual poverty. Their richness has informed the most massive, and possibly the most significant, transformation process in human history – the development of the state and of capitalist industrial society. In navigating between the dynamics of private appropriation and socialized national identity, both state and non-state actors, their actions centered on the development of the nation-state itself, have created the world as we know it today. Whatever the strengths and weaknesses of the nation-state, then, it is the central, active, structuring feature of a rapidly changing global environment. Although its outlines will be blurred somewhat in the future, its structures ever more interpenetrated and its constituent games ever more complex, it is highly improbable that it will actually be replaced by any alternative structure. But it will never be the same again.

Notes

1. Krasner, *Structural Conflict, op. cit.*

2. This section has been adapted from Cerny, 'Political Entropy and American Decline', *op. cit.*

3. Cf. Kennedy, *The Rise and Fall of the Great Powers, op. cit.*; and Gilpin, *The Political Economy of International Relations, op. cit.*

4. Cf. Susan Strange, 'The Persistent Myth of Lost Hegemony', *International Organization*, vol. 41, no. 4 (Autumn 1987), pp. 551–74; Strange, *States and Markets, op. cit.*; and Stephen Gill, 'American Hegemony: Its Limits and Prospects in the Reagan Era', *Millennium: Journal of International Studies*, vol. 15, no. 3 (Winter 1986), pp. 311–36.

5. For the concept of the 'leading economy', see Maddison, *Phases of Capitalist Development, op. cit.*

6. Cf. Marcel Merle, *The Sociology of International Relations* (London: Berg, 1987); and Barry Buzan, *People, States and Fear, op. cit.*

7. See Kenneth Oye, Robert J. Lieber, and David Rothchild, eds., *Eagle Resurgent*, *op. cit.*

8. For example, Robert O. Keohane, *After Hegemony: Cooperation and Discord in the World Political Economy* (Princeton, N.J.: Princeton University Press, 1984).

9. Gill, 'American Hegemony', *op. cit.*

10. Phillip E. Converse, 'The Nature of Belief Systems in Mass Publics', in David E. Apter, ed., *Ideology and Discontent* (New York: Free Press, 1964), pp. 206–61.

Select Bibliography

Sam Aaronovitch, Ron Smith, Jean Gardiner, and Roger Moore, *The Political Economy of British Capitalism: A Marxist Analysis* (London: McGraw-Hill, 1981)

Gabriel A. Almond, *et al.*, symposium on 'The Return to the State', *American Political Science Review*, vol. 82, no. 3 (September 1988), pp. 853–904

Eugene Anderson and Pauline Anderson, *Political Institutions and Social Change in Continental Europe in the Nineteenth Century* (Berkeley and Los Angeles, Cal.: University of California Press, 1967)

Perry Anderson, *Lineages of the Absolutist State* (London: New Left Books, 1974)

William G. Andrews and Stanley Hoffmann, eds., *The Fifth Republic at Twenty* (Albany, N.Y.: S.U.N.Y Press, 1981)

John A. Armstrong, *The European Administrative Elite* (Princeton, N.J.: Princeton University Press, 1973)

Robert Axelrod, *The Evolution of Cooperation* (New York: Basic Books, 1984)

Peter Bachrach, *The Theory of Democratic Elitism* (Boston, Mass.: Little Brown, 1967)

Bertrand Badie and Pierre Birnbaum, *The Sociology of the State* (Chicago, Ill.: University of Chicago Press, 1983)

Michel Beaud, *A History of Capitalism, 1500–1980* (London: Macmillan, 1984)

Jonathan Bendor and Dilip Mookherjee, 'Institutional Structures and the Logic of Ongoing Collective Action', *American Political Science Review*, vol. 81, no. 1 (March 1987), pp. 129–54

Arthur F. Bentley, *The Process of Government: A Study of Social Pressures* (Chicago, Ill.: University of Chicago Press, 1908)

Suzanne Berger, ed., *Organizing Interests in Western Europe: Pluralism, Corporatism and the Transformation of Politics* (Cambridge: Cambridge University Press, 1981)

A.H. Birch, *Representative and Responsible Government* (London: Allen and Unwin, 1964)

Pierre Birnbaum, *La logique de l'État* (Paris: Fayard, 1982)

Pierre Birnbaum, 'The State versus Corporatism', *Politics and Society*, vol. 11, no. 4 (1982)

Pierre Birnbaum, 'Sur la dé-différentiation de l'État', *International Political Science Review*, vol. 6, no. 3 (1985), pp. 57–64

Peter M. Blau, ed., *Approaches to the Study of Social Structure* (London: Open Books, 1976)

Fred L. Block, *The Origins of International Economic Disorder: A Study of United States International Monetary Policy from World War II to the Present* (Berkeley and Los Angeles, Cal.: University of California Press, 1977)

Eileen Boris and Peter Bardaglio, 'Gender, Race, and Class: The Impact of the State on the Family and the Economy, 1790–1945', in Naomi Gerstel and Harriet Engel Gross, eds., *Families and Work* (Philadelphia, Pa.: Temple University Press, 1987), pp. 132–51

Raymond Boudon, *The Uses of Structuralism* (London: Heinemann, 1971)

Pierre Bourdieu, *Ce que parler veut dire: l'économie des échanges linguistiques* (Paris: Fayard, 1982)

Adam Buick and John Crump, *State Capitalism* (London: Macmillan, 1986)

James MacGregor Burns, *The Deadlock of Democracy: Four-Party Politics in America* (Englewood Cliffs, N.J.: Prentice-Hall, 1963)

Barry Buzan, *People, States and Fear: The National Security Problem in International Relations* (Brighton and Chapel Hill, N.C.: Wheatsheaf and University of North Carolina Press, 1983)

Martin Carnoy, *The State and Political Theory* (Princeton, N.J.: Princeton University Press, 1984)

Alan Cawson, *Corporatism and Welfare* (London: Heinemann, 1982)

Alan Cawson, ed., *Organized Interests and the State: Studies in Meso-Corporatism* (London: Sage, 1985)

Philip G. Cerny, 'The "Little Big Bang" in Paris: Financial Market Deregulation in a *dirigiste* System', *European Journal of Political Research*, vol. 17, no. 2 (March 1989), pp. 169–92

Philip G. Cerny, *The Politics of Grandeur: Ideological Aspects of de Gaulle's Foreign Policy* (Cambridge: Cambridge University Press, 1980)

Philip G. Cerny, ed., *Social Movements and Protest in France* (London and New York: Pinter and St Martin's Press, 1982)

Philip G. Cerny, 'Political Entropy and American Decline', *Millenium: Journal of International Studies*, vol. 18, no. 1 (Spring 1988), pp. 47–63

Philip G. Cerny and Martin A, Schain, eds., *French Politics and Public Policy* (New York and London: St Martin's Press, Methuen and Pinter, 1980)

Philip G. Cerny and Martin A. Schain, eds., *Socialism, the State and Public Policy in France* (New York and London: Methuen and Pinter, 1985)

Henry J.M. Claessen and Peter Skalnik, eds., *The Early State* (The Hague: Mouton, 1978)

Christopher Clapham, ed., *Private Patronage and Public Power* (London: Pinter, 1983)

Gordon L. Clark and Michael Dear, *State Apparatus: Structures of Language and Legitimacy* (London: Allen and Unwin, 1984)

Raymond Cohen and Elman R. Service, eds., *Origins of the State: The Anthropology of Political Evolution* (Philadelphia, Pa.: Institute for the Study of Human Issues, 1978)

Stephen Cohen, *Modern Capitalist Planning: The French Model* (Berkeley and Los Angeles, Cal.: University of California Press, 1969)

Jean Comaroff, *Body of Power, Spirit of Resistance: The Culture and History of a South African People* (Chicago, Ill.: University of Chicago Press, 1985)

Phillip E. Converse, 'The Nature of Belief Systems in Mass Publics', in David E. Apter, ed., *Ideology and Discontent* (New York: Free Press, 1964), pp. 206–61

Michel Crozier, *The Bureaucratic Phenomenon* (London: Tavistock, 1964)

Michel Crozier and Erhard Friedberg, *L'acteur et le système: les contraintes de l'action collective* (Paris: Editions du Seuil, 1977)

Robert A. Dahl, *A Preface to Democratic Theory* (Chicago, Ill.: University of Chicago Press, 1956)

Ralf Dahrendorf, *Class and Class Conflict in Industrial Society* (Stanford, Cal.: Stanford University Press, 1959)

Alfred Diamant, *Austrian Catholics and the First Republic: Democracy, Capitalism, and the Social Order, 1918–1934* (Princeton, N.J.: Princeton University Press, 1960)

R. Emerson Dobasch and Russell Dobasch, *Violence Against Wives: A Case Against the Patriarchy* (New York: Free Press, 1980)

Lawrence C. Dodd, *Coalitions in Parliamentary Government* (Princeton, N.J.: Princeton University Press, 1976)

G. William Domhoff, *The Higher Circles: The Governing Class in America* (New York: Random House, 1970)

Maurice Duverger, *Échec au roi* (Paris: Albin Michel, 1978)

Maurice Duverger, *Political Parties: Their Organization and Activity in the Modern State* (London: Methuen, 1954)

Kenneth Dyson, *The State Tradition in Western Europe* (Oxford: Martin Robertson, 1980)

David Easton, *The Political System* (New York: Knopf, 1953)

Harry Eckstein, 'A Theory of Stable Democracy' (Princeton, N.J.: Princeton Center for International Studies, 1961)

Lewis J. Edinger, ed., *Political Leadership in Industrialized Societies* (New York: Wiley, 1967)

Murray Edelman, *The Symbolic Uses of Politics* (Urbana, Ill.: University of Illinois Press, 1964)

Saul Estrin and Peter Holmes, *French Planning in Theory and Practice* (London: Allen and Unwin, 1982)

Amitai and Eva Etzioni, eds., *Social Change* (New York: Basic Books, 1964)

Peter Evans, Dietrich Rueschemeyer, and Theda Skocpol, eds., *Bringing the State Back In* (Cambridge: Cambridge University Press, 1985)

Michel Foucault, *Power/Knowledge: Selected Interviews and Other Writings, 1972–1977*, edited by Colin Gordon (New York: Pantheon Books, 1980)

Jean Fourastié, *Les trente glorieuses, ou la Révolution invisible de 1946 à 1975* (Paris: Fayard, revised edn, 1979)

John Gaffney, ed., *France and Modernization* (London: Avebury/Gower, 1988)

Andrew Gamble, *Britain in Decline: Economic Policy, Political Strategy and the British State* (Boston, Mass.: Beacon Press, 1981)

Lloyd C. Gardner, *Economic Aspects of New Deal Diplomacy* (Boston, Mass.: Beacon Press, 1971)

Richard N. Gardner, *Sterling–Dollar Diplomacy in Current Perspective* (New York: Columbia University Press, revised edn, 1980)

John Gaventa, *Power and Powerlessness: Quiescence and Rebellion in an Appalachian Valley* (Urbana, Ill.: University of Illinois Press, 1980)

Anthony Giddens, *Central Problems of Social Theory: Action, Structure and Contradiction in Social Analysis* (London: Macmillan, 1979)

Stephen Gill, 'American Hegemony: Its Limits and Prospects in the Reagan Era', *Millennium: Journal of International Studies*, vol. 15, no. 3 (Winter 1986), pp. 311–36

Robert Gilpin, *France in the Age of the Scientific State* (Princeton, N.J.: Princeton University Press, 1968)

Robert Gilpin, *The Political Economy of International Relations* (Princeton, N.J.: Princeton University Press, 1987)

John H. Goldthorpe, ed., *Order and Conflict in Contemporary Capitalism* (Oxford: Oxford University Press, 1984)

Diana M. Green, 'The Seventh Plan – The Demise of French Planning?', *West European Politics*, vol. 1, no. 1 (February 1978), pp. 60–76

Sven Groennings, E.W. Kelley, and Michael Leiserson, eds., *The Study of Coalition Behavior: Theoretical Perspectives and Cases from Four Continents* (New York: Holt, Rinehart and Winston, 1970)

Peter A. Hall, *Governing the Economy: The Politics of State Intervention in Britain and*

France (New York and London: Oxford University Press and Polity Press, 1986)

Jon Halliday, *A Political History of Japanese Capitalism* (New York: Monthly Review Press, 1975)

Nigel Harris, *The End of the Third World* (Harmondsworth, Mddx: Penguin, 1986)

Louis Hartz, *The Liberal Tradition in America: An Interpretation of American Political Thought Since the Revolution* (New York: Harcourt, Brace, 1955)

Jack Hayward, *The State and the Market Economy: Economic Patriotism and Industrial Development in France* (Brighton: Wheatsheaf, 1986)

Hugh Heclo, 'Issue Networks and the Executive Establishment', in Anthony King, ed., *The New American Political System* (Washington, D.C.: American Enterprise Institute, 1978), pp. 87–124

Paul Q. Hirst, 'Retrieving Pluralism', in William Outhwaite and Michael J. Mulkay, eds., *Social Theory and Social Criticism: Essays Presented to Tom Bottomore* (Oxford: Basil Blackwell, 1987), pp. 154–74

Eric J. Hobsbawm, *Industry and Empire* (Harmondsworth, Mddx.: Penguin, 1969)

Godfrey Hodgson, *All Things to All Men: The False Promise of the American Presidency* (Harmondsworth, Mddx: Penguin, 2nd edn, 1984)

Stanley Hoffmann, *et al.*, eds., In Search of France (Cambridge, Mass.: Harvard University Press, 1963)

John Holloway and Sol Picciotto, eds., *State and Capital: A Marxist Debate* (London: Edward Arnold, 1978)

Peter Holmes and Anne Stevens, 'The Framework of Government–Industry Relations and Industrial Policy Making in France', Working Paper Series on Government–Industry Relations, no. 2, University of Sussex (June 1986)

R.J. Holton, *The Transition from Feudalism to Capitalism* (London: Macmillan, 1985)

Thomas P. Hughes, *Networks of Power: Electrification in Western Society, 1880–1930* (Baltimore, Md. and London: Johns Hopkins University Press, 1983)

Samuel P. Huntington, *Political Order in Changing Societies* (New Haven, Conn.: Yale University Press, 1968)

Geoffrey Ingham, *Capitalism Divided? The City and Industry in British Social Development* (London: Macmillan, 1984)

Ghiţa Ionescu, *The Politics of the European Communist States* (London: Weidenfeld and Nicolson, 1968)

Andrew C. Janos, *Politics and Paradigms: Changing Theories of Change in Social Science* (Stanford, Cal.: Stanford University Press, 1986)

Bob Jessop, *The Capitalist State: Marxist Theories and Methods* (Oxford: Martin Robertson, 1982)

Chalmers Johnson, *M.I.T.I. and the Japanese Miracle: The Growth of Industrial Policy, 1925–1975* (Stanford, Cal.: Stanford University Press, 1982)

Catherine Jones, *Patterns of Social Policy: An Introduction to Comparative Analysis* (London: Tavistock, 1985)

Kathleen B. Jones and Anna G. Jonasdottir, eds., *The Political Interests of Gender* (London and Beverly Hills, Cal.: Sage Publications, 1988)

Peter Katzenstein, *Corporatism and Change* (Ithaca, N.Y.: Cornell University Press, 1984)

Peter Katzenstein, *Small States in World Markets* (Ithaca, N.Y.: Cornell University Press, 1985)

Peter Katzenstein, ed., *Between Power and Plenty: The Foreign Economic Policies of the Industrial States* (Madison, Wis.: University of Wisconsin Press, 1978)

Tom Kemp, *Industrialization in Nineteenth Century Europe* (London: Longman, 1969)

Paul Kennedy, *The Rise and Fall of the Great Powers: Economic Change and Military Conflict from 1500 to 2000* (London: Unwin Hyman, 1988)

Robert O. Keohane, *After Hegemony: Cooperation and Discord in the World Political Economy* (Princeton, N.J.: Princeton University Press, 1984)

Charles P. Kindleberger, *Economic Growth in France and Britain, 1851–1950* (Cambridge, Mass.: Harvard University Press, 1964)

Walter Korpi, 'Power Resources Approach *vs*. Action and Conflict: On Causal Intentional Explanation in the Study of Power', *Sociological Theory*, vol. 3, no. 2 (1985), pp. 31–45

Stephen Krasner, 'Approaches to the State: Alternative Conceptions and Historical Dynamics', review article, *Comparative Politics*, vol. 16, no. 2 (January 1984), pp. 223–46

Stephen Krasner, *Structural Conflict: The Third World against Global Liberalism* (Berkeley and Los Angeles, Cal.: University of California Press, 1985)

Annette Kuhn and AnnMarie Wolpe, eds., *Feminism and Materialism* (London: Routledge and Kegan Paul, 1978)

Thomas Kuhn, *The Structure of Scientific Revolutions* (Chicago, Ill.: Chicago University Press, 1962)

Jean Labatut and Wheaton J. Lane, eds., *Highways in Our National Life: A Symposium* (Princeton, N.J.: Princeton University Press, 1950)

Joseph LaPalombara, *Interest Groups in Italian Politics* (Princeton, N.J.: Princeton University Press, 1964)

Joseph LaPalombara and Myron Weiner, eds., *Political Parties and Political Development* (Princeton, N.J.: Princeton University Press, 1966)

Peter Laslett, *The World We Have Lost* (London and New York: Weidenfeld and Nicolson and C. Scribner's, 2nd edn, 1973)

Adrian Leftwich, ed., *What is Politics? The Activity and its Study* (Oxford: Basil Blackwell, 1984)

Margaret Levi, 'The Predatory Theory of Rule', *Politics & Society*, vol. 10, no. 4 (1981), pp. 431–65

Arend Lijphart, 'Consociational Democracy', *World Politics*, vol. XXI, no. 2 (January 1969), pp. 207–25

Arend Lijphart, *The Politics of Accommodation: Pluralism and Democracy in the Netherlands* (Berkeley, Cal.: University of California Press, 1968)

Arend Lijphart, 'Typologies of Democratic Systems' (Berkeley, Cal.: Institute of International Studies, 1968)

Charles E. Lindblom, *Politics and Markets: The World's Political-Economic Systems* (New York: Basic Books, 1977)

Theodore J. Lowi, 'American Business, Public Policy, Case Studies, and Political Theory', *World Politics*, vol. 16, no. 4 (July 1964), pp. 677–715

Theodore J. Lowi, *The End of Liberalism: Ideology, Polity, and the Crisis of Public Authority* (New York: Norton, 1969)

Steven Lukes, *Power: A Radical View* (London: Macmillan, 1974)

Grant McConnell, *Private Power and American Democracy* (New York: Knopf, 1966)

Howard Machin and Vincent Wright, eds., *Economic Policy and Policy-Making Under the Mitterrand Presidency, 1981–1984* (London: Pinter, 1984)

Iain McLean, *Public Choice: An Introduction* (Oxford: Basil Blackwell, 1987)

Angus Maddison, *Phases of Capitalist Development* (Oxford: Oxford University Press, 1982)

Jane Marceau, *Class and Status in France: Economic Change and Social Immobility, 1945–1975* (Oxford: Oxford University Press, 1977)

James G. March and Johan P. Olsen, 'The New Institutionalism: Organizational Factors in Political Life', *American Political Science Review*, vol. 78, no. 3 (September 1984), pp. 734–49

Marcel Merle, *The Sociology of International Relations* (London: Berg, 1987)

Keith Middlemas, *The Politics of Industrial Society: The British Experience since 1911* (London: André Deutsch, 1979)

Joel S. Migdal, *Strong Societies and Weak States: State–Society Relations and State Capabilities in the Third World* (Princeton, N.J.: Princeton University Press, 1988)

Ralph Miliband, *The State in Capitalist Society* (London: Weidenfeld and Nicolson, 1969)

Terence M. Moe, *The Organization of Interests: Incentives and the Internal Dynamics of Political Interest Groups* (Chicago, Ill.: University of Chicago Press, 1980)

Barrington Moore Jr, *Social Origins of Dictatorship and Democracy: Landlord and Peasant in the Making of the Modern World* (Harmondsworth, Mddx.: Allen Lane, 1967)

J. Peter Nettl, *Political Mobilization* (London: Faber and Faber, 1968)

Eric A. Nordlinger, *On the Autonomy of the Democratic State* (Cambridge, Mass.: Harvard University Press, 1981)

Douglass C. North, *Structure and Change in Economic History* (New York: Norton, 1981)

Mancur Olson, *The Logic of Collective Action* (Cambridge, Mass.: Harvard University Press, 1971)

Kenneth Oye, Robert J. Lieber, and David Rothchild, eds., *Eagle Resurgent: American Foreign Policy in the Reagan Era* (London: Longman, 1987)

J. Roland Pennock, ' "Responsible Government", Separated Powers, and Special Interests: Agricultural Subsidies in Britain and America', *American Political Science Review*, vol. 56, no. 3 (September 1962)

Michael J. Piore and Charles F. Sabel, *The Second Industrial Divide: Possibilities for Prosperity* (New York: Basic Books, 1984)

Gianfranco Poggi, *The Development of the Modern State* (Stanford, Cal.: Stanford University Press, 1978)

Karl Polanyi, *The Great Transformation* (New York: Rinehart and Co., 1944)

Nicos Poulantzas, *Classes in Capitalist Society* (London: New Left Books, 1975)

William M. Reddy, *Money and Liberty in Modern Europe: A Critique of Historical Understanding* (Cambridge: Cambridge University Press, 1987)

Robert B. Reich, *The Next American Frontier* (New York: Times Books, 1983)

Jeremy Richardson, ed., *Policy Styles in Western Europe* (London: Allen and Unwin, 1982)

William H. Riker, *The Theory of Political Coalitions* (New Haven: Yale University Press, 1962)

Arnold Rose, *The Power Structure* (New York: Oxford University Press, 1967)

Mark H. Rose, *Interstate: Express Highway Politics, 1941–1956* (Lawrence, Kan.: Regents Press of Kansas, 1979)

Peter Rutland, *The Myth of the Plan* (London: Hutchinson, 1986)

Marshall Sahlins, *Culture and Practical Reason* (Chicago, Ill.: University of Chicago Press, 1966)

Giovanni Sartori, *Parties and Party Systems: A Framework for Analysis*, vol. I (Cambridge: Cambridge University Press, 1976)

F.M. Scherer, *Industrial Market Structure and Economic Performance* (Boston, Mass.: Houghton Mifflin, 2nd edn, 1980)

Joseph A. Schlesinger, 'Political Party Organization', in James G. March, ed., *Handbook of Organizations* (Chicago, Ill.: Rand McNally, 1965), pp. 764–801

Philippe C. Schmitter, 'Still the Century of Corporatism?', in Frederick Pike and Thomas Stritch, eds., *The New Corporatism* (Notre Dame, Ind.: Notre Dame University Press, 1974), pp. 85–131

Ilja Scholten, ed., *Political Stability and Neo-Corporatism: Corporatist Integration and Societal Cleavages in Western Europe* (London and Beverly Hills, Cal.: Sage, 1987)

Joseph Schumpeter, *Capitalism, Socialism and Democracy* (London: Allen and Unwin, 1943)

Andrew Shonfield, *Modern Capitalism: The Changing Balance of Public and Private Power* (London: Oxford University Press, 1965)

Theda Skocpol, *States and Social Revolutions* (Cambridge: Cambridge University Press, 1979)

Hedrick Smith, *The Power Game: How Washington Works* (New York: Random House, 1988)

Frank J. Sorauf, *Party Politics in America* (Boston, Mass.: Little, Brown, 2nd edn, 1972)

David A. Stockman, *The Triumph of Politics: Why the Reagan Revolution Failed* (New York: Harper and Row, 1986)

Susan Strange, 'The Persistent Myth of Lost Hegemony', *International Organization*, vol. 41, no. 4 (Autumn 1987), pp. 551–74

Susan Strange, *States and Markets: An Introduction to International Political Economy* (London: Pinter, 1988)

Ezra Suleiman, *Politics, Power and Bureaucracy in France: The Administrative Elite* (Princeton, N.J.: Princeton University Press, 1974)

Abram de Swaan, *Coalition Theories and Cabinet Formations: A Study of Formal Theories of Coalition Formation Applied to Nine European Parliaments after 1918* (Amsterdam: Elsevier, 1973)

Richard Tapper, 'Anthropologists, Historians and Tribespeople on Tribe and State Formation in the Middle East', in Philip Khoury and Joseph Kostiner, eds., *Tribe and State Formation in the Middle East* (Cambridge, Mass.: M.I.T. Press, forthcoming)

Lester G. Telser, *A Theory of Efficient Cooperation and Competition* (Cambridge: Cambridge University Press, 1987)

Charles Tilly, ed., *The Formation of National States in Western Europe* (Princeton, N.J.: Princeton University Press, 1975)

Alexis de Tocqueville, *The Ancien Regime and the French Revolution* (Glasgow: Collins, 1969; originally published 1851)

Ferdinand Tönnies, *Community and Association* (East Lansing, Mich.: Michigan State University Press, 1957; originally published as *Gemeinschaft und Gesellschaft*, 1887)

Alain Touraine, *L'après-socialisme* (Paris: Grasset, 1980)

David A. Truman, *The Governmental Process: Political Interests and Public Opinion* (New York: Knopf, 1951)

Henry Tudor, *Political Myth* (London: Macmillan, 1972)

Sylvia Walby, *Patriarchy at Work: Patriarchy and Capitalist Relations in Employment* (Minneapolis: University of Minnesota Press, 1986)

Immanuel Wallerstein, *The Capitalist World-Economy* (Cambridge: Cambridge University Press, 1979)

William Appleman Williams, *The Tragedy of American Diplomacy* (New York: Dell, 2nd edn, 1972)

Oliver E. Williamson, *The Economic Institutions of Capitalism* (New York: Free Press, 1985)

Oliver E. Williamson, *Markets and Hierarchies* (New York: Free Press, 1975)

Graham K. Wilson, *Business and Politics: A Comparative Introduction* (London: Macmillan, 1985)

Erik Olin Wright, *Class, Crisis and the State* (London: New Left Books, 1978)

John Zysman, *Governments, Markets and Growth: Financial Systems and the Politics of Industrial Change* (Ithaca, N.Y.: Cornell University Press, 1983)

John Zysman, *Political Strategies for Industrial Order: Market, State and Industry in France* (Berkeley and Los Angeles, Cal.: University of California Press, 1977)

John Zysman and Laura Tyson, eds., *American Industry in International Competition: Government Policies and Corporate Strategies* (Ithaca, N.Y.: Cornell University Press, 1983)

Index

absolutism 142, 215–16

access,
  and interest intermediation 165, 166,
    167, 176
  to office 35, 39–41, 43, 52, 130
  and political parties 130–1, 132–3, 137,
    138, 140

accommodation 170–1

accountability 105, 130, 143

action, collective 61–2, 172

action, structured field xi–xii, 21, 43,
    85–90, 91–6, 99
  changes in 114–15, 123–9, 242–3
  and choice 56–7, 81–2, 182–3
  and civil society 187, 195, 200
  critical arenas 104–8, 187
  and interest intermediation 148, 151–2,
    160–1, 178
  movement as 189
  party system as 130–3, 134–5, 143
  and state location 113, 233
  transnational 234

actors, state 15–16, 29–32, 244
  and access 35
  and choice 81, 115–16, 182–3
  and corporatism 162, 164–5, 167–70,
    172–5, 177
  and institutions 116
  and interest agents 60–1, 116, 120–8
  and state apparatuses 43–7
  and state structures 51–2, 53, 120, 197,
    200–1, 233–4
  and transnational structures 204–5
  see also leadership; offices, state

advantage,
  comparative 205
  competitive 199, 205, 229, 237–8, 241

agency,
  and choice 19–20, 26, 29, 56–7,
    61, 233
  and interest intermediation 151,
    172
  patterns 56–82

and political allocation xiii, 4–6, 8–9,
    53, 57, 85
of state 82, 93–4, 108, 237
and structure 90–5, 116, 124–9

Almond, Gabriel and Verba, Sidney 54

Althusser, Louis,
  and class struggle 13
  and state apparatuses 47

analysis/synthesis 88

anarchism 37, 75

apparatus, state 30, 43–8, 53, 116–17,
    126, 168, 177
  and corporatism 154, 156, 160–1

arenas, critical 104–8, 116–17

Argentina 170, 198, 237

aristocracy 36–7, 106

Aristotle 106

Australia, as corporatist state 176

Austria, as corporatist state 172–3

autarchy 51, 199, 213–14, 225, 237

authoritarianism 37–8, 41, 42, 45, 51,
    57, 161

authority,
  of leader 121–2, 123–4, 128–9
  legal–rational 13, 15, 17–18, 43,
    48, 156
  and politics x–xi, 7, 78, 106, 163,
    206, 230

authority theory 106

autonomy,
  of agents 19, 41, 60, 120, 164, 178,
    193, 197, 200
  of local government 198, 228
  of personal leader 120–1, 123,
    124
  of political parties 139
  of state 12–13, 15–17, 85–7, 96–7,
    99–102, 108–9, 165, 178, 200, 212,
    234–5; potential 88–96; relative xi,
    60, 158, 174, 197
  of structures 89, 91–3, 95,
    183

Axelrod, Robert 57, 95

Index compiled by Meg Davies (Society of Indexers)